THE UNTOLD TRUTH

"DON'T ASK, DON'T TELL"

A STORY THAT MUST BE TOLD

THE UNTOLD TRUTH

"DON'T ASK, DON'T TELL"

A STORY THAT MUST BE TOLD

A MEMOIR BY

HOWARD DEWITT LINSON

TO MY FAMILY & FRIENDS

TO THE BRAVE MEN AND WOMEN WHO ARE DEFENDING OUR COUNTRY

&

TO THOSE WHO HAVE AND ARE STILL GOING THROUGH.

CONTENTS

PROLOGUE

My name is Howard Dewitt Linson, an Army Veteran of the United States Army. I have decided some time ago how to approach all of you and explain from my point of view on how the LGBTQ+ people are treated in the military of yesterday and today. So, in turn, I will tell you about my experiences while serving in the United States Army as a bisexual soldier and how it affected my entire career, as well as the reactions of individuals who called themselves heterosexuals. As you start to read about how things were and how they are now, do understand that everything I'm about to tell you all is the truth and untainted stories of my career at every move and turn that I decided to make.

In the time that it took for me to write my book, I realized that my past experiences, that I've been through, were keeping me from moving forward within my life and in writing this book all together. Before I decided to write about my time in the U.S. Army, I found it difficult to relive what I've tried so hard to suppress without it interrupting life. But at times when there were opportunities for me to move forward in life, something deep within myself would bring up a memory of my past and I wasn't able to go through anything without doubting myself. Sometimes while at work, I would wonder if the people in my work environment would be the next dead fall chapter of my life.

There was a time when people would ask me about my problems in the military and I could not keep a straight face without breaking down. At times, I would only talk about the good parts and not the bad, just to keep anyone from knowing what I've been through or to stop myself from breaking down and remembering what I tried so hard to suppress. But not anymore!

As I started to write about the twilight zones of my life, in the U.S. Army, I started to realize that not only was I writing my story, but I was releasing what I was holding onto. At times I found it very difficult to write about my ordeals and to tell them to you correctly without flaws. But something happened that I didn't expect within myself, I was releasing the stressors that were prohibiting me from moving forward. Now I realize that not only did those memories stop me from becoming a better person, but they were also stopping me from realizing who I was. So, now after I have written out everything that I kept within myself, I can now see that I've started to move forward within life, not fearing what I used to fear the most, and that was what people thought about me.

As you start to read about the things that I've gone through, I do hope that everyone will understand that these types of problems that I've faced do not make me the only one, but many more like me, have faced fewer or greater challenges. Unlike myself, some people didn't live to tell you their stories, for they have already fallen into silence.

Now from here, I give you the untold truth, and how I survived the hatred and the continual judgments of the "Don't Ask, Don't Tell" policy.

INTRODUCTION

As PVT Harris approached my truck, I yelled out to him… *"Hey Harris, do you need my truck for something?"* but PVT Harris did not respond back.

Watching him walk around the front of my truck, I asked him again… *"Harris what's up, you need my truck?"* as PVT Harris ignored me.

Opening the driver's door to my truck, I yelled out loud to PVT Harris… *"HEY, LET ME GET MY STUFF OUT FROM UNDERNEATH FIRST!"* By this time PVT Harris had already jumped into my truck and slammed the door closed.

"HEY!" I cried out hoping he would hear me.

Going as fast as I could to throw my MRE out from underneath my truck……. the truck started up.

"HEY! HARRIS DON'T MOVE I'M STILL UNDERNEATH! HEY… STOP!" I shouted at the top of my voice.

"HARRIS…HEY STOP!" Then the truck was put into gear.

"AAAAAWWWWW! … STOP!"

Hearing the engine whining up to full power and seeing the tire I was leaning against started to move quickly… *"AAAAAAWWWWWW PLEASE STOP, NO! STOP… STOP… STOP!"* As my screams were overtaken from the noise of the engine…

THIS PAGE INTENTIONALLY BLANK

JOINING THE MILITARY

When I was seven years old, I started to realize that I liked both guys and girls but didn't understand why I did after I had kissed one on my male best friends for the first time. At times, I had often wondered why I liked both guys and girls, but at that age, I felt that messing around like we did was a normal thing. None of us would stop and look down upon it as something bad, but to us we were just kissing or playing show and tell with one another. We didn't know much about sex at that age, or even where to put it if we even had the opportunity to try. I don't know if my mom knew about my sexuality when I was coming up, but at times I would tell her about some of the things I did with my friends, and I always knew my mom loved me and accepted me for who I was.

After my mother retired from the United States Air Force, we moved from Biloxi Mississippi to Jackson Mississippi, and for the most part, I found myself hating our new way of life. As much as I could remember, I was accustomed to the military lifestyle, where I enjoyed a racially diverse group of friends growing up. But moving into a city where nothing reflected the life I once knew, I found myself in a world that was driven more by fashion, slang and hip-hop in an urban environment that I've never experienced until now.

When I first started to attend Murrah High School, I often wondered if I could date girls and still have guys on the side, as I had done in my previous town. But moving into an area where I didn't know anyone, it took me a while to get used to the kids at that school who behaved wild just to get attention from their peers. Thinking about my past school years, while in the ninth grade, I knew a lot of my friends were diverse and open-minded, and I often wondered if these kids in my new school would be open minded as well.

In my new school I didn't socialize much with my fellow classmates but instead, I kept to myself, for the most part when it came to interacting with anyone. Within my first few weeks at Murrah High School, I realized I was no longer around military kids, and I knew nothing about these types of kids who grew up differently than I did. But for the most part, I didn't like the concept that I had to spend the next three years around kids I didn't like. Seeing that I didn't fit in with anyone around Murrah High School, I never thought about talking to anyone about any kind of sexual encounter, because I felt uncomfortable being in a strange environment around people I couldn't quite understand at that time.

Throughout the ninth grade, life started to become more and more unbearable for me. I was one of those kids who got picked on all the time, and most every day, I was shoved into the wall lockers or slapped in the back of the head when I wasn't looking. Since I was the quiet type, rumors started to go around school that I was gay, and while I was getting picked on and harassed, I was repeatedly called *"faggot"*. During the time I was getting called *"faggot"*, most every day, I would think to myself that these were ignorant kids who needed attention, and the way they got their high for the day was to pick on those who were less popular than themselves or didn't fit in.

As a teenager in Murrah High School, I knew why they called me *"faggot"*, although it had nothing to do with my sexuality, but in my case, I was perceived to be gay because I was hanging out with the kids who were also being labeled as such. My tormentors in high school used the word *"faggot"* as an all-purpose slur for anyone with a different background or demeanor. To them the word of choice for us who were labeled *"different"* and not considered to be *"normal"*, this became their favorite insult every day that always turned out to be the worst insult possible, *"faggot".*

At first, I didn't stand up for myself while I was at Murrah High School, because one of my older sister's, Hillary, stood up for me every time I had a confrontation at school. Both of my sisters, Heather and Hillary would tell me to fight back and to stop letting these kids at school run me over. They would tell me that neither one of them was going to be around to protect me when they both graduated from high school. So, knowing that my sisters were now gone when I reached the tenth grade, I started fighting back when anyone at my school started to harass me or even say something derogatory towards me. So, like a cause and effect, most of the kids started to leave me alone, now that I was labeled *"the crazy kid".*

After a few altercations here and there, I started to earn respect from my peers as someone who was no longer weak or easy to push around. During most of my high school years, thoughts about doing any type of messing around went out of the window quickly. With all

13

the harassment and fighting that was going on, I couldn't even think about messing around with anyone.

By the twelfth grade, during one particular day in my economics class, one of my friends named James came on to me in a way I didn't quite comprehend at the time. Since I didn't mind his actions and I liked him, I didn't say much to him about his behavior. So, after our first encounter with one another, James would bug the hell out of me about joining the Navy with him, and I kept trying to explain to him that deep dark water and I didn't mix. Knowing that I wanted him to follow me elsewhere, I also did my best to try to talk him into joining the Air Force or Army with me, but his heart was set on the Navy and mine wasn't.

So, as graduation approached, I didn't know where I wanted to go within my life, until my mom told me I had to start earning my own way around the house, since I was eating up all the food. In the four months after I had graduated from Murrah High School, my mom told me to come up with a game plan on where I wanted to go in life... *"You will not stay in my house eating up all my food Howard. You got to go. It's time for you to get out on your own son!"* My mom would tell me.

"Where would I go?" I would ask myself, thinking about what I wanted to be in life.

As I contemplated joining the military, I never thought my sexuality was going to be an issue. I knew I didn't act gay or carried myself like some of the gay guys I knew from high school did. So, knowing I wasn't like the ones from school, I thought highly of the military and all that it had to offer. Never did I ever worry about bullies or people who would make my life a living hell, for that was the last thing on my mind at that time.

During this time of my life when I had to think of a game plan for myself, I was working at a local Chevrolet dealership as a service department porter. Every day while I swept the floors, a task I hated so much, I knew somewhere out in the world there must be something bigger and better than this, if only I could step out into the world and find it. During my breaks at work, I would walk back to the vehicle detailing department were most of my co-workers would ask me what I wanted to be in life... *"Hey Howard! Since you've been out of school for the past few months, what are you planning on doing with your life, kid?"*

"I want to be a railroad engineer," I replied. *"I want to drive trains across the U.S."*

Every time I would say this to them all, laughter is all I would hear.

"Boy, you're not going to be working on the man's railroad. You're too stupid and black for them to even hire your dumb high yellow ass!"

As I would walk away in anger, with their laughter following me, while I told myself... *"I'll prove all of them wrong!"*

By mid-August in 1998, my mom was telling me to make up my mind quickly, since her food bill was starting to get out of control... *"Boy, every time I go grocery shopping you eat it all up before I can get some. You got-ta go son! What are you planning on doing with your life, the military or college?"* She would ask me.

"Well momma, I have applied to all of the local colleges, but I'm thinking more about the military," not knowing what to say at that time, just to get the conversation off me.

So come one August morning while I was lying in my bed, I made up my mind and decided to head over to the Air Force recruiter's office to see what my options were to become an Air Force recruit. When I told my mom what I wanted to do, she had an expression of pure joy on her face, when I told her about my decision to go into the military.

In the days that followed and after countless times that me and my mom kept going to see the Air Force recruiters, I told my mom to take me to go see the Army recruiters so I could compare both before I made my decision on which one I wanted to join. So, after a few minutes in the time that it took for my Army recruiter (Staff Sergeant), SSG Brown to explain what the Army had to offer and all its glorious things that I could do, it didn't take me too much time to say... *"Sign me up!"*

At first, I was very nervous and a little bit scared about facing the unknown after I had just told SSG Brown I wanted to join the Army. As a big fan of military movies, I imagined being involved in an exciting covert mission in different countries like in the movies *Clear and Present Danger* or *The Hunt for The Red October*, and silly movies like *Major Payne* and *Boot Camp*. During the time that I was looking over the contract to enlist into the U.S. Army, my nervousness wasn't at all

16

related to the fact that I was a bisexual young man, or if my sexuality would affect my career in the military, during the time I was signing the paperwork for me to enlist into the United States Army.

Seeing that I was a nervous wreck sitting at my recruiter's desk, my mom would comfort me by telling me I would soon overcome my fears, and that she was very proud to have me as her son. Hearing those words coming from my mom made me relax and mentally know I was doing the right thing, at the time.

That night before my formal enlistment, I stayed at a hotel with a lot of other recruits who were joining different branches of the U.S. Military, and just like myself, none of them couldn't sleep that night. So, come the next morning, I stood amongst a group of recruits in a small room as we all raised our right hand to be sworn into the United States Military.

On September 8, 1998, I Howard Dewitt Linson enlisted into the United States Army as an 88M (Transportation Truck Driver, 88 Mike), Private Second Class (E-2/PV2) at the age of 18.

That afternoon, after everyone was enlisted into their military service of choice, all of us had our paperwork in hand about what flights we were going to be on that following day. Since I knew, I was going to Fort Knox Kentucky for basic training, I often wondered what the Army would be like and what basic training was all about, besides watching the movie *Full Metal Jacket* all the time.

Later that night back at my hotel room, my recruiter came to me and asked if I was ready to head out that next morning... *"Are you ready for the journey of a lifetime, Private Linson?"*

"I'm pretty nervous Sergeant Brown." I told him. *"Can I wait another week or two before heading out to basic training?"*

SSG Brown laughed out loud... *"No, you can't Private Linson, but don't worry, everything is going to be all right."*

"AAAWWW!" I kept screaming on the inside after hearing him say that to me. But I knew I had asked for this, and I had to see it all the way through to the end.

Later that night I couldn't sleep... *"What did I just do? What would become of me now?"* I kept asking myself, while trying to watch TV.

Laying on my hotel bed staring up at the ceiling and back towards the alarm clock on the nightstand beside my bed, I kept thinking about my childhood and remembering how things were so simple, and how everything was going to change now that I was leaving the comfort of my momma's home. *"Was this the right thing to do?"* I kept asking myself, looking back at the clock, watching the minutes and hours passing by.

After countless hours of thinking about the life I was about to begin, before I knew it, the alarm clock was going off... *"Damn its 5 o'clock in the morning already! Man, I only had a few minutes of sleep. Well, it's time Howard. Let's do this."* I told myself slowly getting up and out of my hotel bed.

After getting all my personal things together, I started my way downstairs to board the charter bus that was taking us all to the airport that morning. Looking around at all the tired faces and nervous looks, I knew I wasn't the only one who had stayed up all night wondering if this was the best course of action to take at such a young age. After arriving at Jackson-Evers International Airport in Jackson Mississippi, I met up with my mom and one of my sisters, Hillary, alongside with SSG Brown, who kept telling me that everything was going to be alright. At the time I wondered how in the world SSG Brown could see that everything was going to be alright, and I couldn't see it like he could.

I knew I looked scared standing there wondering how in the world did I ended up at the airport checking in my bags. After I had finished checking in, I went and sat amongst the other recruits, who were listening to our last and final briefing from one of the MAP's recruiters. While sitting amongst everyone, I met a recruit named Lee who was also going to Fort Knox Kentucky for basic training. Lee tried to reassure me about everything that was to come, but I kept telling him I wasn't worried about basic training, but more worried about the flight there, since it was my first time on an airplane.

Seeing my mom and my sister walking up with huge smiles on their faces, I immediately jumped up to hug them both as tightly as I could, while taking deep inhales to remember the way they both smelled, and while also remembering how my oldest sister Heather smelled like, before she moved overseas with her husband who was in the Air Force. I kept telling myself not to cry while I held my mom and sister in my arms, while standing around people I didn't know.

"Hang in there Howard. You'll make it. Okay." Both told me as I did my best not to cry while hugging them.

When it was time for us to board our flight to Kentucky, I kept turning around looking back at my family, as I started walking through our gate towards our airplane, wondering should I stop now or keep moving. *"Keep moving,"* I told myself. *"Bye yall"* as I watched them disappear around the corner as I boarded my flight.

After walking onto the airplane, I saw that Lee was in the same row of seats that I was going to be sitting in, where he sat at the window seat and an older lady was in the aisle seat... *"Excuse me ma'am, I'm in the middle."* I said to her.

"Sure, come on in and have a seat young man." She said with a smile on her face, getting up to let me in.

"Hey Lee"

"What's up Howard? You ready for this?"

"Heck naw, Lee!" while my legs started to shake up and down.

Lee started to laugh as he saw how nervous I was to be on an airplane for the first time in my life. As soon as I heard the doors close and the stewardess started to talk on the intercom system, I immediately started to pray… *"Our father who art in heaven, hollow it be thy name, thy kingdom come…. Is this your first time flying?"* the lady leaned over and whispered to me.

"Yes ma'am… OH GOD, PLEASE HELP ME!" as I started to grasp onto the arm rest of my seat.

As I heard the engines starting up, I felt my heart beating in my ears, as if my heart was going to burst out of my chest and break through the window and take off running down the runway.

"OH SHIT! OH SHIT! OH SHIT!" I kept saying repeatedly as the airplane started bouncing up and down on the runway going to line up for takeoff. After feeling the airplane turn to the right and stop, I leaned over and asked Lee what was coming next… *"Just wait for it"* he replied.

"Wait for what?" And as soon as I had said that to him, out of nowhere, a thunderous roar came from the airplane as my body sank back into my seat as I started to scream out loud… *"AAAAAAWWWWW! JESUS CHRIST HELP MEEEEE! AAAWWWW GOD HELP! OH NOOOOO!"* as my legs kept kicking wildly into the seat in front of me.

Boy, boy, boy did that get everyone around me laughing their butts off. I knew I sounded like a little girl screaming at every shake from turbulence and turn the airplane made. Lee on the other hand, had tears running down his face from laughing so hard at me. I didn't care, I was shouting to GOD at the time.

Throughout the whole take off, I didn't calm down till the airplane leveled off at cruising altitude. And during that whole flight, the flight attendants kept asking me if I was going to make it... *"Yes, Yes, Yes!"* I replied quickly in a high-pitched voice.

As we started to turn and descend into Frankfort International Airport in Kentucky, I kept repeating out loud... *"Land, please land! Oh Lord please land this airplane!"* And I didn't stop until I felt the thump of the wheels touching down onto the runway... *"Thank you GOD! Thank you, Lord!"* as everyone around me kept laughing.

I knew for a fact that this flight was the best flight those people ever had, having to listen to me squeal like a stuck pig, from take-off to landing at our next destination.

BASIC TRAINING

After arriving at our terminal gate, I felt another rush of uncertainty about what was to come next. To me, I was starting a career that I had known from television commercials and movies. Walking around the airport trying to find out where I had to go, I was looking around for some tall fella with a large round brown hat, to start yelling at us for no apparent reason, like the Drill Sergeant in the movie *Forrest Gump*. But of course, that wasn't the case after standing around for a few minutes wondering where the USO was located at. (**U**nited **S**ervice **O**rganizations)

Sitting around in the USO, I saw a lot of eager and nervous young adults, like myself, waiting for what was to come next. It seemed like we were all wondering why we were there from some of the looks that I saw from other Army recruits. As we all waited around the USO for the buses to come and take us to Fort Knox, I looked around and kept asking myself... *"Was this the right thing to do? Is it too late to get out of this?"*

Grasping on the concept that there wasn't a way out of this decision that I had made, I quickly recognized all the different types of people who were just sitting around like I was. Laughing on the inside, I realized that I was surrounded by thugs, hippies, country people, skateboarders and preppy individuals from all different parts of our nation... *"Did I really make the same decision as they did?"* I thought to myself looking around at everyone.

After long hours of waiting around the USO for the buses to show up and take us to Ft. Knox, it was around eight o'clock that night when the buses showed up, and we were all told to line up outside in a single file line to board the buses. During the time that I was waiting in line to board one of the buses, I felt like I had done something very wrong, and had been sentenced to jail for some strange apparent reason. After all of us had loaded onto the buses and started our journey out of the airport, I kept wondering what my crime was, as I looked down at the long stretch of dark highway heading towards Ft. Knox.

When the buses finally made it to Fort Knox late that night, the only thing I wanted to do was to see my family again, just so I could have someone that I knew to calm me down from all the anxiety that was building up within me. When we were all instructed to put our things away and what bed we were going to be sleeping in, I couldn't believe that I was going to be sleeping in an open bay area with over 60 other guys that I didn't even know, or for that matter, people who were acting crazy... *"Oh boy, this is nothing like what my recruiter had told me!"* as I kept talking to myself, while putting my things away in my wall locker, while glancing at everyone around me.

But one particular guy that I will never forget who slept across from me named PVT Mooradian who seemed, to me, to be a skateboarder type of guy with a silly personality. After introducing myself to him, we both started to talk about how we felt about being cramped into a large open bay area, with so many loudmouth individuals. Later in basic training, PVT Mooradian became my best friend.

For the first five days of in-processing, we were all split into different groups to get our shots, uniforms and other training gear that we needed for basic training. On the sixth day, we were told that we were going to be meeting our Drill Sergeants from Bravo Company 2-46th Infantry, our basic training Company. Knowing that we were going to be leaving the in-processing holding barracks and starting the real Army stuff, none of us knew what was to come the next day but speculated what was to come.

Come the next day, all of us were formed up into a single file line, as we marched into the gym only to find angry looking Drill Sergeants staring us down... *"Don't laugh Howard"* I kept telling myself, while looking away from the Drill Sergeants.

"When we call out your name, fall outside into your prospective areas by platoon." One of the Drill Sergeants yelled out loud.

"Linson," Drill Sergeant Martinez yelled out loud.

"HERE, DRILL SERGEANT!"

"Third Platoon," Drill Sergeant Martinez replied, as I took off running outside into 3rd platoons' formation.

After everyone's name had been called out for third platoon, Drill Sergeant Martinez came back outside and told us to pick up our gear and personal things... *"Right face...File from the left forward... MARCH!"*

With all my heavy bags in hand, we started marching off in a single file line down the hill towards Bravo Company's location, when out of nowhere, Drill Sergeant Martinez yelled out loud... *"DOUBLE TIME...MARCH!"* And just like that, our Drill Sergeant took off running like a bat out of hell, while looking over his right shoulder yelling at us to keep up.

At that time, I weighed over 235 pounds and carried over 200 pounds of gear and my personal things. You can say I wasn't doing so good.

Looking at the two guys ahead of me that were keeping up with Drill Sergeant Martinez, I knew while struggling to hold onto my bags, I could not keep up with them. So, in turn, I was very slow and was holding up the rest of the platoon, as Drill Sergeant Martinez and the other two soldiers, who didn't have as much stuff as I did, took off and left the rest of us behind.

"Come on Private Linson, keep up! WHAT THE HELL ARE YOU DOING!" Drill Sergeant Martinez kept yelling, as he ran backwards looking at me.

Gasping for air while picking up and dropping my things along the way, I looked back and saw that everyone behind me was struggling as well, but I was the one who kept everyone from keeping up with Drill Sergeant Martinez.

During that short run down the hill towards our Company area, I felt so embarrassed as we came down the hill and took up formation again with the other two soldiers who were already formed up... *"Welcome, Private Linson. What took you so long?"* Drill Sergeant Martinez yelled out towards me, as I kept gasping for air.

Out of breath and sweating like a pig, the only thing I could do in response to his question was to shrug my shoulders up and down, thinking I was in serious trouble for holding up everybody else. Standing around with Drill Sergeant Martinez were two more of our Drill Sergeant's named, Drill Sergeant Brown and Drill Sergeant Padilla, who were also yelling at us to get into formation.

After we all got back into formation, Drill Sergeant Brown walked around the platoon shouting... *"Some of you fat boys are going to have a good time here at Fort Knox! Welcome to Bravo Company 2-46th Infantry, 3rd Platoon Mad Dogs."*

Standing there listening to our Drill Sergeant's explaining what our platoon motto was and what was to come in the next nine weeks ahead of us, I remembered hearing back at MAP's, that Fort Knox was the hardest basic training post in the United States Army. I knew we had it coming but didn't know how hard it was going to be and to what extent.

During the process of putting our personal things away and seeing Drill Sergeant Brown locking it all up in one room, both Drill Sergeant

Martinez and Drill Sergeant Padilla explained to all of us that we had assigned bunk beds, and whomever we bunked with, was going to be our battle buddy for the remainder of basic training.

Hoping that I would get someone who was cool and down to earth, my battle buddy turned out to be this country kid from east Texas named Thomas, a red headed freckled faced guy who always kept me laughing with his deep southern country accent. As that day came to an end, my first night in basic training, I laid in my bed listening to the 9 o'clock bugle sounding off, while thinking to myself... *"Did I make the right choice?"* as the third platoon's sleeping bay fell into silence for the rest of the night.

Early that next morning, most of us were already up before 5 a.m., because we were so nervous after hearing all the rumors about how the Drill Sergeants would come into the bay, yelling and hitting an empty metal garbage can screaming for everyone to get out of bed. So, as time drew closer for us to get up, down the hallway we could hear 2nd platoons drill sergeants screaming for their guys to get out of bed and outside before they counted down from 30.

"Damn, what the hell!" I thought to myself, fiddling my fingers.

As I laid there nervous and excited at the same time, I wondered when it would be our turn to be rushed outside like the other platoon, when suddenly the lights came on... *"You have 20 seconds to get outside and into PT (**P**hysical **T**raining) formation or your asses are mine!"* Drill Sergeant Brown said very calmly.

Jumping up and out of my bed, while hitting my head on the top bunk beds metal frame, I yelled out loud… *"AAWW, SHIT!"*

"Are you okay?" Thomas asked me.

"I'll be alright. Damn, that hurt!" as I struggled to put on my shoes, fearful I wouldn't make it outside in time.

With my eyes filled with tears and I could not see what I was doing, I just put on my shoes and took off running downstairs with everyone else with my shoe's strings untied, just to make it to formation on time.

When everyone made it downstairs and into formation, Drill Sergeant Brown put us all in the front lean and rest position (Push Ups), as he started to yell at all of us… *"Every single one of you in this formation is fucked up! First, not one of you came downstairs as a team, but individually! Second, walking in the center of my floor and not going along the walls, as I had explained to you all on your first day here! Third, where in the hell are you all's flashlights and canteens? KEEP PUSHING!"*

As I looked around, while struggling to do pushups, none of us had them, as I recalled that we were told the night before to bring them down with us for PT. But I guess we were so nervous and not thinking about what was said to us that all of us had forgotten about what we were instructed to do the day before.

Shortly after that day, we started to learn quickly what it meant to work as a team. You can say we got sick and tired of being smoked (pushups, flutter kicks and sprints), all the time.

After our first week of basic training, our Drill Sergeants were explaining to us the road marches that we had to do and the names of the hills that we were going to know by pain; Agony Hill, Cardiac Hill, Misery Hill and Heart Break Hill. These four hills are famously known at Fort Knox for the pain that they caused, and rumor had it, even a couple of deaths, so they say.

During our first 5K road march, we went down Agony Hill and back up Misery Hill. Going down Agony Hill was easy at first for me, but due to its steep downgrade descent, the weight of my gear shot agonizing pain down through my legs. Leaning back as we made our way down Agony Hill, we did our best to keep ourselves from falling forward and onto our faces, or from rolling down the hill with every step that we took. On that long downhill march, we all kept hoping to reach the bottom of this hill to relieve some of the pain, and to find a way back to the barracks without experiencing more pain on top of what we were already experiencing.

When our Company made it down to the bottom of Agony Hill, Drill Sergeant Padilla started yelling to the whole platoon... *"Don't look up! Just suck it up men and keep looking down at the ground! Keep your spacing and don't bunch up!"*

"What is he talking about?" A few of us started to ask one another, as I watched the platoons ahead of us start to turn to the right and around the corner.

Walking around the base of Agony Hill and turning a long right curve towards Misery Hill, of course we all looked up and to me, Misery Hill looked like it was a part of the sky. As I was screaming on the inside… *"GOD NO!"* while looking up wondering who the insane person was who thought about paving this road like this, as I started to pray that I would not pass out or die, as we started walking up Misery Hill.

Listening to Drill Sergeant Padilla and Drill Sergeant Martinez yelling at us to look down towards the ground and not to bunch up, I started to lean all my weight forward into the hill, to take it on headfirst. Going up this hill was unlike anything I had ever experienced in my entire life at that time. At the start of going up Misery Hill, I started to pray for gravity to be on my side, but in this case, it wasn't. Yes, it was hard to come down Agony Hill, but going up Misery Hill was misery to the 10th power.

During the time that I was struggling to make it up Misery Hill, I glanced over at my friends, PVT Mooradian and PFC (Private First Class) Olson who I meet on my first day when we were in-processing, who was also struggling going up the hill. PFC Olson's face was dark purple, and Drill Sergeant Padilla kept yelling at him to breath, while PVT Mooradian was right behind him with a bright red face gasping for air.

Watching our Drill Sergeants walking up and down this hill with ease, while talking to the platoon to keep it together, PVT Mooradian yelled out to some of us that he had to use the latrine (restroom) really bad. While we all tried telling him to hold it in until we got back to the barracks, PVT Mooradian wasn't listening to us when he called out loud Drill Sergeant Padilla's name... *"What Private?"* he replied.

"Dude, I got-ta take a major shit man!"

My eyes almost popped out of my face when I heard him say dude and man, to Drill Sergeant Padilla.

"WHO THE FUCK ARE YOU CALLING DUDE, PRIVATE?"

"Dude, I got-ta go really bad man!"

"WHAT!"

Then without question, PVT Mooradian got off the road and over into the ditch and pulled down his trousers and started to use the wood line (using the tree line outside to relieve himself).

"WHAT THE HELL ARE YOU DOING SOLDIER?" Drill Sergeant Padilla yelled out to him.

"I'm taking a major shit dude!"

In that second, Drill Sergeant Padilla pushed PVT Mooradian into his own crap while he was still in the process of relieving himself. By this time, we were all laughing our butts off to what just happened to PVT Mooradian, as we kept walking towards the top of the hill.

32

When we made it to the top of Misery Hill, we felt like the walking dead, and I often wondered how in the world did I make it to the top of this hill, without passing out or dying.

After arriving back to our Company's barracks location and forming back up into our platoon formations, Drill Sergeant Padilla came walking up with PVT Mooradian who was covered in his own crap and was yelling at him for calling him dude and man. Just looking at PVT Mooradian's face expression made me want to laugh so hard at the both of them, as we all did our best not to laugh again while standing in formation.

Throughout the rest of basic training, most everyone within our platoon would ask PVT Mooradian what he was thinking when he called Drill Sergeant Padilla "DUDE and MAN."

Whenever we were all sitting around making small talk with one another or as a platoon, someone would eventually yell out loud... *"DUDE, I GOTTA TAKE A MAJOR SHIT MAN!"*, which always got the whole platoon laughing their faces off whenever we saw PVT Mooradian walking up.

SOMETHING FEELS WRONG

During one of our 15K road marches in mid-October 1998, I kept telling myself that I had made a good choice in enlisting into the Army as my career for military service, but I also knew something wasn't right. We had been told from day one that we were all the same color, and no matter what race or where we were from, once we had put on the military uniform, we were all the same color. But most of the time, that wasn't the case.

I grew up as an Air Force brat and had all races as friends. We all hung out together with no issues of who was Black or who was White or Latino. Now, here in basic training, both African American and Caucasian soldiers wouldn't hang out with each other, and all my friends turned out to be Caucasian or Latino's and I knew why that was.

As a person with a military family background, a lot of the African American soldiers didn't accept me for who I was as a person. At times I was told I didn't sound African American or didn't carry myself as one. "Red Bone" was the word some African American soldiers would call me, and at every time I would brush it off. I knew I wasn't a reflection of who they were or what they were accustomed to seeing or being around.

In 3rd Platoon Mad Dogs, you could tell which soldiers grew up around other races and those who didn't. My battle buddy PVT Thomas told me; I was the first person of color he had ever talked to in his entire life. He explained to me that he grew up in a part of East Texas where they talked and made jokes about black people using the words... *"Nigger this and Nigger's that!"*

As a result, from everyone's personal background, there are a lot of racial tension and racial segregation in parts of the U.S. Army. Although we were told in basic training that we are all the same and equal, people didn't abandon their attitudes and upbringings just because they were now wearing a military uniform. The Army tries to break those habits in basic training, but how can you break someone's life-long mentality that people will always have the hardest time letting go? In the tense and enclosed world of the military, people cling to their upbringing even more, when faced with any individual or group of people that they do not like.

One day while our platoon was in the barracks cleaning our weapons, my friend PVT Mooradian (who is white), got into an argument with PVT Thornton (who is black), about something small that blew up into something bigger. While PVT Thornton was in PVT Mooradian's face cursing him out, some of the African American soldiers in the platoon surrounded PVT Mooradian, while the white soldiers stood to the side and didn't intervene. PVT Mooradian stood his ground as PVT Thornton threatened him and kept pushing him in his face until he started to bleed from his noise.

Seeing what was going on, I knew PVT Mooradian didn't stand a chance by himself, and being that he was my friend, I wasn't going to let him stand-alone against all those angry soldiers. As quickly as I could, I jumped up and ran towards the group surrounding PVT Mooradian and broke into the circle that had formed around him and stood toe to toe with PVT Thornton... *"Push me instead, ass hole!"* I demanded.

"GET THE FUCK OUT OF MY WAY, YOU HIGH YELLOW WANNA BE NIGGA!" PVT Thornton yelled out loud.

I couldn't stand on the side and watch anyone be treated with disrespect. Especially because of their skin color or who they were.

"This needs to stop and stop now," I told the group of soldiers. *"We're all one team here, and no one in this room is bigger or better than the next man, regardless of skin color, Thornton! We all need to respect each other and work together no matter how much we can't stand one another."*

When the rest of the platoon saw an African American soldier standing up for a Caucasian soldier in front of other African American soldiers, it gave the rest of the platoon confidence to step forward and break up the confrontation.

Never-the-less, I was immediately disowned by most of the African American soldiers in our platoon for the remainder of basic training. Since I wasn't friends with any of them from the start, I didn't care how they felt about me before or after that incident. From that day forth, their attitudes went from... *"Hey, what's up Linson?"* to *"Get the fuck away from me!"*

From that day on, I earned a lot of respect from everyone else, and even from soldiers outside of our platoon who heard about that incident. PVT Mooradian was my best friend in basic training and without question, I was there for him, and he was there for me.

As we got closer to the end of basic training, it was time for our final and last road march before we graduated from basic training. Drill Sergeant Martinez, Drill Sergeant Padilla and Drill Sergeant Brown warned us about Heartbreak Hill that might in fact kill one or two of us, for it is the mother of all hills at Fort Knox. But most of us knew they were only trying to scare us into thinking that we might die on our final and last road march after eight weeks of training.

On a dark and cold morning towards the end of November 1998, Bravo Company 2-46th Infantry formed up for our final and last field training exercise (FTX). While standing in formation waiting for everyone to get ready to head out, I started to look up towards the clear night skies, staring up towards the stars wondering where life would take me after this week was done and over with, and I was on my way to AIT (**A**dvanced **I**ndividual **T**raining).

As our Company Commander started to give a speech about what was to come during our FTX, I felt a rush of adrenalin surging throughout my entire body, as the early morning's cold winds kicked through the formation. After our Company Commander turned the formation back to our First Sergeant, he gave the Company a right face, and in a rhythm sound, we all took off marching while our Drill Sergeants sung cadence to their platoons as we all sung the songs back, while marching into the darkness with our red flashlights leading the way.

While I listened to everyone around me sing the songs that kept us in rhythm with one another, I kept looking back up towards the stars and the full moon, as the heavenly lights were guiding us though the dark back roads of Fort Knox Kentucky. Hearing the cadence and tramping of our feet and the sounds of our weapons and rucksacks jangled together to the rhythm of the march, I could hear the faint cries of the birds singing as we marched pass their trees that morning... *"Has it been almost nine weeks already GOD?"* I asked myself, looking around at everybody.

By that afternoon, sweat was dripping down from my eyelids when Drill Sergeant Brown yelled out loud... *"HEARTBREAK HILL!"*

At the first sight of Heartbreak Hill, I thought to myself... *"How in God's name, am I going to make this hill?"* after getting a full view of this hill from the adjacent hill.

"Suck it up men. You all made it this far, this isn't nothing." Drill Sergeant Martinez shouted. *"When you get to the bottom of the hill and start to make your way up Heartbreak, use your hands to help you walk up the hill!"*

"What! We have to use our hands for this hill? Oh, hell naw!" I whispered to myself.

Making our way towards the bottom on the adjacent hill towards Heartbreak Hill, the other platoons ahead of us looked like ants on the sidewalk, as we continued to descend into the valley below Heartbreak Hill. In that long walk down hill, I kept looking back behind our platoon to see what everyone looked like from behind... *"Turn around Linson. Stop looking back here, unless you want to go back up and come back down again soldier?"* Drill Sergeant Martinez yelled out to me.

"No, I don't, Drill Sergeant!" as I turned my head back to the front.

Walking up that hill felt like death to me. Halfway up Heartbreak Hill, I looked back and wondered who on GOD's green earth built this road.

As we got closer to the top of the hill, I looked up at the platoon's ahead of us as we started to slow down and bunch up, while all the Drill Sergeants started to yell at us to space out from each other. As my weapon started to drag on the ground, I actually had to use my hands to help keep myself from stopping. I knew if any one of us had stood straight up, there would be no way to stop them from rolling back down this hill until they reached the bottom.

After a few more minutes of pain in my entire body, that seemed like a lifetime, I was in disbelief but greatly relieved when I finally crest the top of Heartbreak Hill.

When every platoon was over the top of Heartbreak Hill and two hours later, we finally made it to our FTX location, where we started our four days of training on how to navigate the land using maps and other military equipment for tactical use. After our four days of FTX training was over, the return march back to main post felt easier to me. Knowing that we were all finished with our nine weeks of basic training and looking forward to graduation, it felt good to know that I had accomplished a task that I thought I would not live to see from day one of signing up to join the U.S. Army.

As we made it back to garrison (Main Post), most of us were shouting the cadence with pride as we marched onto the parade field at Brigade Headquarters. Standing in a Company mass formation, we listened to the Brigade Commander telling us how proud he was of our achievements and how the Army was going to change our lives, and how we were going to change the Army in the years to come.

During that thirty minute or so speech that our Brigade Commander gave us, I stood there at the position of "at ease," thinking about how I used to look and act when I first stepped foot into the Army. Standing there reflecting over my past, I remembered how my mental way of thinking had changed and how this Army life would change me for the long run... *"I can't believe that it's almost over."* I thought to myself, looking around at everyone, without turning my head that much.

Knowing that the future is always uncertain, I knew that something big was waiting for me in the Army that would change my life forever.

FORT LEONARD WOOD

After getting all our field equipment cleaned and turned back into CIF (Central Issue Facility), me and all my battle buddies would sit around and talk about the days when we first went into the Army recruiter's office back where we came from. I knew time was short for us and I didn't want to lose any of my friends that I had made while in basic training. But as Drill Sergeant Brown would tell us... *"The Army is a small world. The best time you will ever have, will be in basic training."* Boy, was he telling the truth.

That following day after graduation, most of the platoon had orders to go to Fort Leonard Wood Missouri for AIT. Looking around at everyone who had their own buses to head out to their next training location, I felt like I was leaving my family all over again, as we all were getting ready to go our separate ways. Knowing that I was an 88 Mike, I didn't realize that there were more than twenty of us in Bravo Company 2-46th Infantry, and none of us knew what was to come next when we were told that we were all going to Fort Leonard Wood, Missouri for AIT.

As we gathered around and waited for our bus to show up, Drill Sergeant Martinez asked our group who wanted to be the team leader in charge of the bus ride to our next duty station. Looking around for a couple of seconds to see that no one was raising their hand to take the task, I quickly volunteered to take charge of the group until we arrived at Fort Leonard Wood.

After we boarded our bus, when it arrived at our Company late that night, I decided to sit in the front of the charter bus to get a better view of everyone that was on there. After the bus took off from our Company, I felt an uneasy feeling that something very dramatic was about to take place in my military career. Sort of like the *Twilight Zone,* opening another door into an unforeseen future. *"Something isn't right,"* I thought to myself, but I couldn't put my finger on it, as the bus got onto the highway.

Now that my military career is over and I have the benefit of hindsight and now knowing that many people cannot and will not accept other people who are different from themselves. Especially those who cannot accept others that will not change who they are, in order to make themselves feel better about having someone who is not like them around them. In my case, I can sum it all up in one word, Homophobia.

But currently, none of what I did not see was on my radar. I felt I was going down a dark tunnel and didn't know what was at the end or where I would end up at. I just knew something was lurking in this dark tunnel and I couldn't figure out what it was for the life of me. But I knew something was there, and I wasn't going to like it.

Not a soul was talking on the bus, as we went down the highway that night. In the quietness of that bus ride, I kept wondering if I wasn't the only one who was sad that we were leaving our friends behind, and if anyone else had this discomfort of not knowing what AIT was all about.

That night, the bus ride seemed to last for a lifetime as we encountered a severe thunderstorm that night. As I looked around the bus, everyone was asleep except for me. I felt so nervous because I had never overseen so many people in my life, and I was worried if I had fallen asleep, someone on the bus would have died, and it would have been my fault. So, I was a nervous wreck sitting in the front of the bus, as I forced myself to stay awake for most of the night.

While random flashes of light kept lightning up the sky all around us, I stared out of the front window of the bus watching traffic passing us by, while remembering the days in basic training when we were crawling in the mud during live fire exercises, and the days we exercised for PT early in the mornings. For the most part, just the days of being around my friends is what mattered to me at that moment.

As my eyes started to get heavy, I thought to myself… *"If I could make it through basic training, I could make it through anything this Army could throw at me."* While looking towards the horizon, as the first signs of morning started to crest the skyline, I was sitting in a daze trying to stay awake but before I could think about the days to come, I was dead to the world. (Sleeping)

43

By noon, I had woken up just a few miles south of St Louis, Missouri while everyone on the bus was awake and talking about their basic training experiences and what was to come next after AIT. Since it was around noon time, we stopped at a local McDonald's to get something to eat for lunch, and soon after we were back on the road heading to Fort Leonard Wood.

When the bus first came to the front gates of Fort Leonard Wood, I felt sick to my stomach as we drove onto the base that afternoon. Knowing that this was a new level in my military career, I knew it was time for me to learn my job as an 88 Mike so I could become a better soldier for the U.S. Army. After being dropped off at our new training Company, Bravo Company 58th Transportation Battalion, Drill Sergeant Berry, one of our Drill Instructors, introduced himself to us as our Platoon Sergeant. After reporting into the Company, he welcomed us to Bravo Company 58th Transportation Battalion and explained to us that we were going to be in 3rd Platoon Mad Dawgs. When he told us this, most of us started to laugh and explained to him that some of us had come from a platoon with the same platoon motto, "Mad Dogs" but not "Mad Dawgs."

Drill Sergeant Berry wasn't too happy that we were making fun of how they decided to spell dogs. But Drill Sergeant Berry told us that we would get used to the sound of it and explained to us that we were now in a co-ed unit working around females. As soon as he said that we were all shocked to know that we had to interact with females while in training, yet alone female Drill Sergeants, since we were from an all-male basic training. Still, Drill Sergeant Berry assured us that everything would work out over time, and that we had arrived at the beginning of a four-day weekend, which was our time to go and get some…. "Sex."

During our four days off, I was bored out of my mind walking around post every day, trying to find something to do besides the PX (**P**ost **E**xchange) and the movie theater. On the last day of our four days off, I ran into another soldier who was in my platoon by the name of PV2 Jones, who was also thrilled to start AIT. During that day, me and PV2 Jones talked about our time in the Army and where we came from in the world. To me, PV2 Jones was a little bit of a book worm, but he was a cool guy to keep around from time to time.

Later that night, the Company had an accountability formation to see if everyone had reported back in time when we were told to be back at the barracks at a certain time. After our accountability formation, we were introduced to our new 1st SGT and Company Commander along with the rest of our training instructors. After listing to what was expected of us while in AIT, Drill Sergeant Berry told the entire platoon to meet upstairs in the male's bay area for further instructions.

After everybody had made it up to the male bay area, we all stood around listening to Drill Sergeant Berry talking about what was to come during our six weeks of training, and what he expected out of us while we were there. During his debriefing, I was looking around at all the new soldiers I looked forward to getting to know while I was in training. When Drill Sergeant Berry had dismissed the females back downstairs to their sleeping area, he instructed us males to partner up with a battle buddy for the remainder of AIT. While looking around for a potential battle buddy, me and another good friend of mine named Private McCalister, who was from 2nd platoon back at Fort Knox, we decided to partner up together. PVT McCalister was a jokester along with one of his best friends named PFC Brooks. Every time you looked up, you would see these two knuckle heads always playing a prank on someone. But later during AIT, both PVT McCalister and PFC Brooks decided to play a prank on me that didn't end well.

One day when I was asleep on my bed during the daytime, both decided to put shaving cream in my hand and tickle my face with a feather. After a while, I slapped myself in the face with a hand full of shaving cream. When I woke up, I wasn't in the best of moods and in the processes of cleaning myself up, both PVT McCalister and PFC Brooks told me that PV2 Sizemore (another soldier from my platoon, from Fort Knox), had pulled the prank on me. So, since I was upset and was looking to get back at whoever did this to me, in retaliation I went to PV2 Sizemore's bed and sprayed both his pillow and blanket down with shaving cream.

"Hey Sizemore, come see what Linson is doing to your bed man." PFC Brooks yelled out across the male's sleeping bay.

Standing next to PV2 Sizemore's bed waiting for him to show up so I could curse him out, PFC Brooks started laughing his face off when he saw that PV2 Sizemore's bed was covered in white shaving cream.

46

When PVT Sizemore came to his sleeping area, let's say he wasn't happy with what he saw. In a flash of an eye, me and PV2 Sizemore were in each other's faces, and when I mean we were face to face, I mean we were face to face cursing each other out. After a few seconds of cursing one another, PVT McCalister came around the corner or Sizemore's bed to see what all the fighting was about and seeing that me and PV2 Sizemore were about to come to blows, he decided to tell me that PV2 Sizemore wasn't the one who played the prank on me, but instead it was him and Brooks that put the shaving cream in my hand. But at the time, me and PV2 Sizemore were too angry to listen to their confessions, as we kept yelling back at one another.

Knowing that I was in the wrong, I managed to calm myself down and apologize to PV2 Sizemore and told him that I will clean up his bed. But being the person that he was, PV2 Sizemore kept going off at the mouth and the other soldiers had to separate the two of us after I blew back up at him. After that day, PV2 Sizemore accepted my apology after we both had calmed down from the prank that PVT McCalister and PFC Brooks had played on us. I myself thought the incident was over with, until one of the female soldiers in my platoon heard about what had happened to me and decided to tell Drill Sergeant Berry about the situation that took place. You can say, things took off from there.

Drill Sergeant Berry called the platoon into formation in the male bay area and ordered me to stand in front of the platoon and explain to everyone what had happened. With fire in his eyes, Drill Sergeant

Berry walked up to me and yelled out loud... *"YOU LET THEM PUNK YOU, SOLDIER?!!"*

"No, Drill Sergeant." I replied.

Drill Sergeant Berry was furious that I didn't physically fight back against PVT McCalister and PFC Brooks for playing this prank on me. But by this time, the entire platoon was laughing their faces off, except Drill Sergeant Berry who was standing toe to toe with me.

"Point out the ones who played this prank on you soldier." Drill Sergeant Berry ordered me.

After pointing out the two soldiers who played the prank on me, Drill Sergeant Berry started to verbally lay into these soldiers for playing pranks on their fellow soldiers. After Drill Sergeant Berry had finished chewing them a new butt, he quickly turned and looked at me... *"From now on, your name is PUNK. I can't believe you let these motherfucker's punk you out and you're from Mississippi! Oh, hell naw soldier!"*

Being that I knew Drill Sergeant Berry was also from Mississippi, it seemed that I needed to represent our state with pride and stand up to anyone who got in our way. As I was thinking to myself when Drill Sergeant Berry was yelling at me, trying not to laugh with everyone else... *"What they did wasn't that bad. So why am I getting this ass chewing from you?"* while looking at Drill Sergeant Berry's face expressions shifting from one expression to the next.

48

"All three of yall get downstairs and wait outside my office!" he ordered.

We had no idea what was in store for us late that night with Drill Sergeant Berry. But when Drill Sergeant Berry came back downstairs after speaking with the platoon, he smoked the everlasting crap out of us for three hours and then sent us to bed. PVT McCalister and PFC Brooks made it clear that they were upset with me for ratting them out. At the time I didn't care if they were mad or not, but the only thing I wanted to do was to shower and go to bed.

Throughout the rest of AIT, Drill Sergeant Berry would look at me, with his eyes bulging out of his skull, as he kept screaming *"Motherfucker"* and *"Punk Ass"* towards me, which gave everyone a good laugh, including myself when he wasn't looking.

As part of our training in AIT, we started to drive 18 wheelers and other large, wheeled military vehicles, around this three-mile-long training track. One of the soldiers from back in basic training named PV2 James, who I stood up against when they tried to dog out my friend PVT Mooradian, told me how mad he was, when I ratted out PVT McCalister and PFC Brooks. So, he says.

Most every day from that day on when Drill Sergeant Berry smoked all three of us, PV2 James became more and more hostile towards me, when I was around him. With every confrontation, I stood my ground and refused to back down from his thug street attitude. But every day

49

it seemed I had to deal with his ignorant attitude, when it came time for us to work together.

One day while driving around the training track, I stopped to help the vehicle in front of us that had broken down temporally, and PV2 James was in the truck behind me waiting for us all to get moving again. After I had helped fix their truck, I ran back to my vehicle to take off moving again, when PV2 James and his driver drove around me and according to the rules of the track, no vehicles were allowed to pass another vehicle, stopped or moving. So, knowing the rules and I knew PV2 James knew them also, I really wanted to get my spot back after they went around us.

So, after catching back up with the two vehicles ahead of me, going above the training tracks speed limit, I began to pass PV2 James's truck on a good stretch of road exceeding the speed limit of 30 mph. Watching PV2 James's truck speeding up as well as I began to shift from gear to gear as fast as I could, PV2 James started to yell out loud and hang his body outside of his window furiously cursing at me as I passed them back up on the right side of their vehicle.

When we came to the end of the course, PV2 James jumped out of his truck and ran up to me yelling... *"YOU TRIED TO KILL ME, MOTHERFUCKA!"*

Seeing that he was approaching my location ready to fight, I started to yell back at him... *"You know the rules soldier! And I wasn't trying to kill you, you paranoid motherfucka!"*

"FUCK YOU!" as PV2 James ran towards me.

Before we could come to blows, soldiers in my platoon got a hold of us, and tried to calm us both down. But PV2 James did all he could to get to me, as every soldier did their best to separate us apart.

For the rest of our AIT, PV2 James and I weren't nice to one another to say the least. On the last day of AIT, we finally apologized to one another, but no matter what he had to say to me, I didn't trust him or believe none of his words that he had to say to me that day.

Looking back over my years in the Army, I can truly say that soldiers hold grudges for years on end. In some places within the Army, tension is always in the ranks where soldiers don't get along with one another, and you can see it as clear as day whenever something is going bad within that platoon. In the places that I have been, a lot of soldiers didn't get along with one another about things long since gone, and like most, they tend to react to one another in ways unheard of.

After our graduation from AIT, I wanted to get out of Fort Lenard Wood and get to my permanent duty station as fast as the Army could get me there. During our last mass formation, Drill Sergeant Berry started to call out our names with our next duty stations that followed. After he had called out my name, I was surprised I was being sent to Fort Hood, Texas when I was hoping to get an assignment out in Georgia. **(Fort Hood is now called Fort Cavazos)**

Getting my orders in hand and putting my things into another charter bus, I was more than happy to see that I was leaving Fort Leonard Wood (Nick named, Fort Lost in the Woods), once and for all.

I felt so overwhelmed that I had made it through another level of my military career, and I looked forward to the opportunity to employ my new skills as an 88 Mike at Fort Hood, Texas.

My Nightmare Begins

On the bus ride to St. Louis International Airport, I felt the same unease feelings about what was to come next. *"Keep Moving"* I kept telling myself. There were eighteen of us from AIT who had orders to Fort Hood, but only a few of us went straight to our next duty assignment, while others went home on leave (Vacation Days). While sitting with my fellow soldiers on the bus ride to the airport, I just thought to myself that I didn't care which Division I was sent to, but the only thing I wanted was to be sent to a transportation unit.

Knowing that our flight wasn't until later that day, we all tried to make the best of what time we had, once we arrived early that morning at the airport.

"Delta flight 105 to Dallas is now boarding gate G-15, all seats" as one of the employees came on the intercom system and announced that afternoon... *"Damn, it's about time! Shit!"* I told one of my Army buddies next to me.

Knowing that this was going to be my second time flying in my life, I just knew I had to do my best and not show how nervous I was, and to try my hardest not to sequel like I did when I first flew on the airplane to basic training. *"Hold it together Howard, you can do this. You're a soldier now. Let's show everyone that you're a man and not a little boy*

53

anymore. *Just hold it together."* I kept telling myself, while buckling my seat belt. Let's say my flight to Dallas Texas was a nerve breaking moment for me. But this time around I was very, very quiet.

"So here we are in Dallas, Texas." I told myself stepping off our flight. *"Just one more flight to go and you'll be in Killeen Texas."* I thought to myself.

Shortly after arriving at DFW International Airport, we boarded a connection flight to Killeen, and this time around I was horrified to see the type of aircraft that we were being put into. A twin turbine propeller airplane, with single side seats on the inside of the airplane.

"Oh Christ, this is fucked up! Please GOD, don't let this airplane go down!" I was screaming on the inside, while looking for my seat.

After boarding the airplane and finding my seat, we all looked around at each other and talked about how messed up this airplane was from the word "GO".

This time around, I really kept myself from blowing up and screaming out with fear. Taking off was the easy part, but the closer we got to Killeen, the bumpier it got while flying through a thunderstorm. In the twist and turns and dramatic drops that the airplane did, I felt like throwing up all over the side window... *"Is this how the Army wishes to scare their new soldier? Shit, well they're doing a damn good job at it."* I said to another frightened soldier across from me.

After coming out of this thunderstorm and descending into Killeen's Regional Airport, I looked out of my window to see the town's lights below us, as I thought to myself... *"Well, this is it. Killeen Texas, here we come."*

Touching down and taxiing down the runway, I sat back into my seat and congratulated myself for not making a fool of myself on both flight from St. Louis and Dallas.

Stepping off the airplane in the middle of a cool night in February 1999, I took in a deep inhale to smell the central Texas air and while looking off into the distance to get a better look at the town of Killeen Texas. Standing there while looking off into the distance thinking to myself... *"How will this place that I'll call home turn out to be?"*

Picking up our bags off the tarmac, we all started to walk together into the airport where a 21st Replacement liaison was waiting for us to take us to Ft. Hood. That night, the van ride to post seemed to take forever, and the butterflies in my stomach didn't help to calm me down at all, as we drove onto Fort Hood that night... *"Here comes the real Army, Howard."* I whispered to myself, while looking into the dark at the ghostly like shaped buildings on Fort Hood.

In the week that it took for us to in-process at 21st Replacement, I made a new friend named PFC Plorde, who was a mechanic and was also eager to get to his permanent duty unit as well. When the day came for us to receive our orders, I crossed my fingers hoping to hear 4th ID after my name was called out... *"Linson."*

"Here!" I replied.

"Divarty, 4th ID"

"Divarty, what the hell is that? Humm, that didn't sound like a transportation unit." I thought to myself, listening to everybody else's assignments.

Regardless, just to hear 4th ID in my orders made me happy, but still didn't know what was ahead of me from that day on.

Later that day, a Divarty liaison came to 21st Replacement to pick me up. He explained to me that I was on my way to 3-16th Field Artillery, a unit within the Divarty Brigade. After receiving my orders assigning me to 3-16th FA, I didn't quite understand this assignment, not knowing anything about the Field Artillery, I really had hoped to be assigned to a transportation unit within the 4th Infantry Division, but now, that wasn't the case.

Sitting around Divarty Headquarters for a few minutes, a liaison from 3-16th S-1 office came over to escort me to the Battalion's Headquarters across the courtyard from Divarty.

"Why am I in a field artillery unit?" I asked the liaison.

"I don't know. Division has been sending a lot of different MOS's to us for quite some time now. But I'm sure you'll fall in with the rest of the 88 Mike's we have here."

"Yall have 88 Mike's here?" I replied in shock.

"Yes. Some of them have been here for years now."

"Wow, they never told us we would be assigned to other places besides transportation."

"Well sometimes we have to learn to accept change, even if we don't like it, new bee."

"New Bee?"

"Yea that means new guy. You never heard of that expression?"

"No." I replied, looking around the courtyard.

"Well get used to it, they say that a lot around here. Well, here we are." The liaison opened the door to the 3-16th and 4-42nd FA Headquarters building. *"We'll get you in-processed up here first, then someone from HHB Battery will come to get you."*

"HHB Battery!" looking back at the S-1 liaison confused.

"Yea. HHB is the Headquarter Battery in the Battalion, then its Alpha, Bravo and Charlie Batteries, a total of four batteries in 3-16th FA." the liaison explained to me.

"Wow, I never heard of such strange names for companies around here. Field Artillery I see; do we get to blow shit up?" I replied in a cheerful manner.

"Hahaha. No not you new bee. Only the 13 Bravos (Gun Bunnies), get to blow up things. You'll see, once you go out to the field."

"Well, I can't wait to see that." as I followed the liaison into the S-1 office.

In the time that it took for me to in-process into the Battalion, I quickly dismissed any and all of the butterfly feelings that I had while I was sitting around waiting for someone to come and pick me up over from 21st Replacement.

"Is this him?" a Sergeant asked the S-1 clerk.

"Yes, Sergeant Perez this is yalls new soldier, Private Second Class Linson."

Recognizing that one of my NCO's was here to pick me up, I quickly stood up... *"Hello Sergeant Perez, my name is Private Second Class Linson."*

"Okay. Where's your bags soldier." SGT Perez asked me.

"Outside Sergeant."

"Let's go."

Following SGT Perez out of the S-1 office, two more soldiers were standing outside waiting for SGT Perez to come back out with me in-tow… *"This is Specialist Smotherson and Specialist Mobley. They will help you with your bags and get you settled in over in the barracks private."* SGT Perez said.

"Hello everyone, I'm Private Linson." I replied to the other two soldiers.

"What's up Linson? My name is Smotherson, you can call me smut. I'm a 13 Bravo and this is Mobley one of the 88 Mike's in the ammo platoon." SPC Smotherson replied.

"What's up big 88?" SPC Mobley announced out loud towards me in a joking manner.

"Nothing, Specialist Mobley."

"Private Linson, Specialist Mobley is going to be your battle buddy to help you in-process into the unit all the way, okay." SGT Perez said. *"Do you have any questions for me soldier?"*

"Yes sergeant. I'm an 88 Mike, why was I sent to a field artillery unit when I belong in a transportation unit?"

"Well soldier, your job is needed here as well."

"How so Sergeant Perez?"

"We have trucks here that need soldiers like yourself to drive around helping out with delivering ammo, and your skills are needed here in the field artillery."

"Wow, I wished they told us about this in AIT."

"Well, you're here now soldier, and this is your home now, the field artillery. Don't worry, we will take good care of you." SGT Perez said with a smile on his face. *"By the way I will be your squad leader, and your team leader is Sergeant Ford. You'll meet him later today."*

"Okay, Sergeant Perez." as I looked back at him.

On the way down to HHB, SGT Perez introduced me to other soldiers who were in the Battery and a few soldiers who were also in my platoon. Walking through the front doors of HHB, SGT Perez pointed out our platoon's office location and where my Battery Commander and 1st SGT's office were located on both sides of the ammo platoon's office.

"Who's that Sergeant Perez?" a voice called out from the ammo platoon's office.

"This is Private Linson, Sergeant Madyun." SGT Perez replied.

"Come on in here soldier," SFC Madyun ordered. *"Where are you from Linson?"*

"I'm from Mississippi, Sergeant Madyun." I replied in a nervous tone.

"No need to be nervous Linson, we are all family here, you'll see." SFC Madyun assured me. *"Well, Specialist Mobley is going to help you get around and settled in. Also, it's the end of the day and when you report to PT formation in the morning at 0630, be in your BDU's (Battle*

Dress Uniform) and oh yea, welcome to 3-16th FA... Wait, wait...what's wrong with your boots soldier?" as SFC Madyun looked down at my boots.

"What do you mean Sergeant Madyun?" I replied confused to the question that he just asked me.

"Why isn't your boot's shiny like Specialist Mobley's boot's soldier? Mobley put your boot next too Private Linson's boots." SFC Madyun replied.

"See how Mobley's boots look shiny to where I can see my reflection in them, Linson?"

"Yes Sergeant." I replied looking down at my boots and SPC Mobley's boots.

"Yours need to look just like his come tomorrow morning. Do I make myself clear soldier?" SFC Madyun demanded.

"Yes, Sergeant Madyun."

"Now go get some rest and also, the First Sergeant and Commander will see you tomorrow, okay."

"Yes, Sergeant Madyun." As I walked out of the office confused about why I needed to make my boots look like SPC Mobley's.

"Wow," I thought to myself. *"This sucks! Why do I have to shine my boots like his. The regulation says evenly brush shine, not spit or highly*

gloss shined. Argh, my night is going to be a long one." I thought to myself.

Later that night, while I sat in my empty room in the barracks spit shining my boots, I kept thinking what was next to come, since field artillery wasn't something that I hadn't trained for or even heard of until now. As I listened to the soldiers screaming and yelling out in the hallway, I wondered if I was in the ghetto or projects of Fort Hood. At times, there were random gunshots and military police sirens going off every ten to fifteen minutes during the night.

Before the terrorist attacks on September 11 of 2001, most all Army posts were open posts, which meant that civilians could walk or drive on and off post without being checked for identification. Because of the lack of security, there wasn't much order or discipline in the barracks in east Fort Hood. To my understanding and knowledge at that time, east Fort Hood in particular, was known as the ghetto of Fort Hood. Some soldiers throughout my unit were thugs and drug dealers. From time to time, I would hear stories about how female visitors were being sexually assaulted and soldiers who had beef with each other would settle the matter with drive-by or group jumping's.

From day to day, I often worried about getting shot myself, whenever I was out minding my own business. At times I would leave the barracks only during daylight hours and would return before the sun went down, just so I could see who was walking around and acting up. When I did return to the barracks, later in the day, whenever I saw a group of soldiers hanging around in large groups, I would walk in the opposite direction to stay away from them, and that's even if I had to walk the long way around just to get to my room.

If the tense atmosphere of living in the barracks wasn't enough, I was already upset that I had been sent to the wrong unit. So, I thought at the time. At one point I would constantly complain to SGT Perez that I should have been sent to a transportation unit and not a field artillery unit. Most of the time, that didn't go over too well with SGT Perez and would eventually cause me a few bumps later down the road. In time, I would eventually learn not to complain about the things I couldn't control or change.

I have learned over the years, when you complain in the Army, your leaders make you pay for it. At times, you're singled out or put on extra work details to get you to shut up. Even after you stop complaining, once you're labeled as lazy or lack thereof, you'll always be viewed as such, even if you haven't complained in months or years.

During the first couple of months, in 3-16th, I always kept to myself, and if I wasn't hanging out with my friend Plorde, who worked on the other side of Fort Hood, I was always out chasing trains from town to town. Knowing that I wanted to get out and explore Killeen, I didn't know how to step out into the party world without revealing who I was. Knowing that my new surroundings were intense, due to the nature of the barracks, I was very cautious about anyone finding out that I was a bisexual soldier. Hell, for the most part, I didn't even know what types of night clubs that were around Killeen and the surrounding towns, or what kind of people to hang out with.

Whenever I got off from work, I found myself hanging out alone, whenever I went into Killeen and the surrounding towns watching BNSF (**B**urlington **N**orthern **S**anta **F**e) trains passing through. At times I would chase trains from town to town all day and sometimes night. And whenever I got tired of chasing the same train for hours on end, I would find a nice neighborhood that sat at the top of a hill and sit on the hood of my car and just looked over the town itself, mostly at night, and think about my future as a soldier.

For some reason I can't explain why, but a passing train always took my stress away every time I stood near one as it passed me by. At times I would stand about four feet from a passing train, and if I had reached out my hand to touch it, I could have lost one of my limbs. I know this sounds crazy, but this was something that took my stress away and always relaxed me every time I did it.

No matter what time of the day it was, most of the trains that came through Killeen were 50-60 mph trains that always gave me an adrenaline rush like no other feeling that I know. Getting whipped back by the wind and standing there with my eyes closed and arms wide open, while hearing the sounds of each and every rail car that passed me by, would always put my mind in a state of peace and serenity.

When the last rail car would pass my location, I felt as if my troubles were being taken away with the passing of that train. I don't know what prompted me to start doing this, but whatever my troubles were when that train first approached, by the end of that train, they were all gone...Sometimes.

At times, I would chase trains all the way to Temple Texas, where the BNSF railroad has a good size yard there, and where I would sit for hours on end watching trains going and coming in and out of the yard next to the Amtrak train station. Watching these trainmen working kept my dreams of becoming one of them together, every time I thought about getting hired onto the railroad. No matter how late the time would get, being in that train yard helped me get my mind off the crazy things that were going on back in my unit and in the barracks.

In the first week in March of 1999, we were informed that the Battalion was going on an NTC (**N**ational **T**raining **C**enter) rotation, out in Fort Irwin, California. So, after knowing when our deployment day was going to be, we had already packed up and shipped our field equipment out to NTC, while we waited to deploy out to Fort Irwin.

Standing in formation the day I had to fly out that afternoon, we all were being briefed about if anyone had missed our deployment report time, that the III Corps. Commander, General B.B Bell, wanted to see that soldier and their Chain of Command personally. So, after I was told where to be and what time at the 16th street gym to be processed out to NTC, I got into a severe car accident at the Warrior Way and Tank Destroyer intersection shortly after being released from formation to take care of any last-minute business that morning.

I had a 1994 Nissan Maxima GLE, when a green GMC 1500 pickup truck ran its red light and hit me on the passenger's right rear side, sending my car air born 360 degrees twice in the direction that truck was traveling, totaling out my car and almost me with it. If anyone had been riding with me that day, he or she would have been killed.

After that accident, I suffered four dislocated ribs, a misaligned hip with a lot of back problems. While lying in my hospital bed, watching the clock's hands passing 12 o'clock noon time, I kept thinking to myself, *"I'm dead meat. General Bell is going to have my ass on a silver plate when I get out of here."* I told myself, while lying in the hospital bed in pain.

Not knowing or having any phone numbers to my unit on myself, the only thing I could do was to wait until I was discharged from the hospital to go and tell someone what had happened to me. Although each nurse and doctor kept asking me what unit I was from, and being new to Fort Hood and in shock, I couldn't remember my unit's name for the life of me, but only the location where it was at.

When I was finally released from Darnel Medical Hospital, my doctor told me I wasn't deployable and couldn't wear any heavy gear or lift any heavy objects for a month. Knowing that I had already missed my flight to NTC, no one knew I had been in a car accident that morning, or where I was at. But when someone at the hospital did help me locate my unit in the phone book, SFC Madyun was pissed off that I didn't contact anyone or even have an alert roster with me, so I could have called someone.

After SFC Madyun had picked me up from the hospital, he didn't like the fact that I was injured and nondeployable, because to him, if you can walk and carry a weapon, you're good to go. So, after we got back to the unit, he explained to the Chain of Command that I was in a car accident, and I was good to deploy the next day to NTC.

Later I found out through research, an NCO (Noncommissioned Officer) or Officer, can't override a doctor's recommendations or profiles. But in a lot of places within the Army, some soldiers' Chain of Commands will and can go along with a soldier's NCO's recommendations without looking at that soldier's medical profile.

In most Chain of Commands, the more soldiers they have that are healthy and deployable, the better it looks for them. NCO's who have a lot of sick or injured soldiers in their ranks are less likely to get an excellent NCOER. **(An NCOER is an individual evaluation report that explains how an NCO has performed in his or her past year performance as a leader while serving in that unit, and the well-being and state of their soldiers under their command).**

But for me, I was far from healthy when SFC Madyun ordered me to get my things together to fly out that following day.

SINGLED OUT

Early that next morning, SFC Madyun and SGT Stibbie, another NCO from my platoon, came to my room and personally escorted me to the gym to the processing area to make sure I wasn't going to miss the next flight out to NTC. At that time, I couldn't lift any of my bags and SFC Madyun had my fellow soldiers carry my things and equipment for me, which only made the situation worse.

When we boarded our flight later that day, I didn't even think about how I hated flying or even wondered about what we did out in NTC. The only thing I could think about was the amount of pain I was in and how long it was going to last, being I didn't have any pain medication with me.

After we had landed that night in Barstow California and got on some buses to Fort Irwin, my body was stiff, and my pain levels were beyond anything that I had experienced in my entire life at that time.

Getting off the bus and falling into one mass formation for 3-16th FA, my pain levels were so great that I could hardly walk or talk because of the swelling around my neck and abdomen. So, after everyone had formed up into one mass formation, I stood in the back of the formation since I was the only soldier wearing a soft cap and not a Kevlar, like everyone else was. At the time, I didn't see Command

Sergeant Major Wyatt, our Battalion Command Sergeant Major, standing behind me until he tapped me on my shoulder... *"Why aren't you in full gear soldier?"*

"Sergeant Major, I was in a car accident yesterday and I have a profile telling me that I can't wear any heavy gear." I replied.

"Humm" CSM Wyatt mumbled. *"Is that why you missed your movement yesterday soldier?"*

"Yes, Sergeant Major Wyatt," I replied, while hearing SFC Madyun starting to call out everyone's name.

During the roll call, I was wondering how I would answer "here," out loud like everyone else did, whenever he got to my name. Since I could not speak that loud cause my neck was swollen, I decided to raise my hand when he called out my name... *"Private Linson!"* SFC Madyun called out.

Raising my hand, hoping he would see me all the way in the back of formation.

"WHERE THE FUCK ARE YOU SOLDIER?" SFC Madyun started to yell. *"SPEAK THE FUCK UP!"*

With a harsh soft voice, I did my best to speak up... *"Here!"*

"WHERE THE FUCK ARE YOU PRIVATE LINSON!"

69

Seeing other soldiers around me starting to speak up for me after they heard my faint repeated cries of "here" every time SFC Madyun called out my name. In an instant, CSM Wyatt walked from the back of the formation towards the front and started yelling back at SFC Madyun about his language, and told him that I was in the back trying to answer him... *"Why is this soldier out here Sergeant Madyun?"* CSM Wyatt demanded an answer.

"Sergeant Major, he can carry a weapon!" SFC Madyun replied, shrugging his shoulders.

After SFC Madyun had made that comment, CSM Wyatt started yelling again at SFC Madyun for allowing me to come out to NTC in the shape that I was in, and that he should have told the Chain of Command that I wasn't deployable. After a few minutes of chewing out SFC Madyun in front of everybody, CSM Wyatt started his way back toward the rear of the formation. I was so embarrassed to hear CSM Wyatt yelling at SFC Madyun in front of what was a small group of the Battalion, but I knew I had done nothing wrong and wasn't supposed to be out there in the first place.

I didn't know it at the time, but the ammo platoon soldiers were now furious with me. Believing that it was my fault that their smoke (Smoke, is the nick name they gave SFC Madyun), was being put on the spot because of me. It seemed to them; I was the new soldier who was making it hard for their "Smoke."

(Enlisted soldiers become very bonded to their NCO's and stick together out of loyalty to them. And most of the time, the outcome can be very bad for anyone who is considered to be a troublemaker.)

During those first few minutes in formation, my relationship with the rest of the platoon was going to hell in a hand basket, and I didn't know to what extreme. After roll call, the Battalion marched over to the sleeping area called "Tent City", while I walked slowly behind everyone else. As we got to our designated Battery sleeping areas, some of my fellow soldiers within my platoon were passing me saying... *"Stay the fuck away from us! If you come near us, you're going to get fucked up!"*

"What did I do wrong?" I kept asking myself, that night. But no matter how hard I thought, I couldn't come up with an answer.

Since SPC Smotherson was still my assigned battle buddy for our sleeping tent, he also seemed mad about what had happened to their platoon sergeant. Never-the-less, SPC Smotherson kept helping me with my things.

While everyone was putting up their sleeping tents, SPC Smotherson's friends kept teasing him... *"Hey Smut, you got a faggot sleeping with you. Watch your back man, he's going to ass fuck you while you're sleeping,"* as everyone around us was laughing, including our NCO's. I could tell that made SPC Smotherson very uncomfortable sleeping in the same tent with me, and from being mistreated by his friends.

"Why are they doing this?" I asked myself. But the answer was simple, I was the new bee causing problems for their Platoon Sergeant, and now it's payback time.

Even though I'm bisexual, I knew the *"faggot"* comments had nothing to do with it. I knew they were pissed off at me because SFC Madyun had gotten in trouble for me being out there. I knew that these soldiers were feeding off the negative words that their NCO's were telling them how ate up I was as a soldier. In their minds by calling me degrading names, they showed how they were trying to get back at me for getting their Platoon Sergeant in trouble. Although it wasn't my fault for getting into a car accident and missing my first flight out here.

After getting our sleeping tents all set up, SFC Madyun arrived at the ammo platoons sleeping area and announced out loud... *"NCO's, I don't want that soldier near me at all, and everybody under the sound of my voice better make sure of it!"* SFC Madyun said out loud, while pointing his finger towards me.

"This man is crazy." I thought to myself.

After SFC Madyun finished talking to the platoon about what was to come in the days ahead, he told me that I was going to be put on KP (**K**itchen **P**olice), until the Battalion went out into the Dust Bowl (Field).

In the two weeks that I spent washing dishes and cleaning up after soldiers, I felt trapped in a time warp with no end in sight. As time drew closer to head out to the Dust Bowl, SGT Perez came to the

DEFAC pad 3 where I was doing KP and told me… *"Get your mind set ready for the dust bowl Linson, because it's a bitch out there."*

"What will my job be out there, Sergeant Perez?"

"I don't know soldier but just be ready for anything." SGT Perez replied, before walking away from me.

"Be ready for anything? What the hell does that supposed to mean?" I thought to myself watching him walk away from me.

When the time came for us all to head out into the dust bowl, the Battalion's ammo platoons from each Battery joined together to create one large ammo platoon, working together separating ammo for each Battery in the Battalion. When we convoyed to the AHA (**A**mmo **H**olding **A**rea), SFC Madyun made sure that everyone knew who I was, and why I wasn't in the same battle dress uniform as they were in.

As I looked away from everyone, SFC Madyun expressed his thoughts about me… *"This is one lazy piece of shit soldier, and that's why he's in a soft cap and not as high speed as yall are."*

It seemed that SFC Madyun enjoyed announcing to everyone that I was too weak to work while everyone else was working, while I stood around and did nothing.

"They never showed this kind of stuff in the Army commercials on TV." I thought to myself while being humiliated.

In the summer months of May and June of 1999 out in the Mojave Desert, the temperatures would soar above 110' degrees as early as nine o'clock in the morning and get up to 135' degrees during the day. In the first week of the field exercise, we had to sleep outside the AHA, because some of our leadership feared that the heat might detonate some of the ammunition. But for me, I didn't care if it did or didn't. The only thing on my mind was the amount of pain I felt throughout my entire body, every time I took a step or bent over to pick up trash within the AHA.

I found myself thinking during the nights if I was going to be treated like that fat guy in the movie *"Full Metal Jacket."* After two weeks of standing around and watching everyone else work, my fellow soldiers started to ask me why I wasn't working like they were. I would tell them why I couldn't, but the only reply I would get from some of them... *"Punk ass Sissy! You couldn't even pick up a 155mm round."* (Each round would weigh up to 100 pounds or more a piece.)

These soldiers were busting their asses, and here I was the new bee, just standing around watching them work. None of them knew I was in a severe car accident week's back on the day I was supposed to deploy. But the only thing that they knew about me was that SFC Madyun hated my guts.

At times I would ask SGT Ford, my team leader, if I could help in any way that I could, even if it was to make me look busy. So, knowing I wanted to work with the rest of the soldiers, SGT Perez and SGT Ford allowed me to help put boxes of fuses onto the flat racks after each individual shipment was built for whichever Battery it was made for.

Some boxes weighed up to 20 pounds each and I felt at the time that I could lift them without causing much pain for myself. But that wasn't enough for SFC Madyun, when he saw I was lifting the light stuff and everyone else around me was lifting the heavy stuff.

As the desert's heat grew hotter throughout the days, I found myself working on the other side of the AHA by myself, away from everyone else. I often worried about how the rest of this deployment was going to turn out if I was going to be working by myself most of the time.

One day while I was stacking boxes of fuses by myself, on the other side of the AHA, SFC Madyun drove up in his Humvee and bluntly asked me... *"What the fuck are you doing over here, soldier?"*

"Sergeant Ford and Sergeant Perez, gave me permission to work alone putting fuses on the flat racks, Sergeant Madyun." But the more I tried to explain, the angrier SFC Madyun became.

"I see you want to be your own one-man Army!" He exploded in anger.

"But Sergeant," I tried to respond.

"SHUT THE FUCK UP AND MOVE YOUR PUNK ASS OVER TOWARDS EVERYONE ELSE, SOLDIER!" as SFC Madyun told his driver to drive over to the Battalion Ammo Platoons.

"What the hell did I do wrong this time?" I kept asking myself out loud, watching SFC Madyun driving away, with the dust kicking up from his tires.

Walking towards everyone else who looked like mirages in the heat waves from the far, I kept telling myself, *"Hold it together. Just hold it together Howard, this can't be that bad."*

As I approached everyone, I recognized that everybody was looking at me as I kept hearing my name being repeated over and over again by SFC Madyun.

Before I fell into the formation, SFC Madyun shouted out to me... *"STOP WHERE YOU ARE SPECIAL SOLDIER! Sergeant Ford, step out of formation!"* SFC Madyun demanded.

"Why was this soldier by himself doing nothing while everyone else is working together?"

SGT Ford did his best to explain why I couldn't do much work and why he had me putting fuses together away from everyone else. After hearing what he had to say, I knew immediately, SGT Ford's response wasn't the right one to give SFC Madyun. Being that it was hot as hell already, it soon got a lot hotter.

Pointing towards me, SFC Madyun started shouting at the other soldiers... *"THIS YOUNG PUNK IS FULL OF SHIT, AND SOMEONE NEEDS TO FUCK HIM IN THE ASS TO GET HIM TO WORK!"* as the whole platoon started to laugh at me.

I couldn't believe what I just heard. A lot of soldiers didn't read in-between the lines but took it literally. For the uneducated soldiers in the group, which there were a lot of them, SFC Madyun just announced that I was gay, in front of 60 plus male soldiers.

Everyone was laughing as I felt that same very deep uneasiness feeling that I felt on the bus ride to and from AIT, as I looked over at SFC Madyun and said... *"I'm sorry that I can't help out Sergeant Madyun, but I do try to help out a little."*

SFC Madyun and SGT Ford exploded in unison... *"WHO TOLD YOU TO TALK, PRIVATE?"*

I stood there at parade rest, as I listened to my NCO's cursing me out and putting me down in front of people I didn't even know. Watching everybody in the mass formation laughing, I wanted to take off running into the desert to get away from these guys, until I reached some type of normal civilization. When both of my NCO's finally stopped their tirade, SFC Madyun yelled out to the other NCO's... *"GET THIS FAGGOT TO WORK, NOW!"*

Watching at the corner of my eyes, seeing SFC Madyun storming off to his vehicle, SGT Ford looked at SGT Perez... *"Find something for this soldier to do. He's your problem, not mine!"* as he walked away from me.

Seeing everyone walking back to their working areas, SGT Perez walked up to me... *"Linson, it's time that you learned how to become an ammo dog."*

"An ammo dog, Sergeant Perez?" I responded in distress.

"Yes Linson, its time you started to know what we do, even if you don't like it." SGT Perez responded in a calm voice.

"Oh, GOD!" I screamed in my mind after hours and hours of loading and unloading countless artillery rounds. The pain became unbearable from picking up and putting down, twisting, and turning from each round that I had to pick up. I knew at that moment I had to find something else to do if I was going to stay in the military.

Without seeing or understanding the bigger picture of the mess that I was in, I tried to talk with some of the soldiers and NCO's about what we did as an ammo platoon along with our main mission within the Battalion. Some soldiers and NCO's would explain what we did, and some wouldn't give me the time of day to explain anything to me.

One summer afternoon in mid-June when we were finished for the day, everyone was sitting in different groups outside of the AHA relaxing and bedding down for the night. So, I decided to try to mingle with the different groups of soldiers that I was working around. Trying to figure out which group to go and sit with, I remembered in basic training when Drill Sergeant Brown told us that we were all the same color and that there was no separation within the ranks. But looking around, every soldier was separated into their own nationality groups, and I didn't know what to think or how to approach any of them. So, at first, I decided to sit with the African American soldiers and listen to what they were all talking about.

For about an hour or two, I got sick and tired of listen to them talk about their sexual exploits and how many women they had slept with back in the barracks and how many they had passed on to the next guy after they were finished with them.

I knew that these soldiers weren't raised as I was, and I felt very uncomfortable listening to them talk about how they used women as toilet tissue. After a few more minutes of listening to them talking, I finally got up to walk away, when SPC Howell, my TC (**T**ruck **C**ommander who sat in the passenger seat), asked me a question… *"Hey Linson, how many girls have you slept with in your lifetime?"*

Looking back at this group of guys that were just a few seconds ago who were loud as hell, were all quit and waiting for my response… *"My mom didn't raise me to sit around in public and talk about how many people I been with for my own personal needs. And she also told me that it was inappropriate to talk about such things with people I didn't know!"* I replied.

Boy did that get a huge response out of them all. I guess someone who is African American or is perceived to be African American, wasn't supposed to say something like that in response to such a very blunt question. Perhaps it would have been better if I had just kept quiet and walked away. To me, it seemed in their minds, an African American soldier who spoke well and respected females had to be gay. But ever since I was a child, I always spoke up if something was bothering me or if anything made me uncomfortable.

By now the entire group was laughing out of control, including SFC Madyun. Before I had walked away, I looked dead into SFC Madyun's eyes and walked away towards the group of Caucasian soldiers.

While I was walking away from them, many of the African American soldiers shouted after me... *"Faggot! Gay ass nigga!"*

While walking away, I thought to myself that this was their way of retaliating against what they didn't understand or perhaps feared.

While approaching the group of Caucasian soldiers, a couple of them asked me what had happened, and I told them what I had said to the group after I was asked about my sex life. Some started laughing, while most got up and went to their trucks shaking their heads. While standing there talking with the other soldiers, some of the African American soldiers followed after me, mocking my choice of words shouting... *"Hey punk ass momma's boy."* As the commotion attracted more attention, some of the Latino soldiers came over and joined in the laughter of what was being said about me. Since I was tired of listening to it all, I started off towards my truck to get away from the childish nonsense.

Looking at my truck as I was walking towards it, I was very angry and confused about what I said or did to cause this kind of reaction from these soldiers. As I climbed into my truck, wincing from the excruciating pain in my body, my fellow soldiers continued to shout degrading comments at me... *"Fucking Faggot! Gay ass nigga!"*

Looking towards my NCO's for help, I knew they weren't going to help me because they were laughing along with their soldiers as well. I didn't know what to think or what to tell myself to try to calm myself down, when I saw my NCO's laughing after the degrading words that my fellow soldiers were making towards me.

Sitting back into my seat watching the sun fade behind the distant mountains, I felt the first cool breeze that came off the desert terrain that seemed to whisper into my ears. While looking back towards everyone going back into their groups, I thought to myself... *"Maybe I should just keep to myself and not talk to anyone anymore."*

After a few moments of reflection, I couldn't think of any direction or distance to run to escape my twilight zone nightmare. So, I just stared out towards the desert horizon, wondering where GOD was when I needed him the most.

As I sat in my truck with the windows down, being in a daze and looking at the desert animals walking around in the distance, I kept asking myself, *"Why me?"*

LIFE OR DEATH

That following morning, I woke up to SGT Perez banging on the door of my PLS... *"Get up soldier and get ready to convoy into the AHA."*

"Yes, Sergeant Perez." I replied.

"Would you look at that sight." I said out loud while looking out into the desert... *"Beautiful haze this morning GOD. Looks like fog out in the desert this morning...AAWW SHIT, MY BACK!"* As I continued to stretch out my body in my truck.

"Good morning, Howell." I said to SPC Howell as he climbed into the truck.

"Man whatever!" he replied, getting into his seat.

As our day started off with separating and loading up the flat racks onto our PLS's (**P**alletized **L**oad **S**ystem tactical trucks), the heat of the day seemed to cook us slowly. Through all our moving around and building up our last ammo orders, my pain was unbearable. From time to time, I would have to sit down to keep myself from falling over or passing out from the pain and heat.

(The Palletized Load System tactical truck (PLS) is a 5 axle, 10-wheel drive vehicle equipped with a 500 horsepower Detroit Diesel engine. The PLS is a 33 short ton gross capacity truck and trailer combination; (16.5 tons each) self-load/unload transportation system. The PLS lift system can pick up 36,250 lbs. at the lift hook, alone.)

While sitting down recuperating, the insults began to grow... *"You fucking faggot! Gay as punk!"* As I kept trying my best to ignore my fellow soldiers and the pain in my body, while the heat of the day lingered on.

When it came time for lunch, everyone went into their usual groups to sit underneath their PLS's, to get out of the sun and to eat their MRE's (**M**eals **R**eady to **E**at), while I walked over to my truck. I sat underneath my truck against the vehicles front left tire underneath the driver's seat, as I could hear off in the distance from some of the soldiers... *"What are you eating over there, FAGGOT!"* hearing laughter following after countless remarks... *"Hey dick sucker!"* as more laughter became louder.

Glancing up at everyone who was looking at me and laughing, I just sat back and watched my NCO's and fellow soldiers making hateful remarks over and over again as I sat there trying to figure out why they were doing this to me. During all this childish commotion, I kept looking at everyone trying to find SGT Perez, but my eyes stopped and was fixated on SGT Ford as he yelled over to PVT Harris... *"HEY HARRIS, COME OVER HERE RIGHT QUICK."*

PVT Harris is the kind of person that seemed like the type that was supposed to go to jail, but the judge granted him the opportunity to join the military instead. He was known back at Fort Hood as the drug dealer in the barracks, and when it came to someone getting shot at, they always questioned him first.

Watching SGT Ford talking to PVT Harris and pointing at me, I didn't know what the conversation was about, but I knew it had to be about me.

Everyone around SGT Ford started to laugh as PVT Harris turned around and started walking towards my location.

"Humm, why is he coming over here?" I thought to myself.

As PVT Harris approached my truck, I yelled out to him... *"Hey Harris, do you need my truck for something?"* but PVT Harris did not respond back.

Watching him walk around the front of my truck, I asked him again... *"Harris what's up, you need my truck?"* as PVT Harris ignored me.

Opening the driver's door to my truck, I called out loud to PVT Harris... *"HEY, LET ME GET MY STUFF OUT FROM UNDERNEATH FIRST!"* But by this time PVT Harris had already jumped into my truck and slammed the door closed.

"HEY!" I cried out hoping he would hear me.

Going as fast as I could to throw my MRE out from underneath my truck....... the truck started up.

"HEY! HARRIS DON'T MOVE I'M STILL UNDERNEATH! HEY... STOP!" I shouted at the top of my voice.

"HARRIS...HEY STOP!" Then the truck was put into gear.

"AAAAAWWWWW... STOP!"

Hearing the engine whining up to full power and seeing the tire I was leaning against started to move quickly, *"AAAAAAWWWWWWW PLEASE STOP, NO! STOP... STOP... STOP!"* as my screams were overtaken from the noise of the engine.

In those brief seconds, I knew I was going to be killed unless I did something quick. *"Oh, GOD!"* I shouted, after being dragged a few feet in the sand from the first axle of my PLS that came into my chest. In those few seconds of being drag along the desert ground, I rolled myself towards the middle of the truck, on my back, as I watched my vehicle roll over me, axle after axle passing my face until the body of the truck was gone and I was staring up at the sun as the dust from my truck blew all around me.

My mind was gone as my vision was being blinded by the sun. The next thing I remembered was SGT Ford pulling me up off of the ground by my BDU jacket and shaking me like a rag doll screaming... *"YOU FUCKING FAGGOT! WHY DON'T YOU JUST FUCKING DIE!?! WHAT THE FUCK ARE YOU DOING HERE? JUST FUCKING DIE!"* As he continued to shake me up and down wildly, as I started to come back into my senses.

Starting to realize I wasn't dead and was looking up at my NCO shaken me and throwing me back and forth like a mad man, I reached up for his hands that were locked onto my uniform with a death grip... *"LET ME GO YOU STUPID NIGGA! GET THE FUCK OFF OF ME, MOTHERFUCKER! GET OFF!"* as I kept twisting his arms back and forth. *"GET OFF ME, YOU BLACK MOTHERFUCKEN NIGGA!"*

In the few seconds that I was screaming at him while dodging his fist over and over again, I saw in the corner of my eye everyone was running towards us, and knew I had to get out of his death grip before I was going to be jumped on by everyone.

"FUCKING DIE!" as SGT Ford kept swinging at my face as I managed to get his hand off me and standing up onto my feet again.

While I was struggling to get away from him, SGT Perez and SGT Stibbie grabbed SGT Ford off of me while three other soldiers were pulling me away from him.

SGT Ford did his best to overpower SGT Perez and SGT Stibbie and the other soldiers who joined in to hold him down as he kept screaming... *"WHY DIDN'T YOU JUST DIE, YOU FUCKING FAGGOT!*

I HATE YOU! .... JUST FUCKING DIE! .... YOUR MOMMA IS A MOTHERFUCKING BITCH FOR BRINGINGING YOU INTO THIS WORLD AND IM GOING TO TAKE YOU OUT, YOU FUCKING FAGGOT!"

Struggling to get back to SGT Ford, while crying out of control and screaming back more degrading words towards him, the soldiers who had a hold of me threw me down to the ground... *"Don't you get up faggot! DON'T!"*

As quickly as I was thrown down onto the ground, I quickly stood back onto my feet with over 20 soldiers between me and SGT Ford. Crying my eyes out, I stood there wishing I had a gun to kill everyone around me, while trying my best to stop crying.

A few minutes had passed before SFC Madyun and 2nd Lieutenant Moore (the platoon leader), drove up in their Humvee's... *"What the fuck is going on here?"* SFC Madyun shouted, getting out of his Humvee.

Quickly everyone including SGT Ford started to explain in their own words what took place as I tried to speak up... *"SHUT THE FUCK UP AND GET AT PARADE REST PRIVATE!"* SFC Madyun and 2LT Moore yelled towards me.

As I stood there listening to the other NCO's explain what happened, I kept thinking to myself... *"They want me dead."*

After a few minutes of explaining themselves, 2LT Moore walked up to me and asked me for my side of the story. When I was finished, 2LT Moore replied... *"I heard about what took place and I don't see what the problem is Linson!"*

"Excuse me sir?" I replied, shocked by his remarks.

"You're in the wrong Linson. You shouldn't even be alive and talking to me right now. You should be dead!" he replied with a cold calm voice.

"Fuck you sir!" I replied in a harsh voice, trying not to cry.

I couldn't believe that an Officer in the United States Army had just said that to me. There was no emotion in his expression as he turned and walked away from me. As he started to walk away, I bluntly said to him... *"Sir I want to see Captain Freeman and First Sergeant Burns right now!"*

2LT Moore stopped and turned his head back towards me... *"I don't think so, PRIVATE!"* and started back walking towards SFC Madyun and the rest of the NCO's.

Standing there in disbelief, I had just been denied seeing my Chain of Command, a given right to every soldier regardless of the situation. At the time I didn't know about the Army's Open Door Policy, or any rules and regulations that pertained to my situation.

As I stood there bewildered, SFC Madyun approached me... *"WHAT THE FUCK IS WRONG WITH YOU LINSON? WHY DO YOU KEEP STARTING UP SHIT? WHY?"* while SFC Madyun was jabbing his index finger into my chest demanding an answer.

As I kept looking at him screaming into my face, the only thing I wanted to do was swing away into his face... *"If I was here and saw what happened, I would have broken your neck myself. I'm tired of your bullshit soldier! I'm tired on how you're trying to bring down my NCO's and soldiers with your 'One-Man Army Bullshit'!! Try something stupid out here again and I'll be the one stopping your fucking clock, you hear me you fucking private?"*

I didn't respond as we stood there toe-to-toe with tears running down my face. I tried my best to get one word out to let him know it wasn't my fault, and that PVT Harris had tried to kill me by the orders of SGT Ford. But my body kept shaking and my voice was trembling out of control.

"I don't want to hear another word out of you soldier. Get the fuck out of my face before you see my foot going down your throat!"

As I started back towards my truck where PVT Harris had stopped it, SFC Madyun kept yelling towards me… *"Don't even think about coming back over here until I say so! And don't you even think about relaxing soldier!"*

While making my way closer to my truck, I stopped and turned around to look back towards everyone and saw 2LT Moore and SFC Madyun patting SGT Ford on his back trying to calm him down… *"Oh GOD, I want to kill them all right now!"* as I turned back around heading towards my truck.

Making it back to my truck, I decided to sit on a stack of fuse boxes trying to make sense of what just happened. *"Had this truck rolled me over and killed me, I wouldn't be here right now."* I thought to myself looking at my PLS and staring out into the desert.

As the day dragged on with no shade or any water to moderate the afternoon's scorching heat, I stared towards the soldiers with their human shapes made slithery by the heat waves, as I sat there wondering what was being said about me or even if someone was plotting again to kill me.

After calming myself down, I laid down on top of some 155mm artillery rounds and stared up at the buzzards circling my location, which it seemed like they were waiting for me to pass out or die from the heat. After a few long minutes of recapping what just happened to me, I managed to slip myself into a state of rest and put my mind in a place where I was at peace with myself and the rest of the world. I was imagining myself being back at home and away from the Army, as I put my kevlar over my face to block out the sun.

Later that day, I woke up and saw someone walking towards me from the other side of the AHA. To my surprise it was SGT Perez with some food in his hands and a canteen of water in the other.

"How are you feeling soldier?" SGT Perez asked me.

"I'm okay Sergeant Perez. I'll make it." I replied.

As he passed me the food and water, he sat down beside me... *"Relax and eat something Linson. After you finish eating, I need you to walk over with me towards the rest of the group to go see Sergeant Madyun."* SGT Perez said.

While I was eating, I asked SGT Perez a simple question... *"Why are they doing this to me Sergeant?"*

"I'm not in this Linson," he replied looking off into the distance.

I could tell that SGT Perez was one of the few good NCO's but didn't understand at the time why he didn't step up to help me.

After I had finished eating my food, we both started walking back towards where everyone else was sitting down and eating by their trucks. As we got closer, SGT Perez pointed towards SFC Madyun and 2LT Moore's Humvee's and said... *"Soldier, I don't know what to tell you, but you need to watch your back out here. They are after you! Now go over there and see what they want."*

"Why isn't Sergeant Perez protecting me?" I asked myself, as he turned to walk off to where SGT Stibbie was sitting.

"You wanted to see me, Sergeant Madyun?"

Watching him eat his food, SFC Madyun looked up... *"You need to watch your back soldier. A lot of soldiers out here are upset with you because there's a gay soldier out here in the middle of the desert staring them down."*

That was the first time I felt the term was being used as a specific accusation and not as a general slur. Before this day, I was called *"Gay"* because I wasn't working, but now I'm apparently a homosexual because I was looking at them work? These soldiers still didn't know that I got injured and couldn't work and had nothing to do but stand around and, in their words, "staring at them."

"I'm not gay Sergeant and I don't know why they think I am." I replied.

"I didn't ask you for your opinion soldier!"

At that time, a part of me was worried that my sexuality would be known, but I also knew that none of them knew me for that matter, and none knew I was bisexual in the first place.

"None-the-less soldier, you do know the Army's policy about gays in the military?" he continued.

"Sergeant, I'm not gay!" I kept implying.

"I don't care if you are or not Linson, but the Army has a policy called "Don't Ask, Don't Tell", and I'm telling you here and now soldier, you better start watching your back for now on." SFC Madyun replied bluntly.

"I will Sergeant Madyun." I replied in disbelief to what I just heard.

"Now go back to your truck and bring it over here with everyone else and get ready to convoy out of here for the night."

"Yes Sergeant!" as I quickly turned around to not show how angry, I was... *"I wish someone would put their hands on me again out here. Oh GOD! I wish someone would try to hurt me again, I'm going to kill*

them all! Oh GOD I will…I will!" Talking to myself out loud, walking back towards my truck.

After driving my PLS back over to pick up SPC Howell, he seemed uneasy to be in my presence, yet along in the same truck with me.

That night a strong sandstorm came through the desert like a category 5 hurricane, with no end in sight. That night I sat in my truck staring out into the darkness, wondering who was out there in the howling winds looking to bring me harm again… *"Was someone out there with some type of weapon ready to open my door and kill me?"* I thought to myself as the vehicle rocked back and forth from the strong winds.

"Who's out there? Why me?" I kept talking to myself, as random noises kept coming from my door. *"Oh GOD! Why me?"* I kept screaming in my mind.

The sound of the winds and the motion of the vehicle rocking back and forth made it one of the worst nights in my life, with all the dark thoughts going through my mind. From time to time, I heard someone banging on the passenger door, although SPC Howell was sleeping on the roof of our vehicle, I knew it wasn't him. His friends had teased him before everyone had gone to bed that night, telling him that I would try to rape him throughout the night. To make it very clear to me, SPC Howell told me he didn't like being around me, yet alone within the same truck, and that he was going to be sleeping outside for as long as we were out in the field. But I knew why SPC Howell was behaving like this so he wouldn't be called a homosexual as well.

"It's so cold!" I kept mumbling to myself, as the temperature dropped that night and the wind blew harder and harder, it seemed. My eyes became heavier as the countless hours passed that night and I couldn't see anything outside in the darkness of that deserts storm... *"It's so cold!"*

After a while, I fell asleep with my head on the steering wheel that night. What seemed like an hour later, it was already morning. Looking up to see a mist surrounding our location left by the passing sandstorm, I sat back in my seat and straightened out my body behind the steering wheel and saw that everyone else was still asleep in and around their vehicles. But for me, I was still tired and on edge that morning.

Those following days seemed to go by so slowly, like tree sap running down a tree's bark on a cold winter's day. Most every day after that day I was almost killed, I found myself in countless confrontations with other soldier from other batteries. Day in and day out, they joked about me having sex with other men and "sucking dicks", out in the field. With nowhere to run, I kept telling myself... *"Hold on Howard. Just keep holding on."*

One particular day while we were out in the Dust Bowl waiting for the rest of the ammo truck to come to our location so we all could convoy back to the AHA, some of the soldiers decided to take showers outside of their vehicles with a five-gallon water jug. Seeing these soldiers getting ready to clean themselves, I knew nothing good would come of this as I got up and walked around to the other side of my truck, where I couldn't see anyone cleaning themselves. While sitting on the other side of my truck, two soldiers from Alpha Battery came around my truck and both stood on different sides of me replying… *"Hey Linson look up!"*

Knowing that they were both naked, I kept looking down cleaning my weapon… *"Hey you wanna suck us both off?"* as they waved their penises back and forth in front of my face.

While they were doing this, other soldiers stood by making fun of the nude soldiers waving their penises and butts in front of my face. After a few seconds of trying to humiliate me, one of the soldiers tried to rub his penis on the side of my face, until I stood up shouting… *"STOP, YOU SON OF A BITCH!"*

As I took off walking back around to the other side of my truck, SPC Vasquez, another soldier in my platoon, was cleaning himself on top of his vehicle covered with soap yelling… *"COME OVER HERE LINSON! COME SUCK ON THIS PUERTO RICAN COCK, YOU FAGGOT ASS BITCH!"*

Like a group of kids, escalating out of control, the other soldiers started pulling out their penises one by one, *"SUCK IT, FAGGOT!"* while laughing out loud.

Climbing back into my truck, trying to get away from it all, one of the NCO's from Bravo Battery ordered the soldiers to stop sexually harassing me. While I sat in my truck, looking out into the desert, I felt like starting up my truck and running every soldier and NCO over until they were all turned into oatmeal.

After all the soldiers who were cleaning themselves were finished and the rest of the Battalion Ammo met back up, we started our convoy back to the AHA where the rest of the Battalion Ammo platoons were waiting to start another day of reloading ammo back onto our flat racks.

Later that evening after arriving back at the AHA, I walked up to SFC Madyun and told him what had happened earlier that day, and that I didn't appreciate that kind of behavior from the soldiers around me… *"Okay, Linson. Walk with me right quick."* as he called everyone into formation.

At that moment I believed that he was finally going to do something about my problems. While SFC Madyun got everyone's attention, 2LT Moore walked up behind me… *"Who are you trying to get into trouble now Linson?"*

Wanting to turn around and kill this Lieutenant where he stood, I didn't reply as he laughed walking away from me.

"Private Linson isn't happy looking at naked soldiers taking showers outside of their vehicles," SFC Madyun announced to the formation. *"He'd rather see all of yall take turns butt fucking him, so at least he'll know what it means to work for a living and not stand around doing NOTHING!"* SFC Madyun yelled.

Boy did that get a response from everyone and not the kind I was looking for at all!

Laughter after laughter rose out of the formation, as I looked over at SFC Madyun and 2LT Moore in disbelief. I couldn't understand why my recruiter never told me about this part of the Army, while I looked back at everyone laughing at me.

From that day forth, I didn't use the rest room or try to clean myself, in fearful of being raped or sexually assaulted again. So, knowing that these soldiers were stepping up their insane behavior towards me, I decided to wait to take a shower until we had returned from the field and back to tent city. I figured if I used the community showers with soldiers who weren't from my unit where in there, I would be less in danger from any type of sexual assaults.

Day after day went by without me cleaning myself or changing my clothes around anyone. Of course, everyone soon knew about this and ridiculed my reluctance to undress in front of them, and for me not putting on a clean uniform. On many nights I contemplated stealing a vehicle to drive across the desert until I reached a city or a town far, far away. Sometimes at night, I would cry quietly to myself and pray for GOD to take me away from all this hate.

While the last few weeks passed and the days grew longer, my frustration with the daily humiliation grew to the point of insanity. Whenever we were around the rest of HHB Battery out in the field, I would request to speak to First Sergeant Burns, and every time that I had asked, my NCO's kept telling me that he didn't like talking with homosexual soldiers. At times when I tried to approach 1st SGT Burns out in the field, other soldiers from my platoon would always gather up around me and order me back to my vehicle, just to keep me away from him as ordered by my NCO's. At times, SGT Ford would tell me in front of other soldiers, not to go anywhere near 1st SGT Burns, and if I did, there would be hell to pay for disobeying a direct order from a Noncommissioned Officer. Again, being that I was new to the Army, I did as ordered.

In the two months that we spent out in the field, it seemed like it took years to pass. But when the end of the field exercise came to an end, I knew I had to find a way to tell somebody what was going on out here before I went AWOL (**A**bsents **W**ith-**O**ut **L**eave) or killed someone out in NTC.

UNCERTAIN

Before we had returned out of the Dust Bowl, SFC Madyun came up to me and pulled me to the side from everyone else and instructed that I would be put back on KP again. Meanwhile, I drew up a plan in my mind on how to go AWOL or some other means of escape from hell as soon as we had returned out of the field and back to the main post on Fort Irwin. So, on our first day back, I found out everything I needed to know about Fort Irwin and where and when to sneak off the post and how to catch a ride out onto the west coast of California. But the more I thought about it, the more I knew I wouldn't get too far on foot once someone figured out, I was gone. So, I decided I had to find a way to speak to 1st SGT Burns and pray that he would listen to me.

After the morning breakfast rush, I saw SGT Reaves from HHB's Training Room and asked him where 1st SGT Burns was or where he was going to be located later that day... *"Sure Linson, he going to be at a Battalion meeting until 11 a.m. today. Why, what's up?"* SGT Reaves replied.

"No Sergeant it's okay. I'll wait for him to come out of his meeting." While smiling back at SGT Reaves, with a fake smile on my face.

"Okay, cool. How's KP treating you?"

"I hate it!" I bluntly replied.

"Well, we all been on it throughout our years in the Army, it's just your first. Don't worry you'll see more to come if you stay in long enough." SGT Reaves explained to me smiling.

"Yea right Sergeant Reaves. I don't like cleaning up after soldiers!"

"Well, Linson, we all have to do what we don't like to do in this Army."

"Well Sergeant Reaves, I have to get back to cleaning the dishes, I'll catch back up with you later. Bye." As I turned and walked away quickly from SGT Reaves not to show him, I was mad about his comments towards me.

As I went back to washing the dishes, I knew I had only one chance to make some type of contact with 1st SGT Burns, and that was the moment he left his meeting.

Before noon had approached, I ditched my KP duties and took off running as fast as I could from pad 3 of the mess hall area, doing my best to dodge anyone from my platoon in route. When I arrived near our Battalion Headquarters tent, I found a narrow space between two large containers and hid there. Anyone who had passed by my location wouldn't have seen me, or recognized me in such a very small, confined area. That's how small of a space it was.

I spent over an hour watching everyone coming in and out of the Battalion Headquarters tent, and none of them were 1st SGT Burns... *"Did I miss him already?"* I thought to myself, while sweating my butt off… *"No, no, no…just stay put and wait all day if you have to,"* I told myself as the heat of the day bared on.

As countless soldiers, NCO's and Officers passed my location, I kept my concentration on everyone coming and going out of the Battalion Headquarters tent.

Finally, a little past 1 p.m., 1st SGT Burns emerged out of the tent by himself, tapping his green notebook on his right thigh. As he came closer to my location, I moved some of my body out of my hiding area and proceeded to call out for him… *"FIRST SERGEANT BURNS"* I yelled out loud. *"FIRST SERGEANT BURNS"*

Looking around to see who was calling him, I couldn't help but laugh to myself as he twisted and turned to see who was calling him.

"FIRST SERGEANT BURNS!" I yelled at the top of my voice.

Then his eyes caught the location from which his name was being called out. As he started walking towards me with a confused look on his face, as I motioned him to come towards me with my index finger. After he had recognized who I was, and the fact I was using my index finger to motion him over to me, he kept looking around himself to see who I was talking to before he started walking towards me with anger in his eyes.

"What the fuck are you doing, soldier!" he said in a calm but angry voice.

"I'm scared First Sergeant! If they knew I was talking to you, they said they'll kill me!" I replied trebling and crying out of control at the same time.

1st SGT Burn's angry expression quickly turned into a shocking surprise as he watched me lose control of myself crying and sliding back into my hiding area.

"No one is going to hurt you Linson. Not anymore." as he reached his hand out and put it on my shoulder. *"What's wrong?"*

"First Sergeant, soldiers...already tried to kill me...once already... out in the...field!" as I struggled to get my words out.

"What the Fuck!" he replied in a tone of disbelief.

"They will kill me First Sergeant, they will! I don't.... I don't...know what.......to do." Doing my best to speak straight.

1st SGT Burns looked at the ground shaking his head and then back up at me... *"Calm down soldier and follow me to my tent. I need to know what's going on, okay."* 1st SGT Burns replied.

After a couple of minutes, I managed to get myself back together again before I stepped out from between the two containers to walk with him to his tent. As we walked into the Commanders and 1st SGT's sleeping tent, 1st SGT Burns turned and asked me... *"Does Sergeant Madyun know about this?"*

"Yes, First Sergeant and so does Lieutenant Moore. They both encouraged soldiers to hurt me and rape me." I replied, with tears running down my face.

After we had made it back to his tent, I told 1st SGT Burns everything that had happened to me from day one... *"Why didn't you tell me when you saw me out in the field?"* he asked.

"First Sergeant, NCO's and soldiers warned me not to approach you or there will be trouble. They told me that you didn't want to talk to homosexual soldiers." I explained.

"Don't you know about my Open-Door Policy, soldier?"

"No First Sergeant. What is an open-door policy?"

"Don't worry about it right now soldier, you're here now. Why didn't you just approach me?" he persisted. *"I would have removed you from that situation a long time ago, Private Linson."*

"They told me they would kill me if I told you here or back at Fort Hood." I replied crying out of control.

"Who said they will kill you soldier?"

"Those soldiers in all of ammo platoon, and some of the NCO's said that also out there, First Sergeant."

1st SGT Burns looked down at the ground shaking his head... *"Private Rushlow!"* as he yelled out for his driver.

Standing there shaking out of control, with tears falling down my face, as 1st SGT Burns directed PFC Rushlow to go and find CPT Freeman, SFC Madyun and 2LT Moore.

As I watched 1st SGT Burns pace around his tent, I managed to clean myself up to the best of my abilities. In my mind, I kept asking GOD to be with me from that point on.

After a few minutes had passed, the tent flap opened and in walked CPT Freeman... *"Hello Private Linson, how are you?"* he said with a smile on his face.

"Not good sir! Not good!"

1st SGT Burns told CPT Freeman what I had reported about the incidents out in the field, and I knew this was CPT Freemans first time hearing anything about these incidents from the looks he gave 1st SGT Burns when he explained it all to him.

"So, tell me Private Linson, what's going on?" as CPT Freeman sat down on his cot with a genuine concern attitude.

"I had been told that no one cared about my situation, sir." I explained away.

"Who told you that, Linson?"

"Lieutenant Moore."

After seeing the reaction on CPT Freemans face, I realized that everything that I've been told was a lie as the tears started coming down my face once again.

After a few brief moments of silence, SFC Madyun and 2LT Moore walked in. Before any of them could say a word, 1st SGT Burns started yelling at them to get down in the front lean and rest position. As I watched in shock as the two men who encouraged my tormentors were being ordered to do pushups... *"WHAT THE FUCK HAPPENED OUT THERE, SERGEANT MADYUN?"* 1st SGT Burns shouted. *"KEEP PUSHING TILL I TELL YOUR ASS TO STOP!"*

"First Sergeant, I don't know what's going on here," SFC Madyun replied.

"BULLSHIT!! YOU KNOW EXACTLY WHAT HAPPENED TO THIS SOLDIER!!" 1st SGT Burns shotted back. *"WHAT THE FUCK HAPPENED TO THIS SOLDIER OUT THERE, AND YOU BEST NOT FUCKING LIE TO ME SERGEANT MADYUN AND LIEUTENANT MOORE!"*

"First Sergeant, Private Linson knows he can come and talk to us about anything," 2LT Moore replied.

"DON'T FUCKING LIE TO ME LIEUTENANT!" 1st SGT Burns screamed... *"WHAT IS THIS I'M HEARING ABOUT ANOTHER SOLDIER DRIVING A PLS OVER THIS SOLDIER AND OTHERS SEXUALLY HARASSING HIM, SERGEANT MADYUN AND LIEUTENANT MOORE? YOU BOTH BETTER START THINKING REALLY FAST AND HARD!!"*

While I watched as SFC Madyun and 2LT Moore started to run out of breath from doing pushups, CPT Freeman spoke… *"Get up Sergeant Madyun and Lieutenant Moore,"* CPT Freeman said. *"So, let's have it from the both of yall. You first Sergeant Madyun!"*

"Captain Freeman and First Sergeant Burns, this soldier has been acting up from day one out here in NTC, and he has been causing a disruption within the ranks and…."

"SHUT THE FUCK UP, MADYUN!!" screamed 1st SGT Burns. *"WHAT IS THIS SHIT I'M HEARING ABOUT SOLDIERS PUTTING THEIR HANDS ON THIS SOLDIER AND MAKING THREATS AGAINST HIS LIFE?"*

Now that they were caught, 2LT Moore and SFC Madyun suddenly became quiet.

"First Sergeant Burns and Captain Freeman, what happened out there is something we should have brought to your attention. We should have stopped these actions before they got this far out of control." 2LT Moore explained.

"YOU GOD DAMN RIGHT LIEUTENANT! YOU GOD DAMN RIGHT!" 1st SGT Burns shouted back.

"Sergeant Madyun, go find me SGT Ford and bring his ass to me now!" 1st SGT Burns ordered.

After SFC Madyun walked out of the tent, 2LT Moore told his side of what went on out in the desert… *"I didn't know how to handle this situation because of its intensity,"* he explained away.

CPT Freeman got off his cot and instructed 2LT Moore to walk outside with him.

"This shit should have never happened." 1st SGT Burns said out loud. *"Don't worry Linson, we're going to take care of this. No one is going to touch you ever again!"* 1st SGT Burns reassured me.

In about five minutes, SFC Madyun and SGT Ford walked into the tent... *"GET AT FUCKING PARADE REST SERGEANT FORD!"* 1st SGT Burns shouted as he jumped up off of his cot and rushed up into SGT Fords face... *"PUT YOUR FUCKING HANDS ON ME, MOTHERFUCKA!!!.... COME ON SERGEANT, TOUCH SOMEONE YOUR OWN GOD DAMN SIZE, BITCH!!"*

Seeing SGT Ford looking dumb founded, I watched as this man who ordered another soldier to try and kill me, and tried to beat me up, stood there in absolute silence.

"COME ON SERGEANT, SHAKE ME LIKE YOU SHOOK HIM, I FUCKING DARE YOU!!...DO IT!" Seeing 1st SGT Burns was flexed and ready to fight... *"I DON'T SEE YOU BEING SO TOUGH NOW MOTHERFUCKA!!!"*

After a few seconds of 1st SGT Burns being up in SGT Fords face, 1st SGT Burns finally backed off from SGT Ford... *"You and Madyun fucked up big time Sergeants. What fucking happened out there Sergeant Ford?"* 1st SGT Burns demanded.

"First Sergeant, I have nothing to say," SGT Ford replied.

"WHAT THE FUCK YOU MEAN YOU HAVE NOTHING TO SAY, SERGEANT!" 1st SGT Burns shouted. *"DIDN'T YOU ORDER ANOTHER SOLDIER TO RUN A PLS OVER THIS SOLDIER? AND DIDN'T YOU NOT PUT YOUR HANDS ON THIS SOLDIER, SERGEANT?"*

"First Sergeant, I don't know what happened, but I was wrong for putting my hands on this soldier and to allow the harassment to continue towards him." SGT Ford explained.

"YOU GOD DAMN RIGHT SERGEANT! YOU GOD DAMN RIGHT, MOTHERFUCKA! ... WHAT THE FUCK WERE YALL BOTH THINKING?" 1st SGT Burns demanded.

"First Sergeant, we have nothing to say. But this soldier is out of control, and we tried to set him straight." SFC Madyun replied.

Just then, 1st SGT Burns facial expression turned into a killer's expression after hearing SFC Madyun make that comment... *"ALL OF YALL ARE OUT OF CONTROL, SERGEANT MADYUN! ... HOW IN THE FUCK CAN YOU STAND THERE AND JUSTIFY WHAT YOU DID WAS THE RIGHT THING TO DO? ... HOW IN THE FUCKING HELL ARE YOU EVEN THINKING STRAIGHT! ... You know what, don't even worry about it right now Madyun. As of this moment on, Private Linson is not your soldier anymore, and I will deal with the both of you later. Get the fuck out of my tent before I press charges against both of your asses!"*

After both of my NCO's had left the tent, 1st SGT Burns kept pacing back and forth from one side of the tent to the other, while I stood there trying not to break down again.

"Go and get your shit and move over here next to PFC Rushlow. You do not talk to anyone from ammo platoon, and you do not talk to anyone in this Battery about this. You are now my soldier, and I wish someone would try something now!" 1st SGT Burns replied. *"Rushlow!"*

"Yes, First Sergeant," PFC Rushlow walked back in.

"Walk with this soldier and help him bring his gear over next to you! Now get the fuck out of my face."

I couldn't help but smile at 1st SGT Burns and wonder why I didn't do this a long time ago. Before I left the tent, CPT Freeman walked back in and assured me that nothing like this would ever happen again for as long as he was the Commander.

For the first time in months, I was walking with confidence in my steps, as I felt relieved of my Twilight Zone nightmare. As I gathered my stuff together with PFC Rushlow's help, my fellow soldiers kept asking me why I told on them… *"You need to hurry up and get your stuff out of here before we do it for you."* Some of the soldiers insisted. Out of nowhere, SPC Vasquez started yelling towards me in Spanish as he tried to rush towards me, while most of the ammo platoon soldiers from HHB started to drag him away while I kept packing up my things.

"Don't say a word, Linson!" PFC Rushlow mumbled underneath his breath.

As we walked back to the Headquarters platoon's sleeping area, PFC Rushlow said I was going to be working in the training room for the remainder of my time when we got back to Fort Hood, and I was probably going to be the Commander's driver.

After we had returned to 1st SGT Burns and CPT Freeman's tent as instructed, 1st SGT Burns started to explain to me about my future within the HHB 3-16th FA... *"We're both sorry that you had to go through that experience out in the field, Private Linson. From now on, you're going to be working directly with us and no one else."* 1st SGT Burns explained to me.

After hearing about my new duties as the Commander's driver, I wanted to give 1st SGT Burns the biggest hug of his life. From that moment on, I looked up to 1st SGT Burns as a father figure. He was the only person who I could trust while I was in 3-16th FA.

"Go outside and get SGT Reaves," 1st SGT Burns ordered PFC Rushlow.

After PFC Rushlow reported back in with SGT Reaves, both of them were told by 1st SGT Burns and CPT Freeman that no one from ammo platoon was to talk to me or work with me in any kind of way... *"You will be on the first flight smoking out of here as soon as possible soldier."* 1st SGT Burns said to me. *"Do you have a problem with that?"*

"No, First Sergeant" I replied, with the biggest cool-aid smile on my face.

1st SGT Burns looked back at me with a half of a smile on his face or should I say, more like a smirk... *"I've never seen you so happy before in my life, Private Linson?"* 1st SGT Burns said. *"The only thing you need to do from this point on until we get back to Fort Hood, is to relax and enjoy the rest of your time on this deployment. If you need to go somewhere, let SGT Reaves or PFC Rushlow know where you are going. Do you understand me, soldier?"*

"Yes, First Sergeant," I replied.

After hearing the things that were to come in the near future, I felt like a huge burden was being taken off of my shoulders that day. Exiting out of the tent, I thought about the days out in the field when I contemplated taking a military vehicle and racing across the desert just to get away from all of what I had to endure.

"Now, where will this road take me?" I asked myself while laying down on the rocks beside my stuff. Taking deep inhales in and out while looking up towards the clear blue skies... *"Why did this happen to me? Why?"* I kept asking myself.

Trying my best to piece together all the events that led up to the now, and before I knew it, I was out cold.

THE JOURNEY BEGINS

By the end of July of 1999, was when the day came for me to be processed out of Fort Irwin to head back home to Fort Hood Texas. I felt very nervous when PFC Rushlow helped me carry my bag to the staging area late that afternoon. Not really paying attention to the pain that was still throughout my entire body, I kept thinking to myself... *"Will this episode ever come to an end, or will it get worse or better?"*

"Have a good flight home." PFC Rushlow told me, as he shook my hand before he walked away.

"I guess there are some good people in this military." I thought to myself, watching PFC Rushlow heading back towards Tent City.

As I took a deep in and out exhale, while looking around seeing that I didn't know anybody that was returning to Fort Hood with me, *"Did I really make it this far?"* I mumbled underneath my breath, as I looked around to see other military personnel sitting around joking and having a good time... *"Ha! At least someone out here is doing good."* I thought to myself.

Boarding the bus that took us back to the airport in Barstow, I sat in a seat next to the window as I watched everyone putting their bags onto the trucks and into the cargo area underneath the bus.

"Where did everything go wrong?" I asked myself, looking outwards towards the distant mountains.

After waiting a few minutes for everyone to get settled into the buses, we finally started our journey to the airport, which took an hour or so late that afternoon. In the time that it took for us to make it to the airport, I kept remembering the days when I first got on the bus bound for basic training and AIT.

"I just don't know. I really just don't know." I kept telling myself, looking across the highway at the distant mountains and valleys in the California terrain.

Sitting next to someone who I didn't know really made me feel uncomfortable, and I didn't show that person how uncomfortable I was to have someone that close to me. *"Oh GOD, why do I feel this way?"* As I did my best not to show that person, I was shaking and ready to hit him at a moment's notice.

As soon as we arrived at the airport and drove up next to our airplane, it was already night time when we arrived and everyone was already half asleep, except for me. I was wide awake and on the edge of breaking down.

Hearing the briefings of what we were going to be doing once we landed at Fort Hood, I felt happy and nervous to know I was heading back to where it all began, but this time around I knew it was going to be different... *"Training room, this is going to be fun."* I thought to myself as I walked up the stairs onto the airplane, looking over at the huge engines that powered this bad boy.

Moving through the plane to find an empty window seat where I could look out of the window and see the front of the engines on the wing... *"This is going to be fun,"* I thought to myself.

Taxing down the runway and lining up for takeoff, I looked around to see that most everyone was already asleep. Hearing the engines powering up and feeling myself being pushed back into my seat, I began to laugh to myself about the day when I first left Jackson's International Airport when I was screaming on my first airplane ride. But now, here I was looking out of my window and not having any feelings of being afraid or nervousness as we took off from Barstow, California.

"Humm," as I sat there feeling limp. *"I guess, I'm over my fears of flying now.... Who am I?"* I asked myself, as the plane climbed up to cruising altitude.

During the flight home, it was very quiet on the airplane that night, with only a few light snores and moderate turbulence that broke the silence from time to time. I leaned back into my seat and stared outside of my window towards the dark horizon, where the fading night skies started to give way to the new morning distant light... *"How can anyone say they're having a bad day, when we have this to look forward to every morning, GOD?"* I thought to myself.

As time seemed to slow down on that flight home, my troubles in the desert kept racing through my mind...*"Why did this happen to me? What would happen in the upcoming months ahead?"* I kept asking myself. Never had I wanted an airplane ride to go on forever. I knew I didn't want to face the future, knowing that soon I would have to face the ones who caused my mental pain in the upcoming years.

"What's this on my face?" My attention was quickly broken by something moving down both sides of my face, as I reached up slowly to see what it was. In slow motion, I pulled back my hand and saw that it was wet, as I told myself...*"Stop crying Howard before someone sees you. Just stop crying. Please stop."* as I wiped my face and eyes dry, slightly looking around to see if anyone saw me crying. As I forced myself to regain my composure, I told myself that I would be victorious in the end, but I didn't know when or how that would happen, but I knew in my mind I wasn't going to give up this fight.

When we landed that morning in Fort Hood and I returned to my barracks, none of it felt the same to me anymore. After what I been through out in NTC, I wasn't sure how to put my life back together again. I felt more uneasy and unsure about the Army than ever before. At the time that I was waiting to get my bags, I wished that I could turn back the hands of time, so that I would have never walked into that Army recruiter's office in the first place. But I managed to push that thought away and out of my mind as I made my way towards my room in the barracks.

After putting my things away, I quickly changed clothes and came back downstairs thinking about where I left off, and where do I begin, being that I didn't have a car anymore.

Feeling the morning's breeze racing through my cloths, I started to look around and whispered to myself..."It's quiet out here," while looking up towards the low-level clouds racing across the early morning's blue sky. "Aww, it feels great out here." I shouted, as the cool wind blew through my clothes and across my face, while I stopped and extended both my arms open toward the winds, with my eyes closed and head tilted back, as I felt my tears rolling off the side of my face.

After a few minutes of imagining myself flying up into the sky, I began to walk around my barracks to head towards the Warrior Way PX. I felt so out of place with who I was, as I kept repeating to myself..."Why me?" While I continued to convince myself that joining the Army was the right thing to do.

Knowing that I didn't have a car to go driving around in, I told myself that the first thing I needed to do was to go out and buy another car. And I did, after getting everything cleared up with my insurance company.

After getting myself another Nissan Maxima, I often found myself cruising down Highway 190 and Highway 195 for long countless hours, not really caring in which direction I was going or for how long. When I was tired of heading one way, I would turn around and drive back the same way I came. Sometimes I would drive four to five hours at a time, chasing trains from town to town, wondering if I really wanted to return to the Lion's Den of 3-16th FA.

"No, I couldn't do that to myself or to my family back at home." I told myself. *"I have to keep moving."* I convinced myself.

As everyone started to return from NTC, 1st SGT Burns instructed me to report to the training room to start learning what I needed to learn to become a training room soldier, and as CPT Freeman's driver... *"If anyone from ammo platoon comes around you or starts to give you any trouble, call or come to me ASAP. I don't care what time of the day it is or when,"* 1st SGT Burns added. *"Now get the fuck out of my face and get to work soldier."*

"Yes, First Sergeant." while smiling exiting his office.

Walking out of his office, it felt good to know that someone was looking out for me, and I felt that 1st SGT Burns was being more like a father to me, than any man has ever been in my life.

Walking across the orderly room towards the training room, I reported to SGT Reaves who introduced me to the rest of the soldiers who worked in the training room, SPC Hall, PFC Rushlow and PFC Ray.

"Have a seat Private Linson." SGT Reaves instructed me.

As he gave me a complete rundown of what was expected of me, he told me that they all knew what went down out in NTC, and that nothing like that would happen again back here at Fort Hood, or anywhere else... *"Now just like what First Sergeant Burns had told you, if you have any further incidents with ammo platoon or anyone else, no matter what the rank, you come straight back to the orderly room and report what happened to me or whoever is in here, ASAP. Do you understand Private Linson?"*

"Yes, Sergeant Reaves."

"Now since we're all just getting back and about to go on our four days off, guess what Linson?"

"What?" I replied with a confused look.

"You get to have another four days off again. What do you think about that?"

"Well, I don't know. Why can't I stay here while yall are gone?"

"You're new to the training room, and I don't want you sitting around here doing nothing. So, to save you from being put to work doing something I don't want you doing, you will be off with us, and First Sergeant Burns said you will as well." He replied.

"Well, no augments out of me." as I looked at all of them smiling.

"Now go have a good time Linson while you have the time too, because when we all return, you will not have the time to do much of anything, okay."

"Yes Sergeant." I replied while getting out of my chair heading out of the training room.

As I started off towards the barracks, I began to think about what to do for another four days off that I haven't done already… *"Hmm, what about the club scene?"* I asked myself. *"Where do I want to go?"*

Since the day I've joined the military, I kept a low profile about myself, but now, I had the urge for a more social life… *"Should I go to one of the gay or straight clubs, or just keep chasing trains and wasting money on gas?"* I thought to myself.

I figured since I was 19 years old and no longer had to ask my mom for permission to go out anywhere, I decided to head out to see for the first time, what the "gay world" was all about. *"Would anyone recognize me in the club? Would I be in trouble if I went? Humm, FUCK'EM!"* I said out loud walking up the stairs to my room.

When that night came, I was staring into the mirror, dressed to impress, wondering if this was the right thing to do… *"Am I really gay, or just being told that I am?"* while looking at myself. *"Well here goes nothing."* walking out of my room.

While driving down the highway, I felt so nervous as I came closer to this gay club called Cross Over, in the town east of Killeen called Harker Heights Texas.

"Would I be raped or sexually assaulted by a group of gay guys?" Talking out loud in my car as I saw the club off in the distance... *"Oh no, what am I doing? This feels so wrong,"* I kept saying to myself. But the other part of me knew I had to find out what they were calling me and to see what a "real gay guy" looked and acted like. But then another voice kept telling me to turn around and head back home. For a few seconds I kept fighting with myself, wondering if this was the right course of action to take.

So, to make it look like I was just another person driving by this club, I glanced out of the corner of my eye and saw a few people standing in the parking lot socializing as I drove by. *"Oh no, I can't go through with this. Someone is going to recognize my car and then they'll be right about me. I could just hear it now, we saw Linson's car at the gay club last night! .... No, no, no, go see what this is all about."* as I kept fighting with myself.

After getting myself under control, I made a U-turn and started to pull into the parking lot of the club. *"Oh no, what are you doing?"* I squealed out loud in my car. While starting to sweat like a stuck pig, I said to myself... *"Get out of here and go home quick!"* and just like that, like a madman, I took off out of the parking lot, as if I was in a Daytona 500 race, spinning my tires pilling out of the parking lot.

With the engine whining to the max as I shifted from gear to gear, swerving from lane to lane, doing my best to avoid oncoming headlights as if each driver was a member of my unit, I couldn't stop shaking as I rolled down my window to get some fresh air into my car... *"What the hell are you doing Howard? You should be at that club*

120

right now! … No, you shouldn't Howard!" as I raced off into the distance, looking back to see if anyone was following me. *"Stay in your room and keep chasing trains!"* I told myself out loud.

But I knew something wasn't right and I didn't feel right going home that night. *"You have to break the ice."* I told myself. *"You have to go. This is the only way you can understand what all of this is about. You have to go to that place where people will accept you! I will, I will one day, but not today."* Talking with myself, while speeding back onto Fort Hood. *"Boy that was a close one."* I told myself. *"Just get back to your room and sleep this off. You'll be alright."*

After my four-day weekend of contemplating on where to hang out, it was finally time to head back to work. On my first day working in the training room, SGT Reaves decided to walk me through the motor pool where he introduced me to the mechanics that I would be working with, when it came time for me to work on HHB 5, HHB 6 and HHB 7.

Not long after being introduced to the maintenance platoon, rumors about why I left ammo platoon to become the new Battery Commander's driver were beginning to spread around the Battery. At first, I didn't pay any of the rumors much attention, because I was working in and around an area where other soldiers weren't scrutinizing me. But in the days the followed my return from NTC, 1st SGT Burns had a difficult time finding a soldier who wanted to be my roommate in the barracks. Apparently, most soldiers were not comfortable sleeping in the same room with someone who was rumored to be gay.

So, to deal with this situation, 1st SGT Burns had me moved into PFC Ray's room, since we both worked well together. PFC Ray to me was a silly, crazy kind of guy who always added the words after every cut down, "These Nuts" or when he called out your name, he would say this. PFC Ray always told me he didn't care what everyone was saying to him about me being his roommate.

On our time off, PFC Ray and I would talk about Star Wars and Star Trek, and from time to time we always bumped heads about who was the better of the two and which one seemed to be the future of humanity. PFC Ray would argue that Star Wars was the future, and I believed Star Trek was more realistic to become our future if we really wanted to explore the galaxy. Still no matter how much we would yell back and forth with one another, I still say Star Trek, Ray.

As the weeks passed, the incidents that occurred in Fort Irwin seemed to fade away as I didn't pay too much attention to what anyone was saying about me. Yet, from time to time throughout the weeks to come, I would get into occasional confrontations with soldiers and NCO's about my work ethics and my abilities to do certain things due to my physical capabilities. From the time I had left ammo platoon, I had gotten a reputation of being a lazy soldier from not working a lot out in NTC.

During the times when I was in confrontations with NCO's and soldiers within the Battery, some told me that I should have been court marshaled for "homosexual acts" during our deployment out in NTC. It seemed very evident when I did get into it with soldiers and NCO's about the rumors of NTC, I was always told to stay away from their working areas since hostility from soldiers followed me wherever I went. Yes of course, I would report back to SGT Reaves about the incidents I was in, and what was said and why did it start.

In every confrontation that I was in, something about NTC was the cause of the argument that I was in. It finally got to a point where I just didn't care anymore about who said what or what kind of behavior, I encountered most every day I had to work down in the motor pool. I always concentrated on my work in the training room and while working in the motor pool performing PMCS (**P**reventive **M**aintenance **C**hecks and **S**ystems) on my assigned vehicles. In time, I had to find a way to just deal with the ignorance of people who didn't know the truth about what really happened in NTC.

Within the days that passed from the time that I left the club Cross Over, the urge to go out and experience the gay world kept growing stronger and stronger within myself, whenever I was off from work and sitting around in the barracks doing nothing. Almost every day after work, I found myself chatting with girls and guys off my favorite chatting web site called "AOL", which became a way for me to meet someone for a particular interest. But no matter how hard I tried to say yes to those who wanted to meet up, I just couldn't bring myself to type out the words, "Yes, when and where?" I just couldn't do it.

So, to keep it on the safe side, I decided to keep chasing trains on my time off.

Back at work, I spent most of my time working down in the maintenance bay. During countless days and hours working on my Commanders and 1st SGT's Humvee's, two NCO's who I will never forget, always treated me as if I was one of their maintenance soldiers; SSG Brown and SSG Gonzales.

One day while I was working on one of my vehicles, SSG Brown instructed me to also complete the maintenance for two of the Humvee's that I was in charge of by the end of that day. What he explained for me to do, I knew it was impossible of a task just for one soldier to do by himself, and in response I told SSG Brown... *"Sergeant Brown, that's not going to happen today!"*

"Says who, Linson?" he asked.

"I said so."

What can I say, that didn't settle too well with SSG Brown, as I stood there at parade rest, while SSG Brown chewed me a new one. He explained to me the great importance that enlisted soldiers were not supposed to talk back to their superiors and soldiers are not supposed to be lazy when told to do something.

After SSG Brown dismissed me from my ass chewing, everyone in the maintenance bay was laughing their butts off. But for me, I wasn't too pleased about the situation and decided to stop working and

124

walked back up to the training room to inform SGT Reaves about what I had done for the day, as well as the remaining tasks that I couldn't finish that day.

Since it was towards the end of the day and everyone was waiting around for formation, I figured I wouldn't see SSG Brown until then. But only a few minutes had passed since my return to the training room, when SSG Brown came into the orderly room looking for me... *"Linson, who told you to stop working on those vehicles soldier?"*

"Sergeant, I told you it wasn't going to get done today." I replied.

"Okay, I got something for you soldier. Let me go talk to First Sergeant and I'll be right back. Don't go anywhere." SSG Brown ordered me.

"Hey Sergeant, I'm not going anywhere else today but right here in this training room." I replied, with a smirk on my face.

"We'll see about that Linson!" As SSG Brown headed towards 1st SGT Burns office.

Watching SSG Brown walking into 1st SGT Burns' office, it only took a few minutes until SSG Brown came back out smiling and shaking his head from side to side... *"Hey everyone,"* SSG Brown announced, *"If Private Linson tells you something's not going to get done, then he means what he says---it's not going to get done!"*

As SSG Brown started walking towards where I was sitting at, I was trying my hardest not to burst out laughing at him as he approached me… *"I'm impressed to see a soldier stand his ground on what he will and will not do. Your something else Linson."*

As he reached out to shake my hand, I broke into laughter as SSG Brown started to laugh after I did… *"Sergeant Brown, no hard feelings okay."* while I shook his hand.

"Oh no Linson, none today but you just wait until tomorrow. You will be working on those vehicles you hear me."

"Ha, ha, haaaa, if you say so Sergeant Brown, if you say so." I laughed in reply.

"Keep it up Linson, keep it up." SSG Brown replied laughing as he walked out of the front door of HHB.

I knew from that moment on, I had made a good friend.

SOUTH KOREA

In the month of September 1999, 1st SGT Burns called me into his office to offer me the opportunity to deploy to South Korea with the 4th Infantry Division for the upcoming Fowl Eagle FTX. In hindsight it seemed that 1st SGT Burns was offering me a "vacation" way from my troubles.

"Yes, First Sergeant, I would love to go." I replied after a brief few seconds that I thought about it. After 1st SGT Burns gave me the basic rundown of what my duties were going to be, he introduced me to SGT Hall from POL platoon (**P**etroleum, **O**ils and **L**ubricants), who would be the NCOIC from HHB overseer of me, SPC Payne and SPC Jones, the other two soldiers who I was going with.

At the time I didn't care who these two other soldiers were, I was just excited to know that I was going to a foreign country on the other side of the world. When I got off that day, I called my momma and told her about 1st SGT Burns letting me go on a deployment with my Division to South Korea, to be part of a field training exercise on a detail that loaded and unloaded military equipment in Busan, South Korea.

My mom was excited as well to know I was happy to get the opportunity to head off to another country. My momma would always tell me... *"Keep your head up Howard and keep GOD in your life wherever you go. And remember, GOD will be with you every step of the way, no matter where you might go in this world."*

At the end of every phone conversation with my momma or sisters, I would always tell them... *"I love you!"* And they would always reply the same, which was a reassurance for me to know I was still being loved in this world. No matter how bad my day would be, I knew that my momma and my two sisters loved me as much as I loved them. No matter how far I would be away from them in the world, the love from my family is what kept me together throughout my whole entire military career.

Towards the end of September, we began to out-process to fly out to South Korea at the 16th street gym on Fort Hood where I met another one of my best friends named SPC Hanenburg, who was also eager to go to South Korea as well. SPC Hanenburg was a little taller than me, skinny and filled with energy. He also told me he was from New Orleans Louisiana, and loved his job as a tanker in the 2-67th Tank Brigade, which at that time I didn't know even existed in the 4th ID.

Talking about where we both did basic training and what kind of background we both grew up in, I didn't tell SPC Hanenburg how my life had been since I joined the Army. At the time, I didn't want to make him feel uncomfortable for being around me, even for that matter, I didn't want him to think I was gay because of the problems I've been going through.

128

On the bus ride to the airfield, me and SPC Hanenburg sat beside one another as we kept talking about what was to come and guessed on how the culture of the South Korean's was like. After we boarded the airplane, I asked SPC Hanenburg if he wouldn't mind sitting next to me… *"Of course, not Howard,"* he replied.

"As long as I get to sit next to the window," I added.

"Shoot, I don't care."

I knew from that moment on that this guy was going to be one of my best friends to have for life. As the sun started to set, the plane started down the runway as I started to have flashbacks of the harassment and violence I had experienced on my first deployment. Feeling weary about deploying again so soon, I knew I was heading off to a place where conflict raged from day to day, so I thought at the time.

"Would I be able to avoid new conflicts?" I asked myself while staring out of the window watching the ground disappearing beneath the clouds. No matter how hard I tried to ignore my thoughts, I knew something bad was going to happen in South Korea, but didn't know why I would think this, knowing I wasn't with the ones who cause all my problems in the first place.

After a few hours of chatting with SPC Hanenburg, I fell asleep while looking out of my window thinking about what was to come in South Korea.

"Wake up Howard. Look out your window." SPC Hanenburg replied, shaking me awake.

Seeing the snow-capped mountains and blue and white glacier after glacier as far as the eyes can see, took my breath away. *"Hello Alaska!"* I said while looking off into the distance.

As we descended onto an Air Force base somewhere in Alaska, I was very confused to see that the sun was still up when it was almost midnight there. Then I remembered back in school when my teacher explained to us, during the summer and winter months, the northern parts of the Earth, experienced longer and shorter days than we did, since we were closer to the Equator.

After getting off the airplane and waiting a few hours with everyone sitting around in an airplane hangar, it was finally time to get back into the airplane and on our way to South Korea. By the time we reached cruising altitude, almost everyone was already asleep. But I kept staring outside of my window at the snowcapped mountains as the sky started to get darker ahead of us. Looking over at SPC Hanenburg to see that he was already knocked out, I sat up to look around the airplane at everyone else around me who was either watching the on-board movie or already sleeping as well.

Sitting back into my seat, I kept telling myself to relax and enjoy the flight over to South Korea. Listening to the sounds of the airplane engines, as the plane turned from one side to the next, I closed my eyes and thought about home and in those few minutes of remembering the good days of my life, I was out.

Waking up hours later, I felt a sense of excitement and the biggest adrenaline rush as we started to descend into South Korea. Looking out of my window along with SPC Hanenburg, the only thing we could see was clouds and some lights here and there when there was a break in the clouds beneath us.

"He we go," I said when I looked back at SPC Hanenburg.

"This is going to be great," SPC Hanenburg replied with a cool-aid smile on his face.

While flying through the clouds, I asked SPC Hanenburg... *"Where's the ground?"*

"We been coming down for quite some time now," he replied.

"Man, this is some bull shit!" I answered back, worried about our decent.

Before we knew it, we had touchdown and immediately the engines thrust reversers started to slow the airplane down by the end of the runway.

"Ah, fog" I replied looking out of my window.

"Wow, we made it." SPC Hanenburg replied.

"Well, here goes nothing." While looking around at everyone getting their things together.

That morning, it was cold and foggy as we stepped off the airplane and down the steps. I looked back up towards SPC Hanenburg and said... *"Smell that Korean Air,"* as I took a deep inhale and exhale.

"Yea, it stink's" SPC Hanenburg replied.

"Yea it might, but it's the smell of Korea." I replied, taking in another deep inhale, while we were walking down the steps off the airplane.

My attention was not towards the military personnel telling us which buses to get on, but more on my surroundings and seeing the faint hills and lights through the fog off in the distance.

"So, this is South Korea?" I said to myself. *"Humm. What a beautiful place."*

After getting onto our assigned buses, 1st SGT Thompson who oversaw our detail explained to us that we were going to Busan and what type of work that lay ahead of us. To me, I was excited just to be in another country, and being around new military personnel, is what made the whole deployment worth being a part of. I was very happy to know I didn't have to deal with the ignorance of the ones who made my life a living hell back at Fort Hood. So, I thought at that time.

On the bus ride from the air base, me and SPC Hanenburg sat towards the front of the bus, as we both talked about how the Koreans drove and how crazy everyone's car had a heavy-duty bumper on the front and back of their vehicles. None of us knew anything about the culture of these people, but just to be in their presents was enough for most of us to enjoy being there.

After a couple of hours of riding on the bus, we finally made it to our small base in Busan South Korea, where we were met by Korean and U.S. Military personnel, who explain to us what we could and could not do while being stationed temporarily in South Korea. The biggest thing SPC Hanenburg wanted to do was to try some "Soju," some type of Korean Alcohol... *"Man I can't wait till we can go out into the economy."* SPC Hanenburg replied.

"Dude your crazy. Do you know what kind of trouble you'll be in if you got caught drunk while we were here? Yet alone, we were told not to do any of that by the Commanding General." I told SPC Hanenburg. But of course, he didn't listen to me later in the deployment when he got a hold of some of that stuff and mixed it with some orange juice.

After we had gotten our bags, 1st SGT Thompson formed us up and told us to pick a room to sleep in and that he didn't care who we picked to be our roommates. I knew at that moment that I was not going to be sleeping in the same room with the other soldiers from my unit. Since me and Hanenburg already agreed we would share a room, we quickly found a room where another soldier named SPC Moore bunked with us and who also became another one of my friends while in South Korea.

When we finally started to work at the seaports, we spent hours on end unloading tanks and vehicles off the ship and onto trains that were heading up north to Camp Mobley near the DMZ (**D**emilitarize **Z**one).

It was the beginning of fall in South Korea, and most of the mornings were cold and foggy, and on some days the rain just wouldn't stop. On one rainy day, during our lunch break, we were all sitting down on the wooden docks eating our MRE's when I jumped off and managed to get several splinters in my right hand that hurt like hell. As I quickly tried to remove some of them with my teeth, I realized I had to wait later on that day to use my fingernail clippers that were back at the barracks to remove them.

Come the next day when it was still raining all day again, I was helping load up M1 tanks onto the trains when at times certain parts of my body started to itch badly. Throughout the morning until noon, underneath my rain gear, my whole body was itching like crazy. SPC Hanenburg kept asking me if I was okay and SPC Moore kept teasing me about getting some type of STD from some "local tail" (Girl). Everyone around us was laughing about what SPC Moore had said, but not me. I was so tormented by the harsh itching and scratching that I was doing all over my body. I felt like stripping off my skin and burning it, as I kept twisting and turning trying to scratch every inch of my body.

So, during our lunch break, I went into the restroom and took off my rain gear and BDU jacket to see what I was itching all this time, and to my surprise, there were red bumps on top of red bumps all over my arms and torso leading down pass my belt line.

"What the hell is this?" I yelled out loud, while I kept scratching my arms and torso everywhere.

While I looked at the rest of my body, I recognized that every part of my body down to my feet was covered in these bumps, and as soon as I uncovered them, the itching turned into a burning/itching sensation. As I began scratching all over myself like a mad man, I yelled out to the top of my voice in agony, *"OH GOD, WHAT THE HELL IS THIS ALL OVER MY BODY?"*

As I took off my shirt and started scratching myself all over my body, and in the process of me stripping down, SPC Hanenburg came into the restroom to see who was yelling... *"Oh Shit, dude! What the fuck is up with your skin?"* as he started backing away from me.

"Go get the First Sergeant." I replied in agony.

"Holly Shit dude!" as SPC Moore walked in after SPC Hanenburg and saw that my body was covered in bright red bumps from my neck to my feet.

After a brief few minutes, 1st SGT Thompson walked in... *"What the hell is going on with you soldier?"*

"I don't know First Sergeant. This started this morning when it began to rain." while I stood there in my underwear with my paints down to the ground, scratching myself all over the place.

"What's that on your skin?" 1st SGT Thompson replied.

"I don't know, but it burns and itches like hell. AAWWW!" as I kept twitching and turning trying to scratch every part of my body.

"Soldier get your clothes back on and come with me now to go see the medics."

"I CAN'T!"

"I don't care how, but you're not leaving this rest room like that Private Linson."

"AAWWW!" as I kept scratching everywhere.

"Look, do your best to stop scratching yourself and get your clothes back on okay." 1st SGT Thompson replied.

"Okay, I'll try," as I reached down shaking out of control to pull up my paints and put back on my shirt and the rest of my uniform. *"OH GOD!"* as I started to cry, still scratching myself while putting back on my clothes.

Looking over at SPC Hanenburg and SPC Moore as 1st SGT Thompson escorted me out of the Latrine (rest room), both gave me a look of concern as if I was about to die.

In the car ride over to the clinic, I was scratching myself as if I was an insane person who needed a stray jacket. The driver who was taking me to go see the doctor kept asking me if I was going to make it.

"Yea, I'll make it. I came this far, didn't I?" I replied to him, twisting, and turning in my seat.

"What's wrong with you?"

"I don't know, I had some splinters in my hand yesterday and now I got this. I don't know what it is!"

"Well man don't die on me okay." As he smiled, trying to get my mind off myself.

"Don't worry, I won't die on you. Just get me to a doctor fast before I do." While I tried to return a smile back at him.

After a couple of phone calls to the clinic, the driver told me that the Army doctor wasn't in and that he had to take me to the Korean Army base to be seen by their doctor.

"I didn't care who sees me, as long as I'm seen ASAP." I mumbled.

After being checked into a Korean Military Hospital, a Korean doctor didn't know what I had and couldn't diagnose me. After he took pictures of my body and sent it to other doctors across South Korea, no one knew what I had, and the only thing he could prescribe for me to take was some red steroid pills, for a period of three days to help with the itching and irritation until they knew what I had.

I was so nervous and confused to see that countless doctors didn't know what I had, or even attempted to find out what I did have. After long hours of waiting to see if the steroids would work, the Korean doctor told me to stay out of the rain and keep taking these small red pills to prevent the amount of itching sensation that was going on.

When I had returned to the barracks, the other soldiers started to tease me with sexual STD's jokes about me not using condoms out in South Korea... *"Hey Linson! Would a condom have prevented what you have?"* SPC Moore yelled out loud in front of everyone.

I didn't think that was very funny, but everyone else did except for me and SPC Hanenburg. Later that night when I took a shower with my friends like before, both SPC Hanenburg and SPC Moore were stunned to see how my skin looked and asked me to shower on the other side of the community showers since no one knew if it was contagious or not. While taking a shower with some of the other soldiers, everyone quickly finished up as soon as I started to take a shower near them. From that day on, only SPC Hanenburg would take a shower alongside me.

In time, my skin condition eventually cleared up, but the damage had been done mentally to everyone else. After a while, SPC Moore moved out of our room and pressured SPC Hanenburg to come with him, since I was looked upon as an unknown disease threat. No matter what the other soldiers said to him, SPC Hanenburg didn't budge an inch from his area. After a few complaints about me, 1st SGT Thompson pulled me to the side one day and told me that everyone felt uncomfortable being around me, due to my freakish skin condition. In a sense, who could blame them? If I was in their shoes, I might have done the same thing they did. But the soldiers who came from 3-16th FA, shied away also, as some of the soldiers within our detail kept telling me they were hearing rumors that I was gay from the NCO and two soldiers from my unit.

At times I felt terrible to be alienated and kept away from everyone else because of the outbreak I had, but it wasn't like NTC, where I was told to work away from everybody. To me, this was because no doctor could tell me or my Chain of Command what I had. But only one person stood beside me the entire time, and that was SPC Hanenburg.

During our last week loading up the last few trains, my skin had finally cleared up all the way, but nevertheless, soldiers kept their distance from me every time we had to work or go somewhere together.

The day finally came when it was my turn to head up north with one of the trains that we loaded up. I felt so excited and nervous to be traveling through a foreign country by train for the first time of my life, yet alone in South Korea. As the train departed the port late that night, everyone besides me was knocked out cold from a long day at work. In the passenger car that we road in, one of the Korean conductors who sat right beside me, tried to carry on a conversation in his native language with me... *"Sorry dude, I don't know what you're saying."* I replied to him in a polite manner. But what he said next is something I will never forget.

"You have beautiful eyes." The conductor replied.

"Wow dude." I replied smiling away from him... *"Thank you, sir."* I looked back and replied to him, as he was smiling at me from ear to ear.

Since it was late that night and the rain was still coming down like cats and dogs, I kept trying to make out the landscape in the dark distant lands of South Korean. *"What is this country all about?"* I thought to myself, as the train took off down the tracks at a high rate of speed. *"It's so cold and wet here."* I whispered to myself. *"Try to get some sleep Howard. It's a 14-hour train ride to Camp Mobley."*

During our time up north out in the field, we spent most of our time fighting off millions of gnats and flies, while trying our best not to freeze our butts off at night. Since we were a port detail, and we had nothing to do for the field exercise, our main mission was guard duty out in the field, where 1st SGT Thompson put SGT Hall in charge of the guard duty detail.

Time and time again, someone whom I didn't know kept asking me questions about NTC and told me that some guys from my detail were calling me gay. Since I didn't know any of the soldiers from these other Brigades, I knew only three people that would talk about something they themselves didn't know anything about and that was SGT Hall, SPC Payne and SPC Jones.

Being that SGT Hall shared his tent with the other soldiers from 3-16th FA, I made my way to their location after hearing more and more things about my time out in NTC. Up until then, I had a lot of soldiers who I considered my friends, but I guess that didn't go down too well with SGT Hall's and the other soldiers from 3-16th FA, vindictive high school mentality.

Without thinking, I walked straight into their tent and started to curse out SGT Hall… *"Who the fuck are yall to go around and tell other soldiers anything that you think is true about me motherfuckers!"* I yelled out in their tent.

"Who the fuck are you talking too soldier!" SGT Hall responded in surprise.

"You bitch!"

"Hey Linson, it's okay to be gay, just stay the fuck away from us." SPC Payne replied.

"You know what you ignorant black mother fucker, come and say that shit to my face, punk!" I yelled toward SPC Payne.

"WHAT THE FUCK DID YOU SAY FAGGOT!" as SPC Payne stood up and SGT Hall stood in between us.

"Get the fuck at parade rest, punk ass soldier!" SGT Hall tried to order me.

"Kiss my ass, Sergeant!" as I took a defensive posture.

"YOU WANT A PIECE OF ME BITCH!" SGT Hall yelled back.

"COME GET SOME BITCHES'!" I yelled, as all three of them surrounded me. *"COME ON BITCHES!"* as I took off my weapon and held it like a baseball bat.

"FUCK YOU NIGGA!" as SPC Jones launched towards me.

Swinging away like a mad man, all three guys started ducking as I took aim at all three of their heads.

"What the fuck is going on in here?" as 1st SGT Thompson walked in. *"All of yall get at parade rest!"*

"What the hell is wrong with all of yall? Linson what's the problem?" as he turned and saw how pissed off, I was and my face dripping with tears.

"First Sergeant…." as I explained to him what was going on out in the field and back down in Busan since we arrived in South Korea.

"SGT Hall, what do you have to say about this?" 1st SGT Thompson asked.

After SGT Hall explained his side of the story, 1st SGT Thompson explained to us all that we need to stop spreading rumors around about one another and work as a team. As 1st SGT Thompson gave us his spill about the importance of teamwork, SGT Hall was looking directly at me with a vicious look as I mouthed the words… *"Fuck You, Bitch!"* to him.

After that day, SGT Hall changed up the duty roster and took me off the day shift and started me on the night shift for the rest of the field exercise. In the days that followed, SPC Hanenburg told me that SPC Payne and SPC Jones were going around telling other soldiers out in the field that they had seen me giving another male soldier head (giving oral sex), out in the bushes. But SPC Payne and SPC Jones didn't say who I did it to, but implied that I did.

In the Military, soldiers tend to listen to what their fellow soldiers say about other military personnel without questioning it. And just like high school, they spread it to the next person. It seems the more people who are repeating the same thing; the more the rumors had to be true.

When we got out of the field and returned to Camp Mobley, SGT Hall approached me as I was getting my things in order… *"Private Linson, from this day forward until we return back to Fort Hood, you will stay right beside me at all times, so I can make sure you're not out here doing your own thing."*

"My own thing? What are you talking about Sergeant?" as I turned and looked at him standing there with SPC Payne beside him.

"Soldier! If you talk to me like you lost your damn mind again, I'm going to give you an Article 15." Sergeant Hall implied as he walked up closer to me.

(An Article 15 is a type of disciplinary action that involves a loss in rank, extra duty and or loss of pay.)

"If you say so Sergeant!" I responded in a sarcastic manner, with my fist balled up ready to strike at him if he tried something stupid.

"So right now Linson, you need to get your things together and follow us to the showers soldier!" SGT Hall replied.

"Sergeant, I don't need to take a show right now."

"WHAT DID I SAY SOLDIER! YOU WILL BE AT MY SIDE UNTIL WE HEAD BACK TO FORT HOOD!" he started to yell. *"DID YOU NOT UNDERSTAND ME WHEN I SAID RIGHT BESIDE ME EVERYWHERE I GO?"*

"Sergeant, I heard you the first time with your bad ass, bruise lee kicking breath came my way. I'm not going to stand there and watch yall take a shower!" I fired back.

"Why not? You did it out in NTC!" Sergeant Hall replied, as SPC Payne started to laugh.

"You know what Sergeant." As I stood there looking into his eyes. *"Okay Sergeant, you want to play it your way. Okay let's go take a shower."* As I picked up my change of clothes and followed them over to the community showers.

When we arrived at the showers, just to see it was full, SGT Hall ordered me to take a shower right next to him. After we started to shower up, SGT Hall decided to do something that I almost killed him over... *"Hey everybody, don't drop your soap, we have a gay soldier in here with us."*

After hearing most every person in the showers starting to yell out loud their own thoughts about what SGT Hall had said, I turned towards SGT Hall, as I felt the need to kill him where he stood naked laughing at me... *"FUCK YOU! YOU BLACK ASHEY SON OF A BITCH!"* as I got my things together and stormed out of the showers, while SGT Hall and SPC Payne tried to follow me shouting my name out loud while laughing.

I thanked GOD they didn't catch back up with me, because I would have done my best to kill them both, if they had tried to stop me from walking away.

Back in our tent, while I was putting my things back away in my duffle bag, SPC Hanenburg walked up to me to find out why I was so mad and throwing my things all over the place. After I had explained to him what took place in the showers, I told SPC Hanenburg that I was on my way to the AT&T pay phones to call back to Fort Hood, and to tell my Chain of Command what's been going on.

Before I left out of the tent, SPC Hanenburg replied... *"Man that's fucked up. Even I wouldn't take that shit from my NCO's back at Hood."* as I took off walking out of the tent, trying not to push everyone out of my way.

145

"GOD, I want to kill those mother fucka's so bad." I kept repeating out loud, while I was walking towards the AT&T pay phone center.

Doing my best not to shake so hard while I was dialing the phone numbers off my AT&T phone card, I started to cry as the memories of NTC kept racing back into my mind. *"AAWW, I want to kill those bastard's so bad!"* as I mumbled under my breath leaning my head against the pay phone while listening to the phone ring.

"HHB 3-16th Field Artillery Training Room, this is Sergeant Reaves speaking, how may I help you sir or ma'am?"

"Sergeant Reaves! This is Private Linson"

"Hey Linson, how's everything? I know you're having a good time over in Korea."

"Sergeant, I'm gonna kill Sergeant Hall and those two fucking soldiers that came with me." I replied crying.

"What's wrong Linson?"

I explained to him what had been going on since we arrived in the country and what SGT Hall had said out loud in the showers about me. I couldn't help but cry the whole time while I told SGT Reaves what had been going on and how I felt... *"Private Linson, you listen to me."* SGT Reaves replied. *"Don't go near any of them, and if Sergeant Hall tries to make you do anything, tell him that me and First Sergeant Burns ordered you not too. And if he has a problem with that, then he can wait until he comes back to Fort Hood and try to give you an Article 15. Don't worry Linson, will take care of it by the time you come back home."*

"Thank you, Sergeant Reaves." I replied, putting my face into my arm that was resting on top of the phone.

"Now you have three weeks until you return back to Fort Hood, now go have some fun while you're still over there, okay." As Sergeant Reaves tried to cheer me up before I got off the phone with him.

"I will Sergeant, I will." I replied, while I kept trying to get my composure back.

Walking as slow as I could to the BX/PX (Base/Post Exchange), both SPC Hanenburg and SPC Moore ran up behind me... *"Boo!"* as SPC Hanenburg tried to scare me.

"What's wrong Howard?" SPC Moore asked me.

"Nothing!"

"Did you call back to Fort Hood and tell them what happened?" SPC Hanenburg asked.

"Yea, they told me to stay away from Sergeant Hall and those two fuck-heads before I did something stupid." I told them both.

"Hey punk if you're straight, bi or gay, we don't care. We're your friends and we won't let anyone touch you out here, okay." SPC Moore said. *"Yea that's right!"* as both Hanenburg and Moore put their arm around my shoulder and started shaking me from side to side.

I couldn't help but smile back at them both... *"Yall crazy."* I replied, with a huge smile on my face.

"Come on Linson, let's go see what's playing at the movie theater." SPC Hanenburg replied, as we all started walking towards the main post.

I knew from that point on, that these two guys weren't like the other male soldiers that I've encountered since I've been in the Army. And I would never assume everyone that I ran into while in the Army, was like SFC Madyun or any other NCO or soldiers that's been giving me hell since day one at Fort Hood Texas.

THE RETURN TO FORT HOOD

In the days that followed my ordeal with SGT Hall, it was time for us all to fly back to the states. Come mid-November of 1999, the Foul Eagle rotation had come to an end, and the Busan detail that unloaded and loaded the 4th ID equipment was bound for Fort Hood Texas.

On that flight home, me and SPC Hanenburg sat beside one another and talked about our days to come after we all had returned to our units, and that he wanted me to come over to his house and meet his family. After we had landed back at Fort Hood the next day, late that night, I felt overwhelmed to be back in the United States or just being back in my home country again. One of the conversations me and Hanenburg had on the flight home was which fast-food restraint we wanted to try first when we landed back at Fort Hood and the number one burger was the Whopper from Burger King.

Life seemed good for the most part that I spent away from 3-16th FA, and especially around my new best friend Hanenburg. But of course, all good things must come to an end.

After our four days off and returning to our perspective units, 1st SGT Burns told me that he had heard about the incidents that took place in South Korea. But one thing I will never forget what he told me in his office that day… *"Linson, I know your time here has been rough, but you know what? Your day is coming soon."*

You know in those few minutes that I spent in his office explaining what we did and how much fun I had, I didn't grasp what he meant that my day was coming soon.

A week later while standing in formation, 1st SGT Burns called out my name… *"Private Linson, POST!"* he shouted.

"Post! What is he talking about?" I looked around asking soldiers beside me.

"Get up there." Everyone around me pointed to the front.

"I don't have all fucking day Private Linson." 1st SGT Burns announced out loud.

Falling out of formation and walking in-between the platoons, the Commander who was standing in the rear of the Battery formation shouted… *"RUN AROUND THE BATTERY, AND NOT THROUGH IT."* he announced, as everyone started laughing.

"What the hell!" I mumbled under my breath, not knowing why I was being told to come out to the front of the Battery in the first place.

"Stand beside the Guide-on." 1st SGT Burns ordered me.

"ATTENTION TO ORDERS!" 1st SGT shouted to the Battery, as everyone went to attention.

"Oh GOD, what did I do?" I was screaming in my mind.

Watching 1st SGT Burns doing an about face, SPC Rushlow who was recently promoted while I was gone, started to read off the orders of promotion.

"I'm being promoted?" I began to smile from ear to ear.

"What the fuck are you smiling at Private First Class Linson (PFC, E-3)," 1st SGT Burns replied with a smile on his face, as he started to pull off my old rank of E-2 and pin on my new ones.

I really wanted to cry but I couldn't stop smiling knowing I was going from Private Second Class (E-2) to Private First Class (E-3).

"You know, I'm very proud of you Linson. You have come a long way in the past year, and I want you to keep going and never quit, regardless of what anyone tells you." 1st SGT Burns whispered to me. *"You know, your old Platoon Sergeant didn't want you to get this, but you know what? This is your time and who ever don't like it can kiss your ass."*

"Thank you, First Sergeant. Thank you so much." I replied with a huge knot in my throat.

"By the way, I will be leaving HHB soon and I wanted you to know that your new First Sergeant will be Charlie Batteries First Sergeant,

First Sergeant Kelly." his lasts words were to me, after applying my rank on my collar.

After hearing him telling me he was leaving, the stunned surprise of being promoted went away quickly, and the surprise of him leaving took over fast.

When I was told to fall back in with the Battery, after the Battery gave me a round of applause, I was shocked at the idea of being left alone in this hell hole without the one man who helped me fight off those who wanted me out of the Army.

Knowing that I didn't have much time to get things going in my favor, I asked 1st SGT Burns after formation if I could move off post ASAP. Without explaining the why, I requested to move off post as a single soldier, I knew 1st SGT Burns already had known why I was asking… *"Yes, you can."* He replied. *"Tell Rushlow to help you put your package together and have it ready for me by the end of the week to sign."*

"Yes, First Sergeant." I answered back with enthusiasm.

"I'm not supposed to let any single soldiers move off post because you're not married, but in your case, I will let you." He replied. *"I think you will do a whole lot better away from the barracks. Don't you think?"*

"Hell yea I would First Sergeant!" I replied.

"Okay, get the hell out of my face before I take your rank away soldier." He added as I turned away to head towards SPC Rushlow laughing my butt off.

It took about three weeks from that day until I had my own apartment off 8th St near downtown Killeen, Texas.

One day while I was shopping in the Warrior Way PX, during my lunch break, I saw the hottest Puerto Rican female soldier I have ever seen in my life. So, like a horny guy, I walked up to her and introduced myself... *"Hello, sorry to bother you, but I just want to say that you're the finest girl I've ever seen in my life."* I told her.

"Hahaha, well thank you very much." She replied. *"My name is Perez, and you are?"*

"Oh, my bad. My name is Howard." I told her, while doing my best not to drool all over her. *"Where are you from?"*

"Well, I'm not stationed here if that's what you're wondering." She replied.

"Really, then where did you come from?"

"My unit is out of Savannah Georgia with the 3rd Infantry Division, and my unit is located out in the Black Hawk airfield in East Fort Hood." She explained.

"Wow. Well, welcome to Fort Hood." I added with a smile.

"Thank you, we been here for about three weeks now and so far, it's okay."

"Well, I've been here for almost a year and it's alright, I guess."

"Hey, I live off post with a couple of my friends from my unit. Would you like to come over sometime this week and hang out, if you can?"

"What! She is asking me out," I thought to myself. "Yes, I would love that. Where do you live?" I replied.

"I live in Copperas Cove." as she gave me her address and phone number.

"Thank you, Perez. I guess I'll see you later this week." I told her as we departed our way. "Oh, GOD." as I looked down at the address and phone number, she gave me... "She is fine as hell. I hope we...." As my mind went off into the deep end thinking about what could come next.

It was now Friday, and I was excited to know that after I had gotten off work, I was heading over to Perez's place to hang out with her and her friends... "Let me call her first, to let her know I'm on my way." I told myself while dialing her phone number. I felt so excited to know I was going to have a girlfriend or try to have a girlfriend, that was the finest thing on earth. "Pick up, pick up, pick up," as her phone kept ringing.

"Hello?" she answered.

"Hey Perez, it's Howard from the PX. Do you remember me?"

"Oh, yea Howard. How are yea?"

"I'm doing good. Can I come over today?"

"Yea you can. I've been telling my friends all about you this week, and they want to meet you."

"Sure, I would love to meet them too." I added. *"What's their names?"*

"I'll tell you when you get here okay," she explained. *"Oh yea, Howard."*

"What's up?"

"I didn't want to tell you at first but before you come over here, I need to tell you something."

"Sure, you can tell me anything Perez."

"Howard, I saw how you were checking me out that day in the PX, and I don't want to get your hopes up. But I need to let you know I have a girlfriend."

"Girlfriend? Do you mean like a best friend or like a girl, girl, girlfriend" I replied in shocked.

"Yea, girl, girlfriend."

"What do you mean?"

155

"Come on Howard, I'm a Lesbian."

"Lesbian!" I replied, lost in my own thoughts.

"Yea. Hey, just come over here and I'll let you meet my baby. She really wants to meet you too."

"Sure thing...sure thing. I would like to meet her too."

"Howard, you like guys, don't you?" she bluntly asked me.

"Guys! Yea to hang out with." surprised to the question.

"Howard, I can tell you like guys as well. You must be bi?"

"How did you know that?" I asked her in a demanding way.

"Look cutie, just get over here and we'll talk about it okay."

"Okay oracle, I'll be over there in a few hours okay." I replied in a nervous tone.

"Bye, Howard."

"Bye, Perez." As I stood there in shock after I got off the phone with her. *"How in the hell did she know I like guys also? Did I say something to her?"* I asked myself. *"No, I didn't. What the hell?"* as I got ready to head to Perez's place after printing directions off the website map quest.

I could hear the ice breaking all around my world with every step that I took going out the front door of my apartment... *"Oh Lord, what am I doing? I want Perez so bad, but she's taken by another girl, and not only that, she has gay friends staying with her! What should I do?"* I asked myself. *"Just go,"* something kept telling me in my mind. *"Relax Howard, everything is going to be all right…. I hope so,"* I replied to the voice in my mind.

As I headed down the highway to the town of Copperas Cove Texas, I found myself more confident that I was going to meet gay people, but I really didn't know why I was happy to be going to someone's place when I wanted the person who invited me over in the first place. *"AAAAWWW, just go and leave as soon as you can."* I kept telling myself.

Walking up the stairs to her apartment, crazy thoughts kept running through my mind... *"She's taken by another girl, what the hell…Look just meet her friends and go home Howard!"* I kept talking to myself as I started to walk slowly and slower to her front door.

"Knock, Knock!" Waiting a couple of seconds for someone to answer the door, as I kept looking around to see who was watching me.

After a few brief seconds the door swung open, and there stood this young very attractive, light-skinned young man who was around my age that answered the door. Standing there looking at him, I couldn't find the right words to say... *"I aahh, I aahh…"* I kept fumbling for words.

157

"Well?" he said.

"Oh, I'm here to see Perez. I'm Howard." I said, extending out my hand.

"Oh yea, I heard about you. I'm Ricky, come on in." as he shook my hand.

Never in my life had I ever felt so eager to meet another guy that I didn't know. *"Who is this guy?"* I thought to myself, while following him towards the back rooms. *"Damn, he's hot as fuck."* I kept telling myself, while checking him out.

"Howard!" Perez shouted, as Ricky opened her bedroom door.

"Hey Perez," giving her a huge hug.

"These are my friends," as she started to introduce me to them and her girlfriend.

"These are gay soldiers." I repeated in my mind as all of them introduced themselves to me. *"I don't act like them, nor do I look like them."* The thoughts kept going through my mind. *"Stop judging them, Howard!"* I told myself, as Perez introduced me to her girlfriend. But for some reason, my attention was more on Ricky than anyone else by this time. I did my best not to show that I was checking him out... *"Damn, he is fine as fuck...No, no, no. What are you thinking, Howard? That's a guy, what are you thinking... Oh, I want him, I want him, I want him.... No, no, no! Stop that!"* I kept fighting with myself.

As the hours passed, I sat there and listened to these soldiers telling me where they came from and why they were at Fort Hood... *"Why hadn't they been harassed or beaten up for being gay?"* I asked myself. *"They love the Army, and I don't! Am I in the wrong unit?"*

"Hey Howard," Perez got my attention.

"What's up?"

"Come outside with me for a second."

"Okay." As I got up to follow her outside.

"What's up, Perez?"

"You're fighting with yourself, and I can see it. We all can see it."

"What do you mean?" I replied in a dumb founded way.

"You need to be yourself Howard, and not something you're not."

"What are you talking about, Perez?"

"If you like guys, then be with guys. If you like girls, then be with girls. But pick the one you want because you're sexually frustrated, and you either need some pussy or you need some ass or you need to be fucked, whichever turns you on."

I started laughing... *"Girl, you're silly as hell. I'm good. I don't need anyone."*

"Stop lying, Howard."

"I'm telling the truth Perez."

"Howard!"

"What?"

"I saw how you kept looking at Ricky."

"He's cute."

"Howard!"

"What?"

"Look dude, if you want to talk to Ricky, then walk up to him and talk to him. Don't be afraid, he doesn't bite. Well at least not yet!"

"That's really gross, Perez!"

"Hey, I call it like I see it. Come on, I'll help you get his phone number."

"No, no, I'll do it."

"Are you sure?"

"Yeah, I think so."

After a few more minutes had passed with me listening to Perez describe my inner person fighting with myself, I gathered enough confidence to walk back into her apartment and ask Ricky for his phone number. And to my surprise, he happily gave it to me.

"Wow. That was easy." I thought to myself.

Ricky later turned out to be my first guy relationship in the Army, the first of a couple that I had in my nine years of service. Later, Perez and Ricky introduced me to the gay world, and of course to the gay club that I didn't go into that day when I drove out of the parking lot like a mad man, (Club Cross Over). In the few months that I spent around them, I started to become more comfortable with my identity as a bisexual young man. Perez really helped me break out of my shell and introduced me to the world of hanging out and making friends of all types, and to stop judging people about the things I didn't know.

Before Ricky and Perez left Fort Hood to head back to Georgia, I asked Perez for a one-night outing with her and her alone.

That night while me and Perez hung out together, we were cruising the streets of Killeen and Fort Hood, as I thanked her for helping me to take away a lot of my fears about gay people, and to help me understand what it meant to accept myself as who I am.

"You know what Perez? If I didn't walk up to you that day in the PX, I don't know where I would be today. Not really knowing how much fun I could have had with or without you just makes me feel bad." I told her.

"Howard, you're a great guy. You need to learn to become your own man and not let anyone else tell you how you should be. The main thing you need to stop doing is to isolate yourself away from everyone else. It's not good for you. Keep your head up and don't look down. I love you very much Howard," as she leaned over and kissed me on my cheek.

"I love you too, Perez," while holding her hand, within mine.

"You know what Howard? There is this song that I know and it's you all the way. Let me play it for you."

"Who is it?"

"Her name is Alice Deejay, "Do You Think You're Better Off Alone?"

"I never heard of her or that song." I replied.

As I sat there and listened to this song play, my eyes started to fill up with tears, as the words of this song got to me. And still till this day, I love that song to the core.

After Ricky and Perez left Fort Hood, I found myself going out to the gay and straight clubs on my own. I also started learning what the gay world was all about, and I found myself becoming more comfortable being around the people who I had once feared and hated.

As a young boy growing up in church, I heard from my pastors over the years and members within the church, who were always talking about how people like us all were *"hell bound."* While I was growing up, I didn't like gay people, but I also knew I was like them in ways I didn't quite understand. As I became more mature about life and religion, my feelings also changed. I realized gay people praised and worshipped GOD like I do, and like everyone else who calls themselves saved and sanctified filled with the Holy Ghost. I realized we all praise GOD the same way, but in different ways and in different religions.

I also realized while traveling out into the world, that GOD can bless a sinner like a murder, liar, adulterers or any person who has done sin of any kind in their lives. I know he has and will always continue to bless a sinner like me, as he has done for countless others that are Straight, Gay and Bi, throughout his world. For GOD forever will and always LOVE ME and YOU no matter what the charge, and I will forever praise and worship him no matter what anyone might say or try to do!

UNTOLD SECRETS

While making new friends and learning what it meant to be myself, I soon realized after Perez and Ricky had left, that not everyone in the military treated soldiers who are "different" in the way I've been treated all this time. But I knew at the time, I was still in the wrong unit when it came to how I was being treated.

During this time of my life, I continued to explore both gay and straight clubs around the Killeen, and Fort Hood area. When I went to the so-called straight clubs, I was still being hit on by guys and girls who were more comfortable with the straight scene then the gay scene.

Away from the club life, I enjoyed hanging out with my friends, SPC Charrette, SPC Hanenburg, PFC McDaniel and PFC Plorde since I've been at Fort Hood. But when I did hang out with any of them, I would talk the way they did, and at times acted out as they did just to make sure that they didn't know anything about my other side.

(Not being who you are can really kill a person from within.)

Yes, being in the closet saved me from a lot of trouble over the years, but it was very hard to hide who I was for the fear of being harmed by anyone who called themselves heterosexual. But I knew that I had to stay in the closet because of the military "Don't Ask, Don't Tell," policy.

Every day when I woke up, I realized that living off post was the best move I have made since I decided to join the Army. There was no one telling me what to do or how to clean up my place or for even that matter, having someone making gay sexual jokes towards me.

Before 1st SGT Burns had left the Battery, he assured me that 1st SGT Kelly would know everything about my situation before he took command of the Battery as First Sergeant. I knew a little bit about 1st SGT Kelly while I was working down in the motor pool, and when we had our Battalion formations. He seemed to be the type of First Sergeant who didn't accept failure or excuses from anyone. If he said to get something done, he meant get it done.

To me, 1st SGT Kelly was a silly and goofy guy, with a deep harsh voice as if he was a heavy smoker. Every time he saw me walking around, he would always ask me how my day was going. One of his favorites saying that would always make me laugh would be... *"Every day in the Army is like a day out on the farm...Happy meal and banquets.... Every paycheck like a fortune...Every formation a parade...I love the Army!"*

Every time I heard him say that I would tell him he was silly and that he took those words off the movie Aliens. But I knew 1st SGT Kelly was a great First Sergeant to be taking over HHB after 1st SGT Burns had left, but before 1st SGT Burns did leave 3-16th, I had one last conversation with him before he announced who was going to be the acting First Sergeant before 1st SGT Kelly took over.

"Listen up Linson, stop running from your problems and face them head on. You know that a lot of these NCO's around here don't like you very much, but don't give them any reason to prove them right about you." He explained. *"Sergeant Madyun is going to be the acting First Sergeant after I leave and let me tell you this, he really hates you and you need to do your job and don't, and I mean don't give him any reason to think about taking your rank. Keep your head up and don't let any of these sons of bitches run over you."*

"First Sergeant, I don't want to stay here!" I replied, trying not to show how sad I was.

"Yea I know, that's why I'm working on trying to get you to come with me to Division, but I will have to work that out with Command Sergeant Major Wyatt."

"Well work something out quick. I can already hear the wolves howling off in the distance already."

"Hahaha. Linson, you crazy! Let me say this much, if anyone tries to do anything to you, don't hesitate to come to me or call me, you hear me?"

"Yes, First Sergeant. But still, I don't want to be here!"

"Well for now, just keep your head up and don't let anyone run over you, Linson! You hear me mother-fucka?"

"Yes…First Sergeant!" as I tried not to laugh that hard, after that statement.

"Now go tell Sergeant Reaves to get his ass over here."

"Will do First Sergeant," as I got up and walked out of his office thinking about the future ahead of me.

Come the next morning, SFC Madyun held the morning formation.

"What the hell?" I thought to myself. *"Where is First Sergeant Burns?"*

"As of now, I am the acting First Sergeant." Sergeant Madyun explained. *"Nothing will change but there is another NTC rotation coming up in May with our sister unit 4-42nd Field Artillery. They will need more soldiers to help them with their rotation. I already have a list from the Platoon Sergeants of soldiers who are going over there to help them out, and if you have any questions about it, come and see me after this morning formation."*

"What the fuck!" I said to myself. *"Well just do your job and maybe he won't bother you."*

After formation, I went back into the training room and soon after stepping into the office, SFC Madyun called out my name… *"Linson, come see me!"*

"Yes, Sergeant Madyun."

"*Oh shit, what now?*" I mumbled walking over to 1ˢᵗ SGT Burns office.

Walking into the office, he started to explain why he called for me... "*Linson, I'm sending you over to 4-42ⁿᵈ FA as of time now.*"

"*Sergeant Madyun, I'm needed more over here.*"

"*I don't care if your needed anywhere around here soldier! I just want you out of my face and away from here. Do you understand me soldier?*"

"*Yes Sergeant.*"

"*Now go get Sergeant Reaves.*"

"*Yes Sergeant.*"

Walking out of the office pissed off to the highest of pisstivities, I walked into the training room to let SGT Reaves know who wanted to see the both of us... "*Sergeant Reaves! Punk ass Madyun wants to see us.*"

"*What's wrong?*"

"*That motherfucker is sending me over to 4-42 today.*"

"*What? No, no, I need you hear.*"

"*I don't think he cares Sergeant.*"

"*We'll see about that.*"

Walking back over to his office, I knew no matter what SGT Reaves had to say to him, nothing was going to change that man's mind.

"Knock, Knock." On the door.

"Come in Sergeant Reaves. Is Linson with you?"

"Yes Sergeant."

"Good. Listen up Sergeant, I'm sending this soldier to 4-42 as of time now."

"Sergeant Madyun, I need him here not over there."

"I don't care Sergeant! If you have a problem with that, then I'll send you instead. How do you like the sound of that?" he shouted back.

"Sergeant Madyun, if you send him over there, I will have no one to do the work in the motor pool the correct way…. I need him."

"Are you fucking death Sergeant?! He is going and there's nothing you can do or say about it. Do I make myself clear?"

"Yes, Sergeant Madyun!"

"Good, now make sure that soldier knows where to report to."

"Come on Linson." SGT Reaves replied, as we walked out of the office.

Knowing that Sergeant Reaves was pissed off as well, I couldn't say much about it since I knew I had no choice but to go.

"Close the door behind you Linson." SGT Reaves told me, after we walked back into the training room.

"This is bullshit!" SGT Reaves said, while pacing back and forth through the office.

"What's wrong Sergeant?" SPC Rushlow asked.

"What's going on?" SPC Hale and PFC Ray asked right after Rushlow.

"Linson is going to 4-42 today." SGT Reaves replied.

"What? We need him." Everyone replied.

"Madyun doesn't care if we do or don't! Ray it's now your job to keep up with all the work in the motor pool by yourself now." SGT Reaves explained.

"It's okay Sergeant, I can handle it all until Linson comes back."

"I can't stand that dude." SGT Reaves mumbled.

"Hey Sergeant, you should have told Madyun to suck on these nuts!" PFC Ray replied that got everyone, including myself, laughing.

"Well Linson, I hate to tell you this, but you have to go." SGT Reaves told me, while looking upset.

"I know Sergeant. I know."

"If anything happens while you're over there, let me or someone here know quickly, okay."

"I will Sergeant. Hey, don't worry, I'll be fine." I replied, trying to lighten up the atmosphere.

I knew SGT Reaves was a good NCO's that wanted to take care of his soldiers, no matter what the problem. But long as SFC Madyun was in charge, there wasn't anything anybody could do.

Towards the end of the workday, I started my way over to HHB 4-42nd FA area, hoping that things would turn out for the best… *"Here we go again. Oh GOD, I wish I could grow wings and fly out of here."* I said to myself while looking up towards the sky.

"Excuse me, where is your First Sergeant?" I asked a random soldier walking around HHB 4-42's orderly room.

"Oh, he's in his office over there."

"Okay, thank you."

"Aaawww shit, here we go," as I walked up to the First Sergeant's door… *"Knock, knock!"*

"Come in."

"Hello First Sergeant Johnson, I'm PFC Linson from HHB 3-16th."

"Yea, I heard about you soldier." He replied, looking up at me.

"This is fucked up," I told myself, while trying not to show him how upset I was just for being there.

"First Sergeant Burns told me to keep you away from Sergeant Madyun." First Sergeant Johnson added. *"You're not going to have any problems over here and if you do, don't hesitate to bring it to my attention. Do you understand me soldier?"*

"Yes, First Sergeant." I replied with a much happier tone that I didn't have before I walked into his office.

"Now while you're here, you will be assigned to Ammo platoon where SGT Martinez will be your squad leader. He is already aware of you coming here, but since it's the end of the day, just go to formation and introduce yourself and he'll take it from there, okay."

"Sure thing TOP." (Top is another word that soldiers use to describe their First Sergeant.)

"Now get out of my office."

"Yes, First Sergeant."

Walking through 4-42nd HHB area, I kept telling myself... *"Here we go again with ammo platoon."*

After introducing myself to SGT Martinez and being introduced to the whole platoon before the Battery formed up to go home, I didn't pay too much attention to my new fellow soldiers, based on my past experiences of trying to make conversations with anyone new in my life. The only thing I felt I needed to do was to do my work and go home while I was over in 4-42nd FA.

I knew some things would never change in the Army, and I wondered if I could even make it through my first four-year enlistment. Never-the-less, I was willing to face whatever challenges that came my way, and I knew that this upcoming NTC rotation was either going to make me or break me. But to my surprise, 4-42nd FA turned out to be what I didn't expect it to be. I made more friends than I thought I would in the first month that I worked in 4-42nd FA before the NTC rotation. I didn't realize just a few hundred yards away, there was a field artillery unit where I got along with everyone, and no one looked upon me as they did over in 3-16th FA. But regardless of how much of a good time I was having in 4-42nd FA, I knew I had to go back to 3-16th FA after it was all said and done.

One Friday night while hanging out in the club Cross Over with my friends, as always, I wasn't paying any attention to anyone around the club, until later that night, I looked over at the bar to see who was sitting there... *"Oh shit!"* I almost shouted.

"What's wrong?" my friends asked me.

"Do you see that guy sitting over at the bar drinking?"

"Yea. What about him?"

"That's my new First Sergeant, in the unit that I'm going to NTC with. Holly Shit!"

"Well, why is he in here?" some of my friends asked me.

"I don't care why he is I just know I have to get the fuck out of here before he sees me. Oh shit, my ass is grass!" I added. *"Hey yall I gotta go, I'll see yall later."*

"Bye Howard."

"Bye yall."

"Oh shit, Oh shit, Oh shit. Just get out of here before he sees you." I kept repeating to myself as the music tried to overpower my thoughts. *"Oh, shit!"* I muttered as I made my way along the walls of the club. But every time I took a few steps, someone I knew was stopping me to carry on a conversation... *"Hey yall I gotta go. I will talk to yall later, okay."*

"Okay Howard, see yea."

"Oh shit, where did he go?" as I lost sight of him at the bar. But my attention was more on the front exit doors as I kept walking along the walls of the club, until my attention was broken when someone tapped me on my shoulder... *"Where do you think you're going?"* a voice came from behind me.

I turned around to see who it was... *"FIRST SERGEANT!"*

"Calm down, Linson."

Right then and there I started to make excuses on why I was in that club, but with every word that came out of my mouth, 1st SGT Johnson

174

kept shaking his head from side to side... *"Yeah right, Linson! Yeah right!"*

After hearing a few more *"yeah rights,"* I just got quiet and looked at him... *"Look Linson, I knew you were either gay or bi before you even came over to 4-42."*

"What are you talking about First Sergeant?"

"Sergeant Madyun told me all about you."

"He did. What did he say?"

"We talked about you, and he didn't know if you were gay or bi, but now I know!"

"No, you don't!"

"Oh, yes, I do Linson!... Look, if you were 100% straight, you wouldn't be in here by yourself, and you surely wouldn't be sitting at the same table with those gay girls and guys. So, you're either bi or gay. Which one is it?"

"I'm in here just to have a good time. That's all First Sergeant."

"Look Linson, I'm gay and proud of it, and you should be too. Let me tell you a story. Come sit down at the bar with me."

"Okay."

"When I was a Platoon Sergeant stationed in South Korea, did you know that Madyun was one of my squad leaders?"

"No, I didn't know that."

"Well let me tell you, I used to tear his ass up almost every night?"

"What are you talking about, First Sergeant?"

"Me and Madyun used to fuck most every night, Linson."

"Wait... what! Are you sure we're talking about the same person, First Sergeant?"

"Yes, the one who's your acting First Sergeant over in 3-16th."

"No, there must be some kind of mistake. Madyun hates me!"

"Linson, he's bi."

"Wait! What the fuck!"

"So yeah Linson, be who you are and stop trying to run away from it, okay. Now, are you staying, or do you feel the need to try to sneak out of the club again?"

"You saw me doing that First Sergeant?"

"Linson, I saw you before you knew I was even in here."

"Wow. Well since you put it that way, I guess I'll stay then."

"Look Linson, there are a lot of soldiers in my Battery that are checking you out and I know you don't even see it."

"No, I don't see it, First Sergeant!"

"Well, you need to start paying attention to your surroundings. Sometimes it's good to stop and look around and interact with other soldiers that like you, like that."

"No thanks. I'll just keep to myself First Sergeant."

"Stop calling me that."

"Calling you what?"

"First Sergeant!"

"That is who you are correct?"

"Yes, when in uniform, but when I'm not, call me Johnson, okay?"

"Sure thing First Sergeant, oh I mean Johnson."

"Now, go have a good time and be safe Linson."

"I will Johnson, you do the same."

"I shall." he replied, before I turned around and headed back to my friends table, shocked to who I just got finished talking too.

Walking away from the bar, I couldn't grasp onto the conversation that just took place between me and my First Sergeant, about the person whom I hated so much.

"Was Madyun really bi? No, no that can't be true, he hates me!" I thought to myself. *"What the fuck just happened?"* as I walked back to

the table I was sitting at. *"Oh well, it is what it is."* As I started to explain to my friends what just happened.

After another month had passed, it was time for 4-42nd FA to deploy to NTC, and I knew that this rotation was going to be different than the previous NTC in every way. Everyone in this unit seemed to be more focused on their duties and what was expected out of them. No one teased me or belittled me in any way, during the whole time I spent in 4-42nd FA. For the most part, everyone got along with one another, besides a few bumps here and there when the heat of the desert got to a few of us.

One particular soldier, who was very new to 3-16th FA, was sent over with me named PVT Cruz who was a 13 Bravo (Gun Bunny), who became a good friend of mine while we both were over in 4-42nd FA. Most everyone who did come from 3-16th FA asked the 4-42nd FA Command Sergeant Major, CSM Keys if we could stay in his unit and not go back to ours. But the only reply we got from him was... *"No, I already tried to keep yall, but Command Sergeant Major Wyatt said he wants all of yall back as soon as we returned back to Hood."*

I knew before he even told us, that our request was going to get shot down before we could even get it up and off the ground.

Life to me fell into an uneventful routine of going and coming out of 3-16th FA. I knew I had to go back to a place where NCO's and soldiers were waiting with razor sharp teeth, to bite into me with all that they had, to make my life a living hell.

When it came time for 4-42nd FA to return to Fort Hood in late August of 2000, I knew that my return to 3-16th FA was going to be one of the biggest challenges I had to face. But to my surprise, 1st SGT Kelly was already in charge of HHB.

Before we were released to go back to 3-16th FA, I walked over to let SGT Reaves know when I was due to return to the Battery.

"Linson, I got some bad news for you." SGT Reaves replied.

"What kind of bad news Sergeant?"

"First Sergeant Kelly, has taken you out of the training room and put you back into the ammo platoon."

"WHAT!" I replied in shock, *"No, no...I have to talk to First Sergeant Kelly ASAP!"*

"He's in his office, if you wanna go talk to him now." SGT Reaves replied.

"Yes, I do!"

Walking toward his office, my world started to crumble with every step that I took.

"How did this happen?" I asked myself, while approaching 1st SGT Kelly's office.

"Linson, come on in," 1st SGT Kelly replied before I could knock on his door.

"Can I close the door First Sergeant? I have a lot to tell you."

"Yeah, go ahead."

"First Sergeant, you can't send me back to ammo platoon."

"Why not Linson?"

In the hour that it took for me to explain to him what's been going on with me, I told him everything that I've been through since day one and why I was removed from ammo platoon in the first place. When I was finished telling him why I didn't want to go back, I didn't know that I was crying when I told him about my first NTC rotation with Sergeant Madyun and the ammo platoon.

"I knew a little about what happened in your past here, but I didn't know to what extent of what had happened between you and Madyun." 1st SGT Kelly replied.

"Okay, how about this. How would you like to be Second Lieutenant Valdez's driver?"

"Who is he?" I asked.

*"He is the new HHB XO (**E**xecutive **O**fficer)."*

"Yes, I would love that First Sergeant."

"*Good, tell Sergeant Reaves that you will be the XO's driver and that Specialist Ray will be my driver now.*"

"*Yes, First Sergeant, I will tell him and thank you so much. You don't know how much you saved me from hell again, First Sergeant.*" I replied.

"*Don't worry about it Linson. But welcome back. Go find Lieutenant Valdez and let him know that you will be his new driver for the upcoming NTC rotation here in a month.*"

"*NTC!*"

"*Yeah, they didn't tell yall that we are leaving in a month?*"

"*No. I just came from there.*"

"*I know. Now you're going to help us out. That shouldn't be hard for you since you just left there, Linson.*"

"*Oh no top, it isn't.*"

"*Good, well go take care of what you need to take care of and don't forget to let Lieutenant Valdez and Sergeant Reaves know about the change of drivers okay.*"

"*Will do top.*"

Walking out of 1st SGT Kelly's office, I felt a huge emotional sense of relief, but at the same time I was cautious about what might happen in the upcoming months.

While meeting with 2nd LT Valdez, he explained to me what our main mission would be, helping Ammo Platoon convoy across the desert when it was time for the live fire exercise. Later in our conversation, he began to tell me how he heard a few things about who I was, before I came back from 4-42nd NTC rotation... *"What's been going on with you?"* he asked me.

After telling him everything that I've been through, he was shocked to learn that I was almost murdered on my first time going to NTC with Ammo Platoon. I told him, this is what I've been dealing with since I've been at Fort Hood and in this unit.

"You know what Linson." 2nd LT Valdez replied. *"That will never happen again, and I know for a fact, this time around it will most defiantly not happen again."*

"Yes sir, I know it won't." I replied, rethinking about what I would do if it did happen again.

When we arrived out to NTC, I felt like I never left that place since I was just here a month ago with 4-42nd FA, but regardless, I knew what my job was, and I looked forward to being the Batteries XO driver out in the Dust Bowl. I didn't mind it at first, but as time went on, being 2nd LT Valdez driver became a pain in the ass.

There were times when I didn't want to be his driver anymore. We would convoy from one location to the next location, day in and day out, convoy after convoy. Even at times, 2nd LT Valdez didn't want to be the XO anymore but knowing that this field exercise wasn't going to last a lifetime, we both just sucked it up and kept going with the flow.

By mid-December of 2000, our NTC rotation was over, and we were all back at Fort Hood getting ready for our holiday leave to begin.

Looking back over that year, I gave myself a pat on the back for surviving that year and my mind was now focused on the year 2001 and all it had in store for me.

"Just two more years until I could re-up, (Reenlist).*"* I thought to myself, signing out of Battalion staff duty going home for Christmas.

Despite everything I had been through, I was very optimistic I would stay in the Army at that time.

After the New Year, 1st SGT Kelly announced to the Battery that he was being promoted to Sergeant Major (SGM), and that SFC Madyun was going to be the acting First Sergeant again. Also, around this time, SGT Reaves was leaving the unit as well and CPL Rushlow (Corporal) was going to oversee the training room.

"Oh no!" I thought to myself. *"Not again!"*

Knowing what I knew about SFC Madyun's secret, I continued to behave the same way around him as I always had before. I wasn't sure if what I had been told was the truth or not about him, but like before, Sergeant Madyun called me into his office...again... and gave me another new assignment...again... *"I'm assigning you to POL, Linson. Its time you found yourself a new job to learn."* He explained.

"Okay Sergeant Madyun," I replied.

"Sergeant Small's is going to be your new squad leader from Headquarters Platoon. He is on his way up here now to pick you up and take you down to the motor pool."

"Sure thing Sergeant Madyun." I replied, as if I was excited to leave the training room once again.

"Knock, knock!" at the door.

"First Sergeant you wanted to see me?" Sergeant Small's asked, standing at the First Sergeants' door.

"Come get your new soldier!"

"Oh no, not you!" Sergeant Small's smiled looking at me.

"Put him to some good use while you have him, Sergeant!" Sergeant Madyun replied.

"Come on Linson. Do you know how to fuel up a truck?"

"Yea. Put the nozzle in and squeeze the handle." I replied laughing.

184

"Yeah, that's part of it. But now you're going to learn how to become a 77 Foxtrot, (Fueler).

"Well, I'm yours for now. Teach me all that you know, Sergeant."

"Don't worry, I will and so will everyone else in the squad."

"Yeah, I heard that a lot since I've been here." laughing in response to his reply.

"I see that you've been all over the place, Linson."

"Yep, I'm flexible like that Sergeant!"

"Well, we're about to see how flexible you are."

"Bring it on, Sergeant!"

It didn't take me long to learn the ins and outs of my new job as a 77 Foxtrot. As time passed, I became comfortable being around the soldiers in the POL squad, but now and then when a new soldier came to the squad or Battery, someone would always tell them about my past. Just like a brush fire, the rumors started back up again but died as quickly as they were started.

Come March of 2001, on a cold and very wet end of the day formation, SFC Madyun called me out of the formation to stand in front of the Battery… *"PFC Linson get up here."*

"What the hell is going on now?" I thought to myself, as I fell out of my platoon.

After posting beside the guide on, SFC Madyun announced, *"Attention to Orders!"* as CPL Rushlow started to read out the orders for me to get promoted.

"HOLY SHIT! I'm getting promoted to E-4." I shouted in my mind.

SFC Madyun walked up to me and ripped my PFC rank off my gortex jacket and pinned on my Specialist (SPC), rank... *"Congratulations, Specialist Linson, it's been a long time coming."* He whispered to me.

"Why are you whispering?" I thought to myself. I was a little confused and thrown off by his kindness, but I didn't let my guard down, not for one minute around him.

"Give Specialist Linson a round of applause." He told the Battery, as I stood there with a cool aid smile on my face.

"King Shammer," as soldiers and NCO shouted out loud laughing when everyone was giving me a round of applause.

"Go fall back in so we can go home. It's cold as hell out here, while you're standing there cheesing." SFC Madyun said to me.

When I fell back into formation, I felt shocked to see E-4 rank on my chest and being I didn't know I was getting promoted was the biggest surprise I have ever had since 1st SGT Burns announced that he was leaving the Battery last year.

That night, I called my momma and Sergeant Major Burns and told them both that I had been promoted to Specialist that day... *"It's about time,"* I got from the both of them.

"Yes sir, it's been a long time coming. Yes, sir long time indeed." I told myself. *"Never thought I'd see this day come."* I told myself late that night, before I went to bed.

HATE

Later, in the month of March of 2001, the POL squad received a new soldier from Hawaii named SPC DeJesus. Being that I was the only person in the squad that knew the in-processing procedures, SGT Small's assigned me to be his liaison to help him get to where he needed to be in a timely manner.

SPC DeJesus did his best to introduce himself as a hard ass that came from a so-called tough Infantry Battalion and at every turn, he would tell us countless stories of heroism as if he was GI Joe himself. Knowing that his E-4 seniority was about as equal to CPL Wayne time in grade and service, he came to the unit with promotable status to E-5, as CPL Wayne was also. I could tell that SPC DeJesus didn't like the fact of falling under someone who hasn't achieved as much deployment and field time as he did. But I didn't care much about his military career, since I was the lowest in seniority when it came to all the E-4's within the squad.

After getting SPC DeJesus all fixed up and ready to become the new 3-16th FA soldier of the year, my job of babysitting this man was over and I was more than happy to release him back to SGT Small's. Watching SPC DeJesus, telling SGT Small's how POL was ran over in Hawaii, SPC DeJesus tried a lot of times to implement changes as soon as he could without running it through the squad leader or through the squad on how we felt about changing up how things were done. And let me tell you, a lot of head bumping came from this one-man band.

"Oh boy, here comes another high-strung future NCO. Always wanting to be in charge but never listens to the ones around him for advice." A few soldiers would say whenever they saw him coming.

Sitting back watching the arguments going back and forth between all the E-4's and SPC DeJesus, I knew it was just a matter of time before I was away from all of this drama, of who was the better 77F. Come the next month, it was brought to our attention during a small field exercise that HHB had finally received a new First Sergeant by the name of Master Sergeant Centeneo.

We all didn't know what kind of person he was, since most of the time they just moved the next First Sergeant from one of the other batteries to become HHB First Sergeant. So, whenever anyone went back to the rear for anything, we would ask them if they saw him or could tell us how he looked so we knew whom to look for when we all returned from the field. But the only person who knew what he looked like was SFC Madyun.

Coming out of the field and getting our vehicles washed and back online down in the motor pool (The term "Online" means to get all of the vehicles in a straight single file row, right beside one another, "Flawless."), the whole Battery formed up for the end of the day formation where we met our new First Sergeant. Standing there in formation waiting for SFC Madyun and MSG Centeneo to come out of the back doors, I knew that I had to tell another new First Sergeant about my past, so he wouldn't be thrown off from any future misconduct from anyone within HHB or the Battalion as a whole.

"Here we go one more time." I thought to myself, looking at our new First Sergeant walking out of the back doors with SFC Madyun.

"How are yall doing today HHB," MSG Centeneo asked us, with a heavy Latin accent. *"I know yall just got out of the field, but I just wanted to tell all of yall that everything will be ran the same way it has been."*

"Well, if you mean fucked up, then I guess you like a shit sandwich." I replied just loud enough for a few soldiers around me to start laughing.

Still, I knew I had to tell him why I've been moved around so much. So, after formation was over, I quickly approached MSG Centeneo and requested to speak with him on some very important matters.

"Sure, thing guy." He told me. *"Come see me in my office in about thirty minutes."*

After waiting half an hour to speak with him, I explained my life's story in the 3-16th FA to him, and after hearing me speak of such harsh stories, he assured me that nothing of the past would happen while he was First Sergeant of HHB. But his words fell on death ears at that moment he spoke those words to me. So many times, have I heard those same words from every First Sergeant after First Sergeant since

1st SGT Burns departed two years ago. And just like the rest of the other First Sergeants, I gave him the benefit of the doubt that he meant what he said.

During this time in April 2001, CPL Rushlow was in the process of out-processing 3-16th and getting ready for his next duty assignment at a different post. Walking past the training room, CPL Rushlow got my attention… *"Hey, Linson!"*

"What's up Rush?"

"Hey, I put in a good word for you to become the next NCOIC of the training room after I leave this hell hole."

"Haha. Why you say it like that Rushlow?"

"You just wait and see. This guy is an ass hole."

"He is?"

"Yes! But I know you can handle a lot of crazy people since you've been here and working in here you get all of them. But I don't need to tell you that, you already know this."

"Yea that's true. That's so…so true." I replied, while looking towards the back of the Battery. *"You know what, sure I don't mind coming back to work in the training room. When will this transition take place?"*

"Don't worry about when, I'll keep you informed on what day. But I know it's going to be very soon though."

"Cool beans. I can't wait. POL is boring. That new soldier DeJesus, he is a major ass hole!"

"Well, it's been rough working in here all by myself, since Madyun put you in POL."

"Yea, I saw you doing everything on your own since Specialist Ray left" I replied. "Put it this way, if I'm going to be back working in here, then ill stress it to Centeneo that I need soldiers to help me out."

"Well, I hope he gives you someone."

"We'll see. Hey, just let me know when."

"Okay."

"Talk to ya later, Rush."

"That's Corporal, Specialist!"

"Whatever punk!"

"Hahahaha. Catch yea later Linson."

"Halla," while throwing up the peace sign walking out of the orderly room.

After I had walked out of the front doors of HHB, I thought to myself... "The training room is better than POL and all its drama...Aww boy, let's get your mind back ready for the training room once more, Howard."

By the next morning, CPL Rushlow approached me and told me that today I would know when to report back to the training room, before the end of the day's formation.

"Wow! That was quick." I replied.

"I told you it would be," CPL Rushlow replied, walking away.

Come that afternoon while standing around waiting for the end of the day's formation, CPL Rushlow approached me and told me to report to the training room the next morning… *"Hey, I'm as ready as I'll ever be stud."* I told CPL Rushlow.

"I hope so, because I'm behind in a month's worth of paperwork."

"Oh, so now you need me to fix your shit for you."

"What? My shit…It's now your shit high speed." CPL Rushlow replied laughing.

"You make me sick Rushlow."

"Hahaha. Don't worry, take some Pepto-Bismol," as he kept laughing. *"Out of everyone here, I know you can get it all done faster than I could."*

"Yea right! Without any help, how can I do the PMCS on the vehicles and work in the training room at the same time?"

"Tell First Sergeant that."

"Don't worry I will first thing in the morning."

"Okay, till then I'll see yea later Linson."

"Aight you too, Rush."

Standing there, not liking the fact that I was going back to the training room with no help... *"Damn, here we go again,"* walking away thinking of ways to fix the hell I was walking into.

Come the next morning, I had a talk with 1st SGT Centeneo about the amount of work that needed to be done in the training room, and the three vehicles that I had to take care of all at the same time... *"Okay guy. I'll get you some help soon...I think we had a new soldier that came in yesterday afternoon."*

"Yes First Sergeant, his name is Kuhstoss...He's a 13 Foxtrot (Fister)." (The job of a Fister is to give grid coordinates to the 13 Bravo's (Gun Bunnies) to fire within a particular location.)

"Take him!" 1st SGT Centeneo replied, quickly.

"I don't think his Platoon Sergeant will like that very much First Sergeant!"

"I don't care. Who's the First Sergeant guy?" as his Latin tone got deeper.

"You are!"

"Okay guy, so tell that soldier he belongs in the training room and not over in the Fister's platoon."

"Will do, First Sergeant."

Walking out of his office, I knew that the Fister's would not like the fact of someone coming into their platoon and tell them that one of their new soldiers will be taken away, as soon as they had gotten them.

"What is up with this word "GUY" he keeps saying to everyone?" I thought to myself, walking back to the training room.

When PVT Kuhstoss came to in-process into the training room, I told him and his liaison what 1st SGT Centeneo had said about him becoming his new driver and working out of the training room. Private Kuhstoss didn't show any concerns about becoming the First Sergeant's driver, but when Kurtosis's NCO's found out, that didn't fly to well with none of them.

"Hey guy," I told Private Kuhstoss liaison, *"He's the First Sergeant, and if he says he works in here, then he works in here."*

"I don't care." PVT Kuhstoss replied.

"By the way, get used to the word "guy", I told him.

"Guy?"

"Yea, that's Centeneo's favorite word...Guy!"

"Okay, guy!" PVT Kuhstoss replied laughing.

195

In the upcoming months that it took me to get the training room back to the way it was when I first entered three years ago, life seemed to be somewhat laid back. Running the training room, the way I liked for it to be run, work was quick and fast when someone needed something from us at any time of the day. In the second week of September of 2001, like many leaders before me, I put in a promotion for Private Kuhstoss to be promoted to Private Second Class for all his hard work that he had done since his first day working in the training room.

One morning, 1st SGT Centeneo called PVT Kuhstoss up to the front of the formation and announced... *"Attention to Orders!"* While I started to read the orders for Kuhstoss to get promoted, looking over at Kuhstoss face expressions and seeing the excitement on his face from getting a rank put on his empty collar, made PV2 Kuhstoss smile out of control.

"Did I look that excited when I got my first promotion?" looking around at everyone giving PV2 Kuhstoss a round of applause. *"Has it been that long ago?"* At the time, just to see one of my soldiers that I oversaw getting promoted to his next rank made me feel good.

The next morning after PT, I was at home in my apartment polishing my boots watching Good Morning America when the words… *"Breaking News"* flashed across the screen… *"This just in, there are unclaimed reports that some type of missile or airplane flew into the World Trade Tower!"*

"Ha, another drunk pilot!" I said out loud, as I kept brushing my boots.

Looking up towards the TV and seeing the smoke pouring out of the tower, I called out to my roommate to come and check out what someone did to the World Trade Tower… *"Hey Nick, come check this out…Another drunk pilot did something wrong."*

"Oh yea, I'll be right out." Nick replied.

"Boy, boy, boy, what next?" watching the smoke pour out of the tower I said to myself. *"Hey, that airplane is flying pretty low…. Hhmm"* as I watched in disbelief as the second plane crashed into the other tower… *"WHAT THE FUCK! NICK GET YOUR ASS OUT HERE MAN, ANOTHER PLANE JUST FLEW INTO THE TOWERS!"* shouting out to my roommate.

After Nick ran out of his room, we both stood there watching all of what has become our future unfolding right before our very own eyes. Picking up the phone, I called everyone in my Chain of Command and family to let them know what just happened in New York City. Never in my life have I thought I would live to see something like this as I watched everybody on TV start to run all over the place.

As the day of September 11th of 2001 drew onwards at Fort Hood, life as we knew it in the military just became a reality of what it meant to be an American Soldier. That day at Fort Hood, the whole post went on lock down. No one was let on or off, due to the uncertainty of not knowing if more attacks were coming.

In the day room in the barracks, me and PV2 Kuhstoss sat and watched the day's insanity play out… *"Are we going to war?"* PV2 Kuhstoss asked.

"What do you think dude?"

"This is bull shit! We should go and fuck up whoever is responsible for this."

"Don't worry, give it a few days or weeks and we'll see what will come next." I replied looking back at the TV.

"Man, this is fucked up!" Private Kuhstoss kept repeating to himself.

"Put it this way Kuhstoss, no more easy field exercise or any make-believe war fighting. From this day on, everyone in the military will learn what it means to become a soldier, no matter what branch of service they are in. Life as we know it here in the states is now over."

In the days that followed September the 11th of 2001, life as a soldier changed with every awaking moment, knowing that at any time we could be deployed to go and fight a new enemy that we never heard of or knew anything about. But every morning thereafter, putting on the uniform that represented freedom, made me realize that those who came before me had given their lives and years of service, so that one day I can uphold the honor of serving my country and fight for what we believe in as a nation which is, *"Freedom will ring from sea to shiny sea, no matter where we go in this world. The United States will forever stand for Freedom, Justice and Peace for whom so every fight for it."*

During this time of our lives, PV2 Kuhstoss would tell me that some soldiers in the barracks were calling him gay for working with me, and that he received his rank because he performed a few sexual favors for me. PV2 Kuhstoss didn't know why his peers were calling him gay or for even that matter, he didn't know anything about my past in 3-16th FA. So as the harassment continued for PV2 Kuhstoss, I knew one day I would have to explain to him why he was being treated as such. When the questions came more and more often on why soldiers were calling him gay in the barracks, and seeing that the rumors were bothering him mentally, I decided to explain to Kuhstoss what I've been experiencing and why he was being harassed in the barracks about being around me.

Knowing I didn't want him to go through what I went through, I requested to 1st SGT Centeneo that PV2 Kuhstoss needed to be moved out of the barracks and off post as soon as possible. *"Sure thing guy."*

1st SGT Centeneo replied. After going through the process of getting his paperwork in order, PV2 Kuhstoss was able to move off post and away from the stupid, childish, high school behavior, of living in the barracks.

As the New Year came and went, 3-16th FA was preparing to head back to NTC for another field rotation with the entire 4th Infantry Division that was deploying together. This time around, it was my third rotation to NTC with the 3-16th FA, but four all together, and I didn't mind the fact that 1st SGT Centeneo was putting me back in POL for the upcoming deployment.

Before the deployment to NTC, 1st SGT Centeneo assigned another new fister to the training room named Private Arroyo, who became his driver and made PV2 Kuhstoss, CPT Morgan, the Commander's driver. Since the first day that 1st SGT Centeneo had been in charge of HHB, he made a few changes to the platoons and shuffled around a few sections into other platoons, and now POL was a part of Ammo platoon, which made SFC Madyun my Platoon Sergeant all over again. But this time around, SFC Madyun didn't bother me like he had done in the past. It seemed like he didn't like the fact that 1st SGT Centeneo had moved so many sections around, that cluster fucked the whole Battery.

When we arrived at Fort Irwin, SGT Mack was the new NCOIC of POL and assigned me to be CPL Wayne's driver for the entire NTC rotation, which took four months to complete. Since my return to POL, there was a lot of tension between CPL Wayne and SPC DeJesus over who was in charge of the squad whenever SGT Mack wasn't around. In addition, the normal three-month rotation turned into a four-month rotation, and the squad was on edge from being around each other for such a long period of time.

Towards the end of the third month out in the Dust Bowl, POL was the first squad to return out of the field and back into the motor pool, to set up fuel points for the returning Battalion to refuel their vehicles. During the days that we were all back together again, SPC DeJesus became more aggressive towards all of us. Although we all were E-4's, we all knew that he was soon to be promoted to E-5, and Sergeant Mack allowed him to talk to us in any kind of way, just to show off his new "ate the hell up" leadership style.

Since the squad didn't allow SPC DeJesus to talk to them as if he had lost his mind, Sergeant Mack told us if we were to talk back to SPC DeJesus that he could threaten us with an Article 15. For the most part, I would just sit back and watch everyone go at it, while I waited for the time when I could head back to the training room. But eventually SPC DeJesus made his way to me.

One cold night in the motor pool, we were all parked beside one another, and some soldiers were sleeping outside of their vehicles and some of us, including myself, slept on the inside of our vehicles to keep warm. This was not against regulations and was a common practice.

Early in the morning, SPC DeJesus opened my door and reached over me and turned off my truck while adding a few words to go with it... *"I'm sleeping outside my vehicle, and I'm tired of hearing your fucking truck running!"* as he pointed his finger in my face. *"Don't turn this vehicle back on, faggot!"* claiming out of my truck and slamming my door closed.

After hearing his comments, I rolled down my window and yelled out towards him... *"Who the fuck are you talking to, bitch?"* But SPC DeJesus didn't respond as he got back into his sleeping bag.

Calming myself back down, I eventually fell back asleep. A few minutes before sunrise I woke up freezing my butt off, and so I decided to turn back on my truck to get warm again.

A few minutes later, my door flew back open and SPC DeJesus jumped into my truck and shoved me back into my seat and turned off the truck again. Being that I was already pissed off from the first time, I managed to shove and kick him out of my vehicle. As he tumbled out, I jumped out after him. While SPC DeJesus charged towards me and tried to put me in a headlock, I managed to pick him up and body slammed him onto the ground.

"I'll kill you; you faggot!" SPC DeJesus yelled out loud, with his Spanish accent.

"Try it bitch, try it!" as I kept fighting with SPC DeJesus.

CPL Wayne woke up and ran around the truck and attempted to pull us apart as we wrestled around in the sand. Sergeant Mack and everyone else in the squad woke up to the commotion and jumped in and tried to pull us apart as well. After we were finally separated, words flew back and forth between me and SPC DeJesus. After we were separated far enough for SGT Mack to take charge of the situation, SGT Mack took SPC DeJesus's side and CPL Wayne took mine, as we all argued about what had happened.

"Specialist Linson, you will be brought up on charges for fighting an NCO." SGT Mack told me.

"Fuck that shit Sergeant, he touched me first, and if you think he's going to get away with it, you better fucking think again!" I yelled back. *"He doesn't have Sergeant strips on yet, and if he thinks he can put his hands on another soldier, he has another thing coming!"*

As we exchanged more degrading words towards each other, CPL Wayne bear hugged me and picked me up and pulled me away from both SGT Mack and SPC DeJesus.

"Calm down Linson, it isn't worth it," CPL Wayne replied, holding me in a bear hug. *"Later today just go and tell First Sergeant Centeneo on him."*

"Fuck that Wayne, he put his hands on me and I'm gonna kill him." I replied in anger.

"Don't mess up your career over that dude. He's fucked up as you can see. Just go tell First Sergeant later today Linson…I got your back." CPL Wayne replied.

After I had finally calmed myself down, SGT Mack walked around our vehicle and ordered me to get a hold of myself… *"Linson, I don't know what happened between the two of you, but you need to know that he is getting promoted today to Sergeant and you need to respect him."*

"Sergeant, I'll respect the rank, but never that fucking nut case. I don't care how much rank you have in this Army, you don't put your hands on another soldier, no matter how much you dislike him or her!" I demanded back to SGT Mack.

"I understand that Linson, but you two need to get along with one another."

"Never Sergeant Mack! Never!" I replied yelling back at him. *"Just to give you a heads up, I'm going to see First Sergeant later this morning."*

"Okay Linson, but I don't know if he will be available to talk to you."

"Don't worry about that Sergeant, he will!"

Later that day, 1st SGT Centeneo approached me and told me that SPC DeJesus had been promoted to Sergeant earlier that morning, and that I had to respect him as an NCO.

"I'll respect his rank, but not him First Sergeant!" I replied.

"Don't worry Linson. DeJesus will be punished for what he did to you." 1st SGT Centeneo replied.

"Yea right!" I thought to myself, looking at 1st SGT Centeneo giving me a bull shit reassurance speech. For the remainder of the NTC rotation, 1st SGT Centeneo ordered me and SGT DeJesus to stay away from one another, so we would not get into it with one another again.

But for me, I personally wanted to finish what SGT DeJesus had started. But I knew if I did, that would be the end of my career.

When we all finally returned to Fort Hood, both PV2 Kuhstoss and PVT Arroyo wanted to know what had happened between me and SGT DeJesus, out in NTC. After laughing at their eager faces, waiting for me to tell them what happened, I explained to the both of them that I wouldn't let anyone put their hands on me, unless it was to correct a defect on my uniform. But as a leader and a role model for the two young soldiers that I supervised in the training room, I didn't show them how truly mad I was about the situation. But in every case, I would display a level of professionalism that the Army expected from any soldier or NCO in a leadership position, when it came down to disagreeing or getting into a conflict in front of enlisted soldiers.

THE INVESTIGATION

In the weeks after we had returned from NTC, my problems with 1st SGT Centeneo started to escalate. At times he allowed both PV2 Kuhstoss and PVT Arroyo to go back to the fister platoon and train up on their MOS's, while I worked in the training room and motor pool by myself again. I explained on several occasions that I couldn't work on the vehicles and in the training room all at the same time when the workload was too much and that I often didn't get finished until 9 or 10 o'clock at night. So, at the beginning of March of 2002 1st SGT Centeneo told me that he was bringing a new NCO into the training room to help me out.

"Hey Linson," 1st SGT Centeneo called me into his office, *"Sergeant DeJesus will be your new acting NCOIC of the training room until I can find someone to be in there all of the time."*

"This man is really crazy," I thought to myself as he explained to me who was coming into the training room.

"Linson, you will train Sergeant DeJesus on what is to be done in the training room and how it operates while you'll work more down in the motor pool. Okay guy?"

"First Sergeant, you couldn't find anyone else besides him?"

"Look guy, you two will get along with each other, one way or another."

"If you say so First Sergeant!" I replied. *"First Sergeant, my birthday is coming up and I'm wondering if I can have that day off?"*

"Sure thing guy...Fill out a leave request form and have SGT DeJesus turn it in to me."

"Will do top." I replied walking out of his office.

At first, when SGT DeJesus started working in the training room, our work relationship was deceptively calm. After explaining to him that First Sergeant said I could have my birthday off, SGT DeJesus was grouchy about the request but told me that he will turn in my leave request form to 1st SGT Centeneo.

After a week had gone by, I asked SGT DeJesus if my leave request form had been approved or not.

"First Sergeant Centeneo has it on his desk." SGT DeJesus replied.

Since I was still considered to be the NCOIC of the training room, I walked up to 1st SGT Centeneo outside and asked him if he had received my leave request form... *"No. What are you talking about, guy?"* he replied.

"The one I filled out, so I can have my birthday off, First Sergeant."

"I never received a leave request form guy. I thought I told you to fill one out a week ago?"

"I did First Sergeant, and Sergeant DeJesus said he had turned it in to you already."

"Well, I don't have it, guy."

Returning to the training room a little bit heated, I started to look around my desk for my leave request form, to see if SGT DeJesus missed placed it. After looking everywhere for it and couldn't find it anywhere, I sat at my desk and waited for SGT DeJesus to return to the training room. Upon his arrival, I asked SGT DeJesus has he seen my leave request form, and in a flash of an eye, SGT DeJesus blew up at me... "SOLDIER, YOU'RE NOT GETTING YOUR FUCKING BIRTHDAY OFF! I SHREDDED YOUR GOD DAMN REQUEST FORM!" he shouted. "NOW, YOU NEED TO GET THE FUCK UP AND OUT OF MY TRAINING ROOM!"

"No Sergeant, I will fill out another leave request form and take it to First Sergeant myself."

Just then after I had told SGT DeJesus what I was going to be doing, he came around my desk and grabbed me by my uniform jacket and tried to pull me out of the training room. In the process of him pulling at me while I was still sitting in my chair, I got up and shoved him off of me as he fell over the CQ desk. As quickly as he flew over the desk, I heaved the desk out of the way to get to him, as he tried to get back on his feet… *"That's it you stupid motherfucker!"* as I started to hit him with a left and a right.

Soldiers and NCO's jumped on the both of us, trying to pull us apart as SGT DeJesus kept yelling out loud… *"GET YOUR PUNK ASS OUT OF THE ORDERLY ROOM."* as soldiers pulled me away from him.

"I'M FUCKING TIRED OF YOUR SHIT, BITCH!" I yelled back.

"GET OUT!"

"GET OFF ME!" as I yanked myself away from the soldiers who were holding me back from SGT DeJesus. As I took off walking out of the front doors, SGT DeJesus opened back up the door after I had slammed the door shut behind myself… *"DON'T YOU EVER BRING YOUR PUNK ASS BACK TO MY TRAINING ROOM AGAIN, SOLDIER!"*

Walking towards Divarty Headquarters where SGM Burns worked, I was furious to the point of losing myself while contemplating returning to HHB to finish what SGT DeJesus had started. After I had arrived at SGM Burns office, I told him what had happened between me and SGT DeJesus back at HHB. Let's say SGM Burns wasn't happy to hear what I had to say. *"Come with me."* Sergeant Major Burns told me standing up from his desk.

On the way back from Divarty, we walked into CSM Wyatt on the way down to HHB, where I explained to him what took place in the orderly room… *"We're all on the way down there, so let go see what Sergeant DeJesus has to say for himself."* CSM Wyatt replied.

When we arrived at the orderly room of HHB, CSM Wyatt asked SGT DeJesus what was going on and SGT DeJesus told him his side of the story. After listening to SGT DeJesus explain himself, SGM Burns replied... *"Put your hands on me Sergeant! Call me a punk ass while you're at it!"*

CSM Wyatt wasn't too happy with the situation and sent the soldier who was on duty at the CQ desk, to go and find 1st SGT Centeneo. As soon as the soldier left out the back doors of HHB, 1st SGT Centeneo walked in the front doors and started yelling at me... *"What are you doing this time, Linson? You are always starting stuff! You're nothing but trouble guy!"* he yelled out.

"At ease that noise First Sergeant. Let's all go and talk in your office," CSM Wyatt replied.

"Sergeant DeJesus and Specialist Linson, you both stand at parade rest outside my door." 1st SGT Centeneo ordered us.

Standing beside SGT DeJesus, I wanted so badly to end his life where he stood. But I didn't budge one inch from where 1st SGT Centeneo told us to stand. As CSM Wyatt and SGM Burns walked out of 1st SGT Centeneo's office, we were both called into his office after they had left... *"Why do you always keep running to Sergeant Major Burns, Linson?"* 1st SGT Centeneo asked me.

"He is the only one around here that will do anything about my problems, First Sergeant." I replied.

210

After hearing what I had to say, 1st SGT Centeneo dismissed SGT DeJesus and told me to close the door behind him… *"You keep stressing me out with your issues guy."* 1st SGT Centeneo replied.

"First Sergeant, you knew that DeJesus and I didn't get along with each other before you brought him into the training room." I bluntly replied.

"Look guy, he is the new NCOIC of the training room and you both will have to get along one way or another. Look Linson," he added. *"Stay out of the training room and just work only in the motor pool until everything calms down."*

"First Sergeant, he put his hands on me again just like he did out in NTC, and I told you I don't care about him, but I will respect his rank. I'm sorry First Sergeant I cannot and will not work around him."

"I know guy. Just go down to the motor pool and keep away from him. I'll talk with him about his behavior."

"That's what you said the last time, First Sergeant." I replied before I was dismissed from his office.

In the end, I was denied my birthday off, which is normally granted without question for anyone of any rank, enlisted or Officer.

A week later while I was at home, I got a phone call that didn't show up on my caller ID. So, thinking it was a bill collector, I let the answering machine get it instead. Listening to the answering machine going through its normal routine, someone started to leave a message, as I turned down my television to listen... *"Hey faggot, if you show you're fucking face back up here at 3-16 again, we're going to kill your faggot gay ass.... We know where you live!"* as the phone hung up.

After hearing the comments that someone from my unit had left on my answering machine, I sat there in a daze and speechless. At that time, the only thought that was running through my mind was... *"What the fuck!"*

After bringing myself back into reality, I called SFC Madyun and told him what kind of phone call I just received from someone in 3-16th... *"Did you call the First Sergeant yet?"* He asked me.

"Yes, but I couldn't get a hold of him." I replied.

"Do you have a tape recorder?"

"Yes, I do."

"Make a copy of it and bring it in first thing in the morning and will get the MP's involved (**M**ilitary **P**olice)*."*

"Should I call the cops now, since I'm living off post?"

"No, don't do that," he replied, *"We'll take care of it Linson."*

Looking around my apartment after I had gotten off the phone with SFC Madyun, I started thinking about what I needed to do to protect myself... *"Do I need to go and buy a gun or a bat?"* I asked myself, getting dressed, to head out to Walmart to go look at the guns that they had.

That next morning, I brought in a copy of the recording to let SFC Madyun and 1st SGT Centeneo listen to it. After listening to the recording, SFC Madyun told 1st SGT Centeneo that he needed to contact the MP's and report this situation to them ASAP. But 1st SGT Centeneo had something else in mind, as he brushed off SFC Madyun comment. After SFC Madyun made his statement clear and left the office, 1st SGT Centeneo opened his top desk drawer and deposited the tape inside.

"What are you doing First Sergeant?" I asked him.

"I'll take care of this Linson. You just go back to work."

Walking out of his office and looking back at 1st SGT Centeneo looking at me in a daze, I was very suspicious and felt that 1st SGT Centeneo would cover up this incident.

Later that evening, when I had talked to a few close friends of mine down in the motor pool, they told me that I needed to go above the First Sergeant's head and go talk to CSM Wyatt and Lt Col Williams about what happened. So, using the open-door policy, I told 1st SGT Centeneo that I wanted to go and talk with CSM Wyatt about this matter.

"Sure thing guy. I'll let him know you're on your way up to see him."

"Thank you, First Sergeant."

"Knock, knock." As I stood outside CSM Wyatt's office, pissed off.

"Come in." he replied. *"Linson, how are you?"*

"I'm doing okay for now Sergeant Major. I need to talk to you ASAP."

"Does your First Sergeant know you're up here to see me?"

"Yes Sergeant Major, I just left his office before I came up here."

"That's good. Have a seat. What can I help you with?"

As I took a seat in front of his desk and told him what was going on with me since I've been in his Battalion all the way up to the now, he asked me one question… *"What did First Sergeant Centeneo say about this death threat?"*

"He said he'll take care of it Sergeant Major."

"That's the wrong answer soldier!" he replied as he stood up from his desk. *"Follow me now!"*

As we walked back down to the orderly room, CSM Wyatt told me… *"You should have been coming to me in the first place. None of this wouldn't have gotten this far, Linson!"* For a moment I felt CSM Wyatt was going to take care of this issue now and for good, but I questioned myself about why I didn't come to him years ago, if he was telling me he would have taken care of my issues a long time ago.

"Every First Sergeant after Burns told me that they told you everything, Sergeant Major."

CSM Wyatt looked at me in disbelief... *"No, they haven't!"*

From that point on, it was a quiet walk down to HHB after he said that to me.

Walking into the orderly room, CSM Wyatt and I walked right into 1st SGT Centeneo's office and closed the door behind us... *"Where is the tape recording, First Sergeant?"* CSM Wyatt asked 1st SGT Centeneo.

"What recording, Sergeant Major?" 1st SGT Centeneo looked at CSM Wyatt as if he didn't know what he was talking about.

"The one Specialist Linson gave you this morning First Sergeant!" he replied.

"Specialist Linson didn't bring me anything Sergeant Major," he answered back, *"nor did he tell me that he was going up to Battalion to talk to you."*

CSM Wyatt and I exchanged startled glances. I looked back at 1st SGT Centeneo... *"First Sergeant, I brought you a tape recording of the message that I received last night, and you and Sergeant Madyun listed to it, and you put the tape in your center top drawer of your desk."* I explained. *"And also, I told you I was using Sergeant Major's open-door policy about this situation."*

First Sergeant opened his desk drawer to show CSM Wyatt that there was no tape in it.

"You removed it from your drawer," I immediately replied.

1st SGT Centeneo stood up and stepped from behind his desk… *"Linson, sit behind my desk and go through all my desk drawers and try to find this make-believe tape you're talking about."*

Walking around and sitting behind his desk, I started looking through all the drawers and around the top of the desk, and I couldn't find it anywhere.

As I stopped looking through his stuff, after a couple of minutes of messing up everything on and around his desk, I looked up at CSM Wyatt with tears running down my face… *"I gave him the tape this morning Sergeant Major."*

Looking over at 1st SGT Centeneo, as he stood there with a smirk on his face, I quickly thought to myself… *"Why do I continue to have faith and trust in my Chain of Command?"*

"See Sergeant Major, this is what I've been putting up with since I became First Sergeant here." He explained to CSM Wyatt. *"Specialist Linson is always late to formations, and he always shows up with unpolished boots and a messed-up uniform, Sergeant Major Wyatt!"*

I kept trying to butt in to tell Sergeant Major that he was lying to him… *"If First Sergeant was telling the truth, why isn't there any counseling reports about my behavior, Sergeant Major?"* But CSM Wyatt was paying more attention to 1st SGT Centeneo than me.

(In the military, people always listen to people who have more rank and not to those who don't.) You are guilty until proven innocent, and I had no way to prove I was innocent, since 1st SGT Centeneo hid or destroyed the tape, I gave him.

1st SGT Centeneo kept up his litany of criticisms as I sat there behind his desk, and I knew any defense I made would be disregarded.

"GET YOUR ASS UP FROM HIS DESK SOLDIER!" CSM Wyatt yelled out loud.

Walking around from his desk, I passed 1st SGT Centeneo as he smiled at me as if to say... *"I got you."*

While standing at parade rest, I asked CSM Wyatt if I could say a few words, but CSM Wyatt erupted into my face... *"WHEN YOU ARE AT PARADE REST, YOU ARE NOT TO BE TALKING AT ALL SOLDIER!"*

"You see Sergeant Major; this is what he does. He's a bad soldier. He's been telling lies all these years since he's been here." 1st SGT Centeneo said while laughing.

"What is your problem, soldier?" CSM Wyatt demanded.

"I don't have a problem and I'm not lying to you Sergeant Major; he is." I replied, holding back my anger.

"Before the end of the year is up," CSM Wyatt replied, *"you will be demoted too private, and the First Sergeant and I will see personally to that! Now get the hell out of here before I rip your rank off you now Specialist Linson!"*

"Stand outside my office at parade rest until I come out soldier!" 1st SGT Centeneo replied.

While standing at parade rest outside of 1st SGT Centeneo's office, a few NCO's and soldiers that were in the orderly room told me to keep my head up and not to worry about what was going on. I couldn't say anything in response because I was pissed off beyond words.

"Come talk to me Specialist Linson." Captain Morgan stepped out of his office to motion me into his office. After entering his office, I closed the door behind myself... *"What's going on Linson, and why were you getting your butt chewed out in there?"*

Thinking that CPT Morgan had any real interests in my problems, I explained to him the death threat and the tape that just disappeared from 1st Sergeant's desk... *"Keep your head up and don't let this get you down."* he replied.

"Where is Linson!" We heard the First Sergeant calling out my name outside the Commander's office.

"Hey First Sergeant, we're in here." CPT Morgan opened the door and told the First Sergeant to come in.

"What's wrong with you, guy?" First Sergeant asked me when he walked into the Commander's office.

The only thing I wanted to do when he walked up to me, was to hit him dead square in his face as hard as I could as he approached me. To get the conversation off of me, CPT Morgan asked 1st SGT Centeneo what he had planned for me... *"Me and Sergeant Major Wyatt, recommends that Specialist Linson receives a mental health evaluation ASAP, and he will receive an Article 15 for lying to a Senior Noncommissioned Officer, and he will not be eligible for reenlistment."* 1st SGT Centeneo replied.

"That sounds like a good idea, First Sergeant," CPT Morgan quickly agreed to the Sergeant Majors and First Sergeant's recommendations, and then turned and looked at me... *"We're going to get you some help soldier, so you will stop lying to your Chain of Command."*

"You fucking bastards!" I thought to myself looking pissed off at the both of them. I couldn't believe what CPT Morgan had just said to me. It was more than strange that one moment he was telling me to keep my head up and next, he was calling me a liar.

Not to cause any more problems, I just nodded my head, as if I agreed with their recommendations. After I was dismissed from CPT Morgan's office, three NCO's from another platoon in HHB told me to walk with them outside, so I could calm down. They knew what I was going through and wanted to help me out. They told me to contact my Senator from my home state and let him or her know what was going on, and that all my problems would go away quickly.

I thought to myself while listening to these three NCO's telling me what I needed to do... *"If the Army can't help me, how can an elected official help me out?"* Never-the-less, I spent all night typing a letter to my Senator, Senator Thad Cochran of Mississippi. I described in great detail what had been going on since my first day I've arrived at this unit, and how I couldn't deal with it anymore. I also informed my Senator that my Chain of Command wouldn't let me re-enlist to stay in the Army, and that I was facing an Article 15, or some type of disciplinary action. After I had emailed the letter to him, I wondered what kind of response would come out of this and whether he could help me out at all.

Come the next day, CPT Morgan gave me my appointment time and where to go and see the mental health evaluator. Before I was escorted to the mental health clinic, 1st SGT Centeneo read me my Article 15 charges that were based on lying to a NCO and placing false judgments on my fellow soldiers, NCO's and Officers within the HHB 3-16th FA. After hearing what I was being charged with, First Sergeant ordered SGT DeJesus to escort me to the 4th ID Mental Health Clinic, where a full bird Colonel was waiting to evaluate me.

In the two hours that I spent talking to this mental health evaluator and explaining everything to him, he couldn't believe what I've gone through since my first day at Fort Hood. Towards the end of my evaluation, I asked the Colonel a simple question... *"Colonel sir, if you were my Commander and you knew what I was going through, what would you have done differently to make sure I was safe and didn't have the issues that I have today?"*

"I wouldn't know what to do with this kind of situation, soldier. I wouldn't know where to begin to tell you the truth." He replied looking back down at his notes, fumbling his pen.

Looking at him flipping through his notes, not knowing what to write down, here sat a Colonel in the United States Army, admitting to me that the United States Army was unable to deal with this type of sexual harassment, death threats and attempts on a soldier's life from other military personnel.

"Sir," as I got his attention. *"I guess I'm screwed!"* as he looked up at me and gave me the deer-in-the-headlights look that confirmed my answer.

At the end of the evaluation, the Colonel, told me that there was nothing mentally wrong with me that he could diagnose... *"I know sir, but my Chain of Command doesn't think so."* I replied.

"Well, I don't know what to tell you soldier, or your Chain of Command." He replied, shrugging his shoulders up and down.

When I arrived back at HHB and gave CPT Morgan and 1st SGT Centeneo the Colonel's evaluation report stating that I wasn't mentally ill, CPT Morgan looked over at 1st SGT Centeneo and said... *"We're going to proceed with the Article 15 to the max, regardless of what this letter says!"*

After I listen to my Commander and First Sergeant putting everything out on the table, I kept thinking to myself... *"Yall just wait, this isn't over with yet!"*

When I got off and went home that afternoon, before I could put my keys down on my table, I received a phone call from an angry CPT Morgan, who told me to report back to his office ASAP. On the drive back onto post, I knew that his anger had to be about my Senator reporting my issues to a much higher command structure within the Army.

When I arrived at CPT Morgan's office, 1st SGT Centeneo and SFC Madyun were sitting in his office waiting for me to show up.

"Why did you contact your Senator, Specialist Linson?" CPT Morgan asked me. Before I could reply, he quickly interrupted me... *"Don't answer that."*

"Why is my name in this Linson?" SFC Madyun spoke up. *"We haven't had any problems in years."*

"Sergeant Madyun, I told him about everything since day one. That's why you're in here." I replied.

"Yea but I shouldn't be."

In truth, it had only been a year since he stopped harassing me. I guess he felt the need to exaggerate his innocence. As I stood there in silence, no one in the office said a word to one another. Here was my Chain of Command trying to figure out how to handle the investigation prompted by Senator Thad Cochran of Mississippi. If they proceeded with the Article 15 at this point, it would confirm that I was right about everything, and if they didn't proceed with it, then what motivated their original case against me? But the biggest question was why wasn't I being investigated for suspicion of homosexual activities, which the Army had the right to do under the DADT policy? After all, I had been harassed and accused of inappropriate behavior with other male soldiers for years now. Why investigate me for apparently lying to a senior NCO, and why not go to the heart of the matter and launch an investigation into my accused sexuality? Was it because my tormentors had no case against me? I thought to myself, while standing there looking at everyone.

After a few minutes had passed, CPT Morgan looked up at me and said... *"We have a Congressional investigation on our hands, and now I'm in the hot seat about why all of this has been happening to you, and I wasn't even here back in 1999."* As CPT Morgan pleaded.

"Look guy," 1st SGT Centeneo interrupted, *"we were going to let you re-enlist and we weren't going to give you the Article 15. What makes you think we're out to screw you, guy?"*

To keep myself from laughing, I didn't say a word back to none of them as the room fell quiet once again. Then CPT Morgan broke the silence... *"The III Corps Commander needs answers in the next 48 hours about what took place now and over the years. Your Senator, Thad Cochran needs these answers back to him ASAP!"* he explained.

After I was dismissed out of CPT Morgan's office, I felt a huge sigh of relief that now it's their turn to sit in the hot seat, as I walked out of the HHB orderly room.

After I made it back home, I called my mom and told her that Senator Cochran had come through for me, and now my Chain of Command was afraid to answer him.

During the next two days, an appointed investigating Officer from Divarty, went through the Battalion asking questions about my accused affairs. A week later after the investigation was complete, I received a letter in the mail from Senator Cochran, confirming the truth of what I had reported to him, and what proper action that would be taken in the days to come... *"If you ever need anything else from me,"* he added, *"you shouldn't hesitate to contact me again."*

Shortly thereafter, the Article 15 proceedings were dropped, and I was raising my right hand to re-enlist to stay in the U.S. Army.

While I stood in front of my old Executive Officer, 1LT Alvarez, as he read out loud my enlistment pledge, while I repeated after him, I kept asking myself... *"How in GOD's name did I make it this far, after four years of hell?"*

NOWHERE TO RUN

During the month and a half that it took for me to out-process out of 3-16th FA, I realized that I was heading to a co-ed unit, where I would have a new start in the 1st Infantry Division, over in Germany. I told myself while I was on my thirty days of PCS leave, that I would talk more with my fellow soldiers, and I wouldn't be so uptight when it came to socializing with anyone. But the biggest thing I loved most about leaving 3-16th, I was starting over with a clean board in a new location.

At the end of January 2003, I flew into Frankfurt International Airport in Frankfurt Germany, wondering to myself why I chose to come over here and not Egypt, when it was a part of my reenlistment choices. None-the-less here I was looking out the window, at the snow-covered ground, wondering what life laid ahead of me.

While being bused over to Wurzburg Germany, I felt that my future would take another dramatic turn for the worst, but for some reason I couldn't understand why I felt this way since I was starting over in a new location, or more like a new country I never been too.

Knowing that I was heading to a co-ed Company called Bravo Company 701st MSB (Main Support Battalion) in the 1st Infantry Division. I looked on the internet and saw that this Company was a

Transportation Company where my MOS was in every platoon, something that I've been longing for since I first left AIT.

When all of us new soldiers arrived at the 1st Infantry Division in-processing location on Leighton Barracks in Wurzburg, I was in a nervous wreck thinking about why I reenlisted to stay in and why didn't I get out when I had the chance. But I told myself that no matter what happened in my last unit, this one would be different and believe me, it was. After all of us were separated by post locations, there was another new soldier to the Army who was going to the same Company in the 701st, and his name is PFC Giavatto, who told me his job was a heavy wheeled mechanic.

After another bus arrived to take some of us to Larson Barracks in Kitzingen, to be in-processed further into the 1st Infantry Division, my new Platoon Sergeant named Staff Sergeant Griffin came and picked me up and drove me over to Harvey Barracks, where the 701st MSB was located. On the drive there, SSG Griffin explained to me that 701st was heading to Turkey to be a part of the Iraqi invasion and that I needed to have my head on straight and ready since they were already loading up everything to head over there.

Being that his words didn't make me afraid or nervous about war, I simply responded... *"I'm ready to deploy Sergeant, bring it on."*

I knew SSG Griffin wasn't expecting that kind of response from me, when he looked over at me with a distasteful look. To me, all I wanted to do was to get off on the right foot and show my new Platoon Sergeant that he wasn't just getting the average soldier into his ranks, but instead he was getting someone who was willing and able to do whatever kind of job he had for me. Now, when I look back over my years in 701st MSB, that was a fortune cookie I should not have broken open.

It took two weeks to in-process into Bravo Company 701st, under the command of CPT Yabarra and 1st SGT Agard, who was out on sick leave and the acting First Sergeant was Sergeant First Class Hinds. During my in-processing time, me and three other soldiers who were new to Bravo Company were put on the rear-d (**R**ear **D**etachment) barracks across from Bravo Company's barracks, since we were not ready to deploy with the unit when their time had come to deploy. So, since I only knew the soldiers that came with me, I hung out with the three new soldiers named SPC Helm, SPC Head and PFC Giavatto, the only soldiers that I knew at the time. During our off time, the four of us would walk to downtown Kitzingen, to try out the natives' foods. At times we had fun walking around site seeing around Kitzingen, looking at the German way of life and trying to learn how the Status of Force Agreement (SOFA), effected our way of life.

Thinking that things were going good for me, my problems first began when PFC Giavatto, who shared the bathroom with me on the other side in a different room, started to spread rumors around about me singing in my room to "girly music" as he put it. Whenever I took a shower, I would sing to myself, and some days it would be Gospel or R&B music. I didn't know at the time that PFC Giavatto would round up SPC Helm and SPC Head and anyone else he could in his room, to listen to me sing while I took a shower. I found this out when another soldier in the rear-d barracks told me that they were going around telling other soldiers that I was singing to "girly music in the shower."

I didn't realize that singing in the shower constituted my latest homosexual act, but to me I was a happy male soldier who liked to sing in the shower, but for a lot of people in the Army, "real soldiers" did not do these kinds of things. I guess my plan of keeping a low profile wasn't going to happen for me, but at first, I didn't care, because I had been through worse. So, I thought.

When I had finished in-processing into 701st, SSG Griffin asked me if I had any experience that could benefit the unit while I was a part of the rear detachment group. Since I didn't know much about anything that pertained to a transportation company, I told him about my experience working in the training room back in my last unit, and to my surprise, he was enthusiastic about me helping in that area of the Company. So later that day, he told me that he had talked with SFC Hinds about me helping in the orderly room and that she had agreed to me coming into an all-female training room. At first, I didn't catch onto the *"all female training room,"* comment until later.

After reporting to SFC Hinds that next day, she explained to me… *"I'm putting a lot of trust in you Specialist Linson to go in there and work and not sit around like the rest of those soldiers,"* she explained. *"Just because everyone else around you is lazy, that doesn't mean I'm giving you the okay to be lazy as well."*

At that time, I assured her that I would perform my job better than all of them combined, and that I would not disappoint her on any level. For me, this was my first experience with a co-ed unit, and I knew I had a challenge on my hands to perform in ways I didn't know how too when it came to working around female soldiers.

For some reason in Bravo Company 701st, the females generally did the administrative work, while the male soldiers did physical assignments and details. But in most units in the Army, the genders were more integrated, and the work was equally delegated to everyone. But for this Company, it wasn't.

After being excused out of the First Sergeant's office, I reported to the NCOIC of the training room, SGT Gonzales, who was surprised that SFC Hinds had sent her a male soldier to work in the training room. When I asked her why she seemed so surprised to see me working with them, she told me that 1st SGT Agard didn't like male soldiers in his training room, and that he wanted men to do men's work and for females to do what he called female work. After she had told me this, I replied... *"That sounds preposterous and ignorant, Sergeant."* But I took it with a grain of salt and ignored the ignorance of one man's opinion.

"Hey Sergeant, I'm in here to do a job and not waste anyone's time." I told her.

"I'm impressed that you are not afraid of office work Linson."

"Hahaha. Sergeant Gonzales, if you knew where I just came from, you would understand why I'm not."

During my first week in the orderly room, I received a lot of compliments from SFC Hinds and CPT Yabarra, on the great job I was doing. Being that I was new to the unit, and I had already picked up on what needed to be done, it felt good to be accepted by my new Chain of Command. But out of all of them, I really wanted to show 1st SGT Agard how efficient and effective a male could do this job alongside with female soldiers.

As the weeks went by, a lot of soldiers and NCOs came by the training room to see this new male soldier who was running the training room after a short period of time. At that time, it didn't matter to me to see countless soldiers and NCO's coming by the training room looking at me, just to see who I was. At times, I kept wondering if 1st SGT Agard was ever going to return to the Company after his surgery.

Throughout the day when I had to take paperwork to CPT Yabarra, for him to sign, he would tell me... *"I know whenever First Sergeant Agard returns; he would be happy to keep you in the training room Linson."*

To hear those words from my new Company Commander made me feel good about things to come.

One Saturday afternoon, I decided to head back to the training room and catch up on some much-needed work, when I heard a voice yell out to me... *"What's up yo!"*

When I looked up, I saw a short female who was barely taller than the counter desk, looking at me.

"Hello."

"Who are you?" she yelled back.

"Specialist Linson."

"I heard about how good of a job you're doing in here soldier. What's up, yo!"

"There's nothing up."

Wanting to get a better look at who this person was, I got up from my desk and walked around to get a closer look at this curious person, who introduced herself as SGT Cardwell.

"I heard about a male soldier working in the all-female training room and I had to come see this for myself." She explained. *"You know First Sergeant Agard doesn't like male soldiers working in his training room, and he has told us that any male who worked in an office had to be gay."*

I started laughing at SGT Cardwell's remarks as she joined in laughing with me... *"Well Sergeant, if that's the case there are a lot of gay office workers in the Army!"* as we both kept laughing together. From that day on, SGT Cardwell became a good close friend of mine.

That following Monday morning, SGT Gonzales told me that 1st SGT Agard would be in later that day, and that he wanted to see me personally. Knowing that this was my time to show him that I could run his training room better than the soldiers he already had in there, I felt excited and nervous to even want to meet him. So come lunch time, I went back to my room to relax and to think about what to say when I first met my First Sergeant. After I had returned from our lunch break, SFC Hinds told me that 1st SGT Agard was in his office and that he wanted to see me later that day.

"Here we go, Howard." I thought to myself, sitting back down at my desk.

Working and typing away, while slightly nervous, SSG Griffin came up to my desk and told me that 1st SGT Agard wanted to see me in his office. Being that I was already nervous, I quickly stood up from my desk and started off toward his office to meet this man who I didn't have a clue about.

"Knock, Knock!" at his office door.

"Come in soldier!"

"Specialist Linson reporting as ordered First Sergeant."

"First of all, welcome to Bravo Company 701st Main Support Battalion soldier."

"Thank you, First Sergeant," I replied standing in front of his desk at the position of "at ease."

"Why are you going around my barracks having sex with my male soldiers Specialist Linson?"

"Hold up! What are you talking about First Sergeant?" I replied in shock.

I had been in Germany two and a half months now and I hardly knew anyone and hardly made any friends, yet alone had sex with anyone since I've been there. But now I stood in front of my First Sergeants' desk dumb struck by the accusation 1st SGT Agard had made.

"It's a simple question Specialist Linson. Why are you engaging in homosexual acts in my barracks?" He shot back with his voice more irritated.

"First Sergeant, you have the wrong person. I'm not doing that in your barracks. And first of all, I don't even live in your barracks. I'm over in the rear-d barracks." I quickly responded.

"DON'T IGNORE WHAT THE FUCK I JUST ASKED YOU SOLDIER!" he shouted back.

I stood there pleading with him... *"I don't know what you're talking about or where you got the idea that I was sleeping with your male soldier's First Sergeant!"*

But no matter what I said, 1st SGT Agard wasn't buying it. He just sat back in his chair and stared at me, and after a few moments of silence... *"I want you out of my training room and back in third platoon with Sergeant Griffin! And while you're walking out, I'll decide if I want to have you court marshaled for violating the Don't Ask, Don't Tell policy soldier. Now get the fuck out of my office before I call the MP's and have your ass arrested for spreading STDs around my barracks!"*

As I turned around and started out of his door without waiting for him to dismiss me, I felt my heart hit the ground as I walked back towards the training room where SGT Gonzales was standing there smiling at me. I quickly realized that my nightmare of my past had returned to my new unit, but this time around it was on the other side of the planet with nowhere to run too.

"What's wrong, Linson?" SGT Gonzales asked me, as I walked past her looking mad.

"I'm out of here. I was just told to go back to third platoon ASAP!" I replied, walking out of the orderly room. As I was walking out, SFC Hinds overheard me telling SGT Gonzales that I was leaving the training room and asked me what happened when I went to talk to the First Sergeant. After I had told her everything that was said, she was furious with 1st SGT Agard's accusations... *"Go back to your room while I get this situation fixed."* She told me.

While I was walking back to my room, I started looking around my surroundings and kept asking myself... *"Why in the hell did I re-enlist for this shit again?"*

As I laid on my bed in my room, looking at the wall next to me, a familiar thought kept racing through my mind, *"Why me?"* and after a few hours of trying to think of a reason why, I heard a knock at my door. When I opened it, SGT Gonzales told me that SFC Hinds wanted to see me in her office down in the motor pool ASAP. Not knowing what was said and who said it, when I had entered the motor pool bay area, I quickly became the center of attention, as I walked through the entire Company as they stood around waiting for the end of the day dismissal formation.

As I entered SFC Hind's office, she instructed me to close the door behind myself and sit down in front of her desk... *"The Company just had a formation with First Sergeant Agard, who told the entire Company that you were going around the barracks having sexual contact with other male soldiers and that it was a crime to violate the Don't Ask, Don't Tell policy."*

"What the fuck!" I replied, as tears started coming down my face. At that moment, I felt my heart skip a few beats as I did my best to hold back my tears as I kept shaking my head from side to side, tapping my hand on the arm rest of the chair. I could tell in those few quiet seconds that SFC Hinds shared my disbelief, as she asked me to keep my composure. She told me that other NCOs within the Company had reported this matter to the Battalion's EO (Equal Opportunity) NCOIC, SFC Ford.

As I struggled to control my emotions, I told her I wanted to see him immediately, and SFC Hinds quickly replied, *"Her."* Struggling to form a smile on my face, I apologized for calling her him, as she smiled back at me. After a few moments of silence, SFC Hinds got up from her desk and told me that she had to hold the final formation and instructed me to wait in her office until she had returned.

After a couple of minutes had passed, SFC Hinds came back into her office with several other female NCO's who were outraged about what 1st SGT Agard had said about me to the whole entire Company. They all told me that he had done similar things to other soldiers who were now gone from the 701st or out of the Army. If a female soldier became pregnant, they said, 1st SGT Agard would call her a "hoe" in front of the entire Company, humiliating her in the same way he had done me. After hearing about 1st SGT Agard's method of operations, SFC Hinds asked SSG Bush to find one of her NCOs, to escort me over to go see SFC Ford over in the DTA building (**D**river **T**raining **A**cademy).

While this female NCO, named SGT Powell, walked me over to go see SFC Ford, she kept telling me everything was going to be alright. But while she did her best to reassure me good days to come, I kept repeating in my mind, *"Yea right!"* I've been down this road too many times to believe the same old words that any person in the Army would say to me, or to make me feel better about something like this.

After we arrived at SFC Ford's office, she introduced herself and told me that she had heard what 1st SGT Agard had said about me to his entire Company. After SGT Powell left the office, SFC Ford asked me to recount what was said in 1st SGT Agard's office that day.

"Why would First Sergeant Agard get the idea that you're a homosexual, Linson?" she asked me.

"I've been told that First Sergeant didn't like males in his training room, and that he thought any male working in an office position was gay." I replied.

SFC Ford was shocked to learn that 1st SGT Agard was circulating such opinions to enlisted personnel. She told me that she was going to speak with CSM Cook, the Command Sergeant Major of 701st MSB, about what 1st SGT Agard had said about me to the entire Company... *"First Sergeant Agard will be taken care of quickly. Keep your head up Linson, it's not the end of the world yet."* She replied. *"You'll be okay. Don't let this get you down soldier."*

"What the fuck ever!" I thought to myself while looking up at her, while thinking about my past. Only if she knew what I've been through already, she would not have said this to me.

As I started walking back towards my barracks, I felt hopeless and useless. I had been in Germany almost three months and the nightmares were happening all over again. I didn't know where to turn or run to. When I made it back to my room, I fell face first into my pillow crying and later passed out while still in my uniform.

Come the next day I found myself standing in third platoon during the morning's formation wondering to myself... *"What would become of me now?"* To my surprise, my squad leader was SGT Powell who told me that rumors were flying around about me, and that I needed to be myself, and the problems would go away.

Listening to her talk, I wished her words were true, but I knew they were not, and I knew my future in the 701st was going to be hell from that moment on. Later that week, SFC Ford requested me to see her in her office again. When I had arrived, she asked me how things were going for me since 1st SGT Agard had created a major problem for me... *"Quiet for now, and hardly any of my peers would talk or work around me."* I replied.

"Don't worry about that Linson. Put it this way, First Sergeant Agard won't be bothering you anymore from this day forward or anyone else for that matter."

I was confused after she had said this to me. *"What do you mean Sergeant Ford?"*

"First Sergeant Agard was forced into retirement." She replied.

I was shocked to hear the news, but by this time I didn't believe the Army could do the right thing anywhere I had gone.

"Thank you."

"You're most welcome," she replied. *"The Army doesn't tolerate this kind of behavior from senior NCO's and Officers, Linson. And in the future, I want you to come straight to me if you have any more problems, and I will take care of it quickly for you,"* she explained to me.

"How many times have I heard that before and nothing was done?" I thought to myself, while looking at her explaining what I needed to do. But this time around, something had been done and perhaps it was possible that my new Chain of Command would take care of things the right way. So, I thought.

After our orders were canceled to go to Turkey, SFC Hinds informed the Company that we were getting a new First Sergeant by the name of Master Sergeant Dennis in a few days, and that she could not wait till he got there, so she could go back to being a Platoon Sergeant again.

In April of 2003, the rear-d soldiers were all re-assigned to new rooms within the Bravo Companies barracks, and my new roommate became SPC Mendoza, who made it very clear that he didn't like me as a roommate. While I was his roommate, he did his best not to get undressed or take showers while I was in our room, but for me there were benefits to this situation. Most of the time, the room was all mine, and I didn't have to look at him every morning and afternoon, when I didn't feel like being bothered by anyone.

Trying to take my mind off my new problems, SGT Cardwell invited me out to socialize with her and her friends who were stationed over in Bamberg and Stuttgart Germany. While hanging out with SGT Cardwell and all her friends, she told me that she knew which soldiers within the Company were gay or bisexual themselves, because she was bisexual herself. She also had explained to me who to stay away from and who was cool to chill with. After hanging out with her and her friends at times, I eventually told her I was bisexual and didn't want to be caught up with anyone in the Company. Being that most of the time I was alone in the barracks or whenever I decided to head out into the surrounding villages, she introduced me to this silly female soldier named PV2 Strittholt, who is still today my friend.

After a while, me and Strittholt would hang out together when we went to the club AKW, which is pronounced "Aue Kea Vea", or just to go driving around Germany into villages we never been to, to go site seeing for fun. Later she introduced me to some of her friends named PVT Bailey who was her roommate, and PV2 Nickels and PFC Ortero.

But to have new friends that I could hang out with, life in the barracks was becoming unbearable for me. Most nights, soldiers would bang on my door and take off running whenever I would open it, to see who it was. Sometimes in the morning I would find used condoms filled with semen taped to my doorknob, and every time someone would do this, I would report this to my Chain of Command, and the only response I would get out of them would be, *"we'll look into it"*.

While the harassment continued, I went and spoke to 1st SGT Dennis about what kind of harassment I've been encountering while living in the barracks. He told me that he knew all about the incident with me and 1st SGT Agard, and that he was sorry to hear that I was going through a lot of problems. *"I will speak to Command Sergeant Major Cook and Lieutenant Colonel Ross* (The Battalion Commander), *about moving you to a new Battalion."*

Although I knew I would miss my new friends, I was once again eager for a fresh start somewhere else, far, far away from the 701st MSB. A few days later, after I had talked with 1st SGT Dennis, he told me that CSM Cook didn't want to approve a transfer from his Battalion to another but suggested that I work over at the gym with the MWR (**M**ilitary **W**elfare and **R**ecreation), for the time being, until they could find another means to fix my problems.

"The gym," I thought to myself after agreeing with my new assignment. *"Well, at least I get to work out whenever I can."* I thought to myself, walking over to the MWR building to report to the civilians in charge of the gym.

After a week of working in the gym, I found my new job very appealing to me. I could work out autonomously when I wanted to, and I could work and participate in the MWR activities when it was feasible for me. Life was good, so I thought. I didn't experience any harassment on the job while working in the gym, although it continued back in the barracks. I kept telling myself to do my best and ignore the soldiers in Bravo Company and enjoy my new surroundings working in the gym.

As the days and months passed, it became more and more evident that we were going to be deployed to Iraq. I often wondered what my job would be, since I had not done much Army work in almost a year as a soldier. Since I've been in Germany, I've been working around mostly civilians, but I knew one day I would have to put back on my uniform and do what I was meant to do as an 88 Mike.

At times when I saw CSM Cook working out in the gym, I would approach him and ask what my job will be when we all went to Iraq... *"We're going to move you over to Delta Company, where your job would be delivering military equipment throughout Germany for the time being, Linson. And also, First Sergeant Griffin of Delta Company knows all about your problems, and he has assured me that nothing like this will be tolerated from his soldiers or NCOs in his Company."*

"Yea that's what your mouth is saying Sergeant Major," thinking to myself, looking at him explaining to me my future within the 701st.

Listening to him talk, I kept thinking about all my time in the Army, and how many times have I heard this same old bull shit speech before. But once again I gave my new Chain of Command the benefit of the doubt of taking care of things, the way they said they would.

Come October of 2003, the 701st MSB had a mass Battalion meeting in the gym about our deployment to Iraq at the beginning of 2004. After the meeting was over, 1st SGT Griffin approached me and introduced himself to me as my new First Sergeant and told me that I will be moving from Bravo Company to Delta Company that following week and introduced me to Delta Companies Company Commander, CPT Ruckman.

Before I physically met 1st SGT Griffin, I was told from countless soldiers of all races, that 1st SGT Griffin was labeled as the head leader of the KKK (Ku Klux Klan) of 701st MSB. So many people told me while I was not in his Company and when I was in his Company, that he hated

African Americans and Latin Americans soldiers that were in his Company and throughout the entire 701st MSB. Most soldiers and a few NCOs in Delta Company told me that the 12th Chemical Company, that was a Company within the 701st, that their First Sergeant was 1st SGT Griffins best friend and that he was also a part of the KKK whom also hated races other than his own as well. But while talking with 1st SGT Griffin, I didn't care about what his personal beliefs were, but only wondered how this man would be as my new First Sergeant, regardless if he liked or disliked people of color.

"Command Sergeant Major Cook and I had talked about the move, but no one had told me when it would happen, First Sergeant?"

"Well, I'm telling you now Linson," 1st SGT Griffin replied.

As I looked around at the faces of Delta Company, I quickly asked myself... *"Do I really want to go through this shit all over again?"* But knowing I did not have a choice in the matter, I told myself, *"Here we go again. Keep Moving Howard, just keep moving, and hold your head up."*

In the week that I had to report over to Delta Company, I got myself back into the mindset of being a soldier again and getting ready for whatever surprises waited for me.

Walking over to where Delta Company was located, I felt like I was opening another door to another door within the Twilight Zone.

243

While I stood around Delta Companies orderly room, waiting to talk to 1st SGT Griffin, a few soldiers introduced themselves to me as if I had just arrived in Germany as a new soldier.

"AAWW, this place is a hell of a lot different than Bravo Company," I thought to myself, looking around at all the bright faces of Delta Company.

After a few minutes of waiting around, I met with 1st SGT Griffin and CPT Ruckman, who assured me that none of the harassment that I had received in Bravo Company would go on here in Delta Company.

I knew while listening to them explain what I was or wasn't going to be experiencing, I knew they weren't telling me the truth. I have been down this road too many times before to believe anything that they had to say to me. But like a good soldier, I put my faith in my new Chain of Command and believed that things would be different for me.

After hearing what Delta Company was all about, 1st SGT Griffin introduced me to SSG Wright, my Platoon Sergeant who was in charge of the Supply Warehouse platoon, who in turn introduced me to my squad leader, SGT Bass. At first SGT Bass seemed to be a quiet person when I first met her, but later I saw that she was anything but quiet.

After SSG Wright drove me over to the warehouse to meet the rest of the platoon and my new squad of 88 Mike's, things didn't get off on the right foot as I had hoped it would. First, none of the lower enlisted soldiers in my transportation squad didn't like the fact that I outranked their senior E-4, Specialist Vasquez, and since they didn't know anything about me, I got a lot of back talk when I was instructed to tell them what to do. At first most of them didn't want to listen to me give orders when SGT Bass left me in charge of the squad. Most of the time they complained to SGT Bass and SSG Wright that my leadership style was more of a Sergeant First Class (SFC) leadership, than of a Specialist E-4, of not knowing what to do.

SPC Vasquez didn't like taking orders from me or when he had to move down one position within the squad whenever we formed up, nor did the second senior E-4 in the squad SPC Thompson, who would argue with me every chance he got. In my new squad, everyone was easily offended, no matter how small the situation was, everyone argued with each other over stupid issues. For me, it was still hard to get used to a co-ed unit, and to learn how to be nice to soldiers who been in these types of co-ed units all their military careers, and who didn't receive any harsh leadership styles like I did back in the Field Artillery.

Before we were on our way to Iraq, we received two more new soldiers into our squad, which one of them turned out to be our new squad leader, named SSG Kerlly and the other soldier named Specialist Simmons, who out ranked me because he was in promotable status.

When SSG Kerlly took over as our squad leader, boy did hell break loose within the squad because of it. Most all the soldiers were very loyal to SGT Bass, and when SSG Kerlly took over, everybody gave him hell most every day that he called himself our squad leader. But since I came from places where new NCOs came into the ranks, I gave SSG Kerlly the respect he deserved of becoming my new squad leader. But SGT Bass did not from day one when she was demoted to team leader.

When I moved all my things into my new room in Delta Company's barracks, I shared this tiny room with a soldier named SPC William from the maintenance platoon. From time to time, he would ask me what happened over in Bravo Company and explained to me that rumors were circulating about what happened to me and the assumed reasons why I was now over in Delta Company. He kept explaining to me that the rumors didn't bother him, because he had a lot of gay friends back at home in the states, although he wasn't gay himself. After our conversation, I thanked him for being so frank, and it meant a lot to me that he wasn't hostile towards me because of what other soldiers were saying about me. Never-the-less, I watched my back around him and his friends that came into our room to hang out, not knowing if they were all Homophobic individuals or not.

As our Iraq deployment got closer in January of 2004, I found myself praying every day for peace in my life. I knew it was inevitable that I would be around soldiers who wanted to kill Iraqis as soon as we entered Iraq. I often wondered would anyone of them would turn their weapon towards me when I wasn't looking.

On the 23rd of January 2004, I boarded a flight bound for Kuwait, where some of us in Delta Company believed that one or two of us might not come back to Germany alive. In my case, I was quite certain I would be killed from a result of friendly fire from one of my fellow soldiers, or a result of a fire fight with the Iraqi's. Never-the-less, here I was heading over to the Middle East to do my part in the U.S invasion of Iraq.

THE BEGINNING OF MY WAR

Shortly after arriving in Kuwait at a camp called "Camp New York," I realized in this time of my life, this place was either going to make me or break me really quick. Looking around into the Kuwaiti desert landscape, I remembered telling myself when I was a young boy, that I would never step foot over here where Desert Storm took place, but here I was standing around wondering, *"Why are we here?"*

A few weeks had passed before we were all getting ready for our movement up north into Iraq, when the soldiers within my squad became more intolerable towards one another. When it came to working as a team, I found myself hanging out with SGT Bass when the squad started going at each other. In our squad we had one female soldier by the name PFC Barrea, who raised hell night and day about who she wanted to work with and who she did not want to work with. At first, me and PFC Barrea worked well together when it came to who I got along with. After getting to know PFC Barrea, she showed me a picture of her gay brother back at home and expressed to me how she thought we would make a good couple as boyfriends or husbands.

For the most part, I would tell her that I wasn't gay, but the more I denied the fact, the more she pushed the fact. So, thinking of a way to get her off my sexuality, I told her I would be happy to meet him. *"Great I'll let him know,"* she would tell me. But I knew this girl was on a mission, but a mission to what means, I didn't know at the time. But as usual, I found out later down the road.

There was another soldier who I called my friend from my squad named PFC Parson, who is an attention deficit hyperactive (ADHD) individual. Back in Germany, we would hang out from time to time, but not as much as me and my friend Strittholt did.

Within the platoon, most everyone knew I had this foot-long Rambo knife that I carried on myself for a means of protection from Iraqi's or any other type of aggressors. One day while in the middle of a squad meeting, PFC Parson was standing next to me and quickly reached over and pulled out my knife. As I reached up and tried to grab the handle before he could pull it out all the way, and of course my hand didn't make it fast enough to stop him, but instead, my hand grabbed onto the blade itself as he was pulling it out of its holster. Let's say, that knife cut into my hand deep!

"AAAWWW SHIT! WHAT THE FUCK PARSON'S!" I shouted, holding my hand in a fist position, as my blood started to come out through my fingers.

"Oh, I'm sorry dude. This is a nice knife." PFC Parson kept looking at it.

"Give it back, bitch!" I demanded.

"You both need to stop horse playing around. Look at what you did Parson" SGT Bass said.

"Oh, my bad Linson. Damn, this is a sharp ass knife dude."

"Yea no shit Sherlock, that's why I got it." I replied.

After giving it back to me, SGT Bass ordered me to head to the medics to get someone to look at my hand to see how bad it was. Looking back at PFC Parson as I was walking out of our barracks, he had the biggest smirk on his face as I did my bed not to smile back at him because of his crazy looks.

For the whole time that I've had that knife, the only blood that it has taken from anyone was from its owner, "ME". Later, down the road, after not learning my lesson the first time around, I was playing with my knife one day and accidentally dropped it and it went into my leg. Boy, you can say, I learned quickly not to play with any of my knives from that day on.

While still in Kuwait, I didn't receive any harassment from anyone from Delta Company, since I believe I was still new and no one knew who I was, but some speculated why I was moved over to Delta Company. But within my squad, me and SPC Thompson started bumping heads more often than most, when it came time for me to instruct everyone what we had to do, when instructed to tell the squad what needed to be done. But like high school kids, you're liked by some, and you're disliked by some.

During this time of getting ourselves prepared for our push up into Iraq, we were all told to do the stupidest thing I had ever heard any Chain of Command order their soldiers to do. We were instructed to take out our driver and passenger door windows and fill the doors up with sand and fill up sandbags and place them all along the floorboard and in the back of our seats to help lower the possibility of IED (Improvised Explosive Device) shrapnel to penetrate our vehicles. Let's say, this was the number one talk amongst the enlisted soldiers and NCO's, about some of the stupid things we had to do while waiting around in Kuwait. While we were all stripping down our vehicles, we all talked about what we were doing... *"Why would you take the desert and put it into the vehicles that weren't made to handle such jimmy rigged, retro fitted, bull shit desert armor?"* But like good soldiers, we did what we were told to do.

When the day approached for the 1st Infantry Division to start to push north to our prospective locations within Iraq, SSG Kerlly told SGT Bass to assign TC's (Truck Commanders), for our first convoy up into Iraq. I don't know why she did this, but SGT Bass assigned SPC Thompson to be my TC, knowing that me and him were not on the best of terms with one another from the start. It seemed to me, intentional punishment to have to drive this crazy ass soldier around, and to hear him bicker and bitch about everything that was going on around him. SPC Thompson was an extremely opinionated person, and he didn't care who he offended, not for one second. But I sucked it up and did as order by SGT Bass.

As the convoy left Camp New York and headed for the Iraqi border, SPC Thompson and I were going back and forth at one another non-stop. He'd tell me, how he hated being in a truck with a *"gay ass driver, who sucked dick for a living"*, and I'd fire back at him about his roadkill ugly looks, and that his mother got fucked by Mr. Ed. (The Horse)

In the process of cutting down SPC Thompson, he must have thought up the idea of handling the situation differently, because he was over on my side of the truck trying to put me into a headlock. Let's say that didn't turn out too well for him. Blacking out for a few seconds, I quickly found myself on the passenger side of the truck, choking the everlasting life out of SPC Thompson, while the vehicle was going down the highway swerving from side to side, out of control. When I finally came to my senses, I jumped back into my seat and managed to get back control of the truck and slammed on the brakes to bring the truck to a stop. In the process of stopping the truck, SPC Thompson jumped out and took off running back towards SGT Bass's truck that was behind us, before I could bring the vehicle to a grinding halt.

In the short time that it took for me to stop the truck, I was already jumping back onto his side of the cab and was about to head out his door after him, when I realized that the rest of the convoy was leaving us behind. So, getting a hold of myself, I slammed his door shut and took off to catch back up with the rest of the convoy.

When we came to our last check point before crossing over into Iraq, we staged our vehicles so we could get ready for the next convoy into Iraq. When I climbed out of my vehicle and walked back towards SGT Bass's truck to explain to her what SPC Thompson had tried to do, after calling me a homosexual, SSG Kerlly approached us and asked me why did he see SPC Thompson running down the middle of the highway like a mad man, a few miles back?

Doing my best not to laugh, I again explained why SPC Thompson had jumped out of my truck, and SGT Bass told SSG Kerlly that SPC Thompson had told her that I jumped on him for no apparent reason.

"That's bull shit Sergeant Bass!" I told her. *"That ignorant fuck head tried to put me in a head lock while I was driving, and so I fucked him up!"*

"Look Linson, you both need to stop fighting each other and realize that we are about to cross over into Iraq where we'll be fighting Iraqi's and not each other." Sergeant Kerlly explained.

"Sergeant Kerlly, I didn't assign that crazy ass soldier to my truck in the first place, and he's not getting back into my truck. Someone needs to find me another TC and not him." I shouted back.

"Okay, you can have my TC." SSG Kerlly replied.

"Who's that?"

"Sergeant First Class Latham."

"Okay, well that's better than that numb nuts over there!" pointing towards SPC Thompson.

While looking at SGT Bass's truck with SPC Thompson sitting in her seat, I wanted to jump into that truck and snap that boy's neck so badly. But I knew this guy had issues with himself and I told myself to let it go before I did something stupid.

As we headed across the Iraqi border, you could see all over the roads, sandbag after sandbags, from everyone throwing them out of their vehicles. Looking over at SFC Latham who was out cold and snoring, I kept yelling at him to stay awake and watch the right side of our truck. But no matter how many times I would yell at him to stay awake, it was useless, he'd be right back asleep after a few minutes of staring outside of his door.

I figured if someone had gotten shot; it would have been him, since he was not looking out for anything. For myself, it was a quiet ride into southern Iraq, as the sun began to set that day. After a few hours of driving on the empty open roads of Iraq, vehicle after vehicle started to break down. At every break down, we would form up into a vehicle formation called a Box Formation, where we formed our vehicles around the disabled vehicle in a box like formation, to provide protection from any hostel activities.

In every box formation, I kept my attention toward the horizon looking out for Charlie, as they called it, but the one thing that caught my attention the most was I could not believe that I was in Iraq watching my first sunset as I remembered telling myself as a kid, I would not come here. Here I was watching the sun disappearing beneath the flat desert horizon, wondering why we were in this country. One of the most important things I have learned in my life is that you can never say what you will or will not do or go for that matter. After a few more minutes of waiting for the disabled vehicle to be towed, we were all back on the move again.

During our first convoy north, several times we had to turn around because our Convoy Commander kept getting lost. For the first two days non-stop, we drove all over the place and vehicle after vehicle kept breaking down. To me, I was excited just to be in Iraq, a country that's been torn apart from countless wars in the past.

Driving at night in southern and central Iraq, seemed like a black hole in space, with only our headlights leading the way. Being in that first convoy heading north made me really open my eyes to a whole new world of reality, and to see what kind of people are out in the world. In some locations, there were still blown and burned up vehicles from the Desert Storm War that we saw from location to location. Just to see all of this made me nervous to what was to come, while being in the war zone in Iraq. Nothing what I actually saw would mount up to what I really experienced in Iraq.

After long days and nights on the road, it took us four days to reach our FOB (Forward Operating Base), Camp Speicher that is in Tikrit Iraq, Saddam Hussein's hometown. But later, it took three additional weeks of convoys back and forth from Kuwait to bring all the 1st Infantry Division's assets to where they needed to be.

During this time, I was in countless conflicts with soldiers, both from my Company and from other companies within the 701st, as the rumors about me being gay started spreading around Delta Company for the reason why I left Bravo Company.

It was a never-ending battle of mental abuse and hatred daily. During almost every convoy, SSG Kelly and SGT Bass had the hardest time trying to get a soldier to ride with me, wherever we convoyed too. During the name calling and threats that I received, I knew I had a long way to go before I would get away from these Homophobic soldiers.

This abuse went on for weeks and months on end, and at every turn, I went up the Chain of Command to inform SSG Wright and 1st SGT Griffin about my hostile working environment, and what I was going through. In response, the only thing my Chain of Command would tell me after reporting my harassment... *"This deployment is not all about you Specialist Linson! Start growing thicker skin like a cow and not like a little girl!"*

"I hate these people! GOD, please get me out of here." I would yell within myself every time I was told to stop complaining like a little girl.

Time seemed to slow down to a crawl after we were finished convoying back and forth from Kuwait, and every time I had a problem, I would tell SGT Bass and SSG Kerlly, as instructed by 1st SGT Griffin and CPT Ruckman to report any harassment to my Chain of Command. *"But how can anyone run from hate in the middle of Iraq?"* I would ask myself, while convoying around Iraq.

In every corner, there was someone who disliked me and made threats against my life, all in the name of homophobia. *"If they really knew who I was, they wouldn't say these things about me."* I told myself. *"Keep it together Howard, no matter what happens, you keep moving!"* a voice kept repeating in my mind.

In the times that I had to myself, I would walk over to the MWR phone center and call my mom and tell her that I was doing okay, and I would not let her know about how stressed I was or how I was being treated. Knowing that my mom was already stressed about me being over in Iraq in the first place, I did not want her stressing about my current state of mind that was on the brink of collapsing. Later during the deployment, I told my mother everything that was going on with me.

During the day, and at night, mortar rounds constantly came into our camp and exploded all around us from enemy fire. To protect ourselves from shrapnel, we had to wear our battle gear whenever we had to work or when we had to go somewhere within a FOB. The stress from that alone was overwhelming for me. I thought obsessively about going AWOL for the most part, but I knew someone on the outside would find me, and then I would be the next person getting their head decapitated on national television.

So, to keep myself up in spirit, I kept reading my Bible and kept telling myself to hang in there, and that everything will be alight in due time. But during that time, time was not on my side, not for one minute.

Come June of 2004, my situation began to spiral out of control. Working around my squad members became more hostile by the day. PFC Parson stopped hanging around me, because he was being called gay himself for being my friend, and SPC Vasquez and SPC Thompson made it very hard for me when I oversaw a task that had to be done. SSG Kerlly and SGT Bass would have to put another E-4 in charge just to calm things down within the squad almost every day. Every time when I was working down in the motor pool or in the maintenance bay, someone would confront me about a rumor that had their name in it, and this kind of behavior became a natural occurrence in the motor pool whenever I was around.

One day, PV2 Barrea started to spread rumors around the Company that I wanted to get married to her gay brother, and that I liked working around certain male soldiers within the Company. When confronted by soldiers whose names were brought up in these rumors and most of them were guys I used to hang around with back in Germany, I would do my best to tell them what they heard was false and that Barrea was lying. No matter how many times I plead with some of these guys, most of them would tell me to stay far away from them, with a threat behind every demand. At every turn, I would report my problems to SSG Kerlly and SGT Bass and there on up the Delta Company Chain of Command, and as always, nothing was done about it.

During the peak of the rumors and death threats, PV2 Barrea told a lot of soldiers and NCOs, that I wanted to sleep with half of the males within the Company. So being that things were getting to the point where I was told to stay away from other sections within Delta Company, SSG Wright approached me and asked me if it was true about me going around making sexual suggestions about other male soldiers within the Company. At that time, all I could say in my defense was to tell the truth and deny the rumors.

SSG Wright just shook his head and stared at me, while I tried to explain to him that I was not doing what was being reported to him. During my time of trying to explain this to him, I knew he didn't believe me... *"Private Barrea wasn't the only soldier who reported you for making sexual comments and looking at people in a funny way Specialist Linson."* SSG Wright replied.

I looked back at SSG Wright and wondered if he really understood what he just said to me... *"If more than one soldier is spreading rumors about me Sergeant Wright, how can I prove that I'm innocent?*

"The only thing that I know Specialist Linson, is that a lot of people are not happy when you're around them, and you need to start watching your back from now on."

"Watch my back!" I replied. *"Sergeant Wright, I'm not out here doing what these people are accusing me of doing! Since we been out here, I have been approached by a lot of male soldiers to give them oral favors or other sexual favors. And every time I report it to the Chain of Command, yall keep telling me to stop complaining."*

"Linson, like we said before, this deployment isn't all about you soldier."

"Sergeant Wright, so you telling me that it's okay for these soldiers to approach me like this and yall will not correct it because I'm not doing what they want me to do? No, fuck that, Sergeant."

"Linson, you have been causing problems since you arrived at 701st, and now here we are in the war zone, and everyone doesn't want you around them. Explain that to me?"

"Sergeant, if I could explain someone else's paranoia problems, then we wouldn't be standing here talking about this right now, don't you think?"

"I don't know what to tell you soldier, but a lot of soldiers are upset with you."

"Sergeant, the only thing I can tell you is I'm not out here doing anything that they are saying I'm doing. I can't make you believe me, that's your job too, not mine."

"We'll see Linson, we'll see."

As I returned his gaze, I wondered what happened to the policy of taking care of soldiers and making sure conflicts like mine didn't get out of hand or even start. I guess that policy didn't apply to me, and it never did, since my first incident within the 701st MSB.

As the days went by after me and SSG Wright had our conversation, the harassment kept going and once again, I used the open-door policy and spoke to my First Sergeant countless times over, about what was going on within his Company. Like before, the only response I would get out of him... "I'll look into it and see what I can do. But until *then, keep your noise clean and out of trouble."* And just like before, nothing came of it, and the harassment continued.

At the time, the only person I could trust and talk to was SGT Bass. Every day I would vent my troubles to her, and she would tell me ways to counter react my issues. One day when we were talking in her sleeping area, she asked me a question... *"Specialist Linson, do you know why we didn't send you to the promotion board back in Germany and now out here we will not? Have you ever thought about that?"*

"Sometimes I do. Why?"

"Well," she replied. *"When you came over from Bravo Company and into Delta, word spread quickly about why you were moved over to us. And your fellow soldiers told SSG Wright back in Germany that they didn't want a gay NCO in charge of them. They told him that they were afraid you would use your rank to gain sexual favors from them."*

After hearing that, the only thing I could do at that time was look at her. When I finally came back to the present, I fired back... *"Sergeant Bass that is bullshit. Did any NCO stand up for me?"*

"Yes, but Sergeant Wright felt the same way about you and no one, even the other NCOs in the platoon, wanted you to get your Sergeant rank for fear that you would abuse a soldier sexually."

"Sergeant Bass, what kind of bullshit is that. I would never do that. That's like saying I would abuse a child or some shit."

"Well Linson, that's why no one wants to send you to the promotion board. They think you will do something sexually to one of the male soldiers under your command."

"I'm sorry Sergeant, but that is wrong, and they are all full of shit and you know it. How can anyone assume what someone will do when they are in a leadership position? You can't!"

"I hear what you're saying, but I'm not the one stopping you from succeeding, Linson. They are."

"Okay Sergeant, they want to play like that. My day is coming soon."

"Yea it might be but not fast enough Linson."

"It will." I replied in anger.

Walking out of SGT Bass's area, I realized that my fight was bigger than I expected it to be. Never did I once think for one moment, that I would be labeled as a "gay male soldier who would be a potential soldier sex offender." *"Where did all of this go wrong?"* I thought to myself. For the most part, I knew that a few members of my squad didn't make my situation any better.

From that day on, it was hard for me to go to work around people who thought of me as a person who would force himself onto someone of a lower rank. I just could not grasp onto the concept that I was viewed as the kind of person who would do something like that.

How can I work around anyone knowing what they were thinking about and what their personal feelings were about me? If I ever tried to become more than what I am today, they would stop me.

"Why me GOD?", while holding back my tears as I made my way back to my sleeping area.

FIGHTING TWO WARS

A few days after I had spoken with SGT Bass, I realized that my Chain of Command didn't want me around on several levels that pertained to unit cohesion. I was looked upon as someone who soldiers reacted negatively to whenever I was around, and it seemed that the root of the problem was me and anyone who wanted to get a good rise out of bad situation.

During one of our convoys to Tikrit, I was a part of a convoy that my First Sergeant oversaw. My TC at the time was PFC Ross from my squad, who was forced to ride with me in this convoy. After we had left FOB Speicher and convoyed our way towards the downtown area of Tikrit, my truck's fuel line exploded, and fuel started to pour into the cab on the driver's side around the accelerator. After the truck went dead and came to a stop, we radioed the Convoy Commander's vehicle, which was 1st SGT Griffin, and told him about our problem. After he had brought the rest of the convoy to a halt about a mile away, he ordered PFC Ross to ride with the mechanics and told me to run up to his vehicle alone.

After hearing him telling me to run up to his vehicle, I replied over the radio... *"Delta seven, can the mechanics bring me up to you so I can have some type of cover? Over."*

"No! You will have to come up here by yourself and be quick about it, Delta Seven out!"

"What the hell Ross, he thinks I'm gonna run up there with no one with me?"

"Hey Linson, better you then me." PFC Ross replied, climbing out of the vehicle.

"That's fucked up Ross. Better you than me, what kind of bull shit is that?" as I climbed out of my disabled truck as the mechanics came along side to take charge of my vehicle.

As I started off walking towards my First Sergeant's vehicle, that was engulfed in the heat waves off the asphalt ahead of me, I realized that this was their time to get rid of me. I could hear it now, *"Specialist Linson was the only one out of the entire Company who got killed by an Iraqi insurgent."*

As I got further away from the mechanics, I looked back to see what everyone was doing before I took off running down the highway. As I looked back, everyone had stopped doing what they were doing and was watching me... *"OH GOD!"* I shouted. *"They want to see me get killed!"* as I took off running towards the First Sergeants Humvee with my weapon at the ready.

After running for a half of a mile, I looked around and saw countless Iraqi's watching me from the roof tops of their homes and business, while some had come out of their stores and cars as I started to slow down and began to walk towards the rest of my convoy.

I realized as I started to look at everyone around me, that this was not going to be the day that I would fall, as I put my weapon on my shoulder and started walking down the center of the road, waving at the Iraqi's while some returned my wave back. *"This is it! Will I die here on this road?"* I asked myself while looking down at the hot pavement.

Looking ahead at the rest of the convoy that stayed stationery, with no one moving to come to pick me up, I kept asking GOD... *"Don't let me fall here and now, GOD."* as the sun started to beat down upon me.

While I kept looking at the Iraqi's as more and more of them came out of their buildings and stood there watching me walking by, I spoke to myself out loud... *"Okay First Sergeant, you want to play it like this. "Okay, I see what you all are waiting for and that will not happen today!",* while I continued to look down the road towards the stopped military vehicles.

Looking back again towards the mechanics who were already hooked onto my truck and were slowly moving towards my location, as if they were waiting for the kill... *"Just another quarter of a mile and I'll be there."* I told myself. *"Hello everyone."* as I continued to wave at the Iraqis around me. *"These motherfuckers are not coming to pick me up!"* as I looked onwards at the gunners of the vehicles ahead of me, only to see the top of their heads sticking out of the top, looking back towards me. *"Five vehicles and not one decided to come and get me? Okay First Sergeant, I'm not finished with you either!"*

As I walked up to my First Sergeants Humvee, I heard him yell out his window for me to get into the seat behind him as I walked around the back of the vehicle to get in... *"AAWW, I see you made it Linson."* First Sergeant Griffin said. *"Okay let's get out of here."* He ordered his driver to take off. *"Everyone form back up and continue on."* As 1st SGT Griffin radioed the rest of the convoy to come up to his location.

"These people want me dead." I told myself, looking at the back of 1st SGT Griffin's head. *"The Iraqi's didn't shoot at me or try to jump me. Thank you, GOD."* I whispered to myself while looking outside the door window. *"Will there be a next time when my vehicle will break down or will someone try to kill me? GOD help me please!"* as I started to tremble in the back seat of my First Sergeant's Humvee.

After returning to FOB Speicher that afternoon, I told myself that their plan had failed and now it was time for them to rethink another way of getting rid of me. *"But how would they do it the next time around?"* I asked myself. *"Watch your back and everyone around you."* I told myself.

"Linson, you made it back." SSG Wright said to me as if he had just seen a ghost.

"Yea Sergeant, the plan failed."

"What plan, Linson?"

"Don't worry about it Sergeant Wright. Why are you surprised to see me back?"

"Oh, I just heard that your vehicle broke down that's all. I thought something bad had happened to you."

"No! Not this time around and not the next, Sergeant!" as I gave SSG Wright an evil look, while he returned a worried expression back at me.

Come the next day when my vehicle was in the maintenance bay getting worked on, I asked the mechanic, PFC Iverson, how the fuel line broke, and his response was... *"It didn't bust; someone had loosened it up that's all. I put it back on and now it's good to go."* He replied. *"What happened out there?"*

"Oh, nothing. The main point is that I made it back in one peace." I replied, walking away in anger.

"Someone purposely broke my vehicle. Those sons of bitches!" As I made my way out of the maintenance bay and started walking towards the truck line.

I knew from that day on, that GOD was with me, and that evil was hard at work all around me working through these people who called themselves leaders in the United States Army.

After that day, when I found out that my vehicle was set up to break down, me and SPC Vasquez got into a major altercation in the maintenance bay, about me not working well with others... *"WHO THE FUCK ARE YOU TALKING TO, YOU PIECE OF SHIT?!"* SPC Vasquez shouted at me.

"GO FUCK YOURSELF YOU IGNORANT DUMB FUCK!"

"What the fuck are you going to do about it faggot!?!" as SPC Vasquez got into my face.

"You better get the fuck away from me before I fuck you up, Vasquez."

"Bitch ill stab you!" as SPC Vasquez pulled out his knife and held it towards his right side, ready to stab me.

"Do it motherfucker!" as I stood toe to toe with him.

"KILL THAT FAGGOT VASQUEZ!" someone shouted in the maintenance bay.

Before I was about to shove SPC Vasquez away from me, SPC Thompson stepped in between us... *"Children, children calm down. Vasquez we all know you'll beat the shit out of this gay ass faggot, but it's not worth it. None of us want to see this faggot's blood all over the place. Just walk away from this faggot ass fool."*

While SPC Thompson started to shove SPC Vasquez away from me, everyone around us including the NCO's started to laugh out loud. As SPC Vasquez turned and walked away so did I, but my destination was towards the motor pool, where SPC Simmons was working on one of our vehicles with PFC Ross.

As I approached them, SPC Simmons asked me if I could help them work on the vehicle, but I had something else in mind... *"I'm heading over to mental health to talk to someone, before I lock and load my 30-*

round magazine and kill everyone around me." I told him, while tears started to come down my face.

SPC Simmons stopped working and looked up at me... *"What happened this time?"*

"I'm just letting you know where I'm heading off too, before something really bad happens here!" In the middle of me telling SPC Simmons what I was going to do, I heard SPC Vasquez yelling out my name off in the distance... *"HEY LINSON!"*

As I took off walking towards SPC Vasquez with my weapon in one hand and magazine in the other, SPC Simmons trailed after me yelling... *"WHAT HAPPENED LINSON?"* SPC Simmons kept asking.

"Not now." I waved him away, while my focus was on Vasquez.

"Do I need to take your weapon away from you?" SPC Simmons asked me, as he caught up and walked along side of me.

"No, I'm good for now. But the only thing you need to do is keep that motherfucker away from me, before I blow his fucking head off!"

"I got this." As SPC Simmons position himself between me and SPC Vasquez, as I walked past him as he kept calling out my name... *"I KNOW YOU HEAR ME LINSON!"* SPC Vazquez shouted.

"Leave him alone Vasquez!" SPC Simmons shouted back at him.

As I kept walking pass the warehouse and Delta Companies Headquarters location, I kept talking to myself... *"What would happen if I opened fire on the ones I hated? What would I do afterwards when I ran out of ammo? How would I explain myself after it all? How would my family react to the news of me killing most everyone in my Company? Should I?* I kept contemplating on what to do, while I locked and loaded my M16 with one 30 round magazine and put my weapon from safe to burst ready to start shooting everyone that I saw.

When I made it to the clinic, it was around 1700 hours (5 p.m. in the afternoon), and a Sergeant First Class female was locking up the clinic doors, when I asked her… *"Is the clinic open?"*

"No, come back tomorrow morning soldier."

"I don't think so Sergeant. You need to take that lock off those doors and open this clinic back up NOW!"

"Excuse you soldier?" as she turned and looked at me.

"Are you death Sergeant? If you don't unlock those doors now, a lot of people are going to be dead before the sun goes down tonight and their deaths will be on your hands and not mine. I promise you that, starting with you first!"

Before she could respond to my threat, she looked into my eyes and saw that my face was dripping with tears as I grabbed my weapon at the ready, locked and loaded and the safety switch to burst and finger on the trigger.

After seeing that I was at my breaking point, she quickly turned around and took the lock off the doors and replied… *"Hello, we're open. What can I do for you today?"*

"Take this away from me before I lose it quick!" as I extended my weapon towards her as she took it away from me and disarmed my M-16 rifle.

After she took my weapon, SPC Doubs came in the doors wondering why the clinic was still open. (He was one of my friends from back in Germany.) *"Hey Linson, how are you doing?"*

"Not good," I replied. As his smile shifted to a worried look when he saw his NCO with my weapon and me standing there flexed.

After about ten minutes of waiting around, the Mental Health Officer showed up to talk with me. When we went into his office, the first question he asked me... *"Why did you threaten to kill my NCO if she didn't keep the Clinic open, soldier?"*

"I told her, if she didn't let me in, a lot of deaths would be on her hands sir." I replied.

"Simple enough, so tell me what's going on with you?"

For the next hour or so, I spilled out everything that was going on around me. After I had explained to him what was going on, he asked me if any of this had been happening stateside before I was sent to Germany, which was followed by the same question that everyone always asked me... *"Why do you think this keeps on happening to you wherever you go, Specialist Linson?"*

I explained to him... *"People are too judgmental about someone when they first see or meet them, sir. When people look at me, the only thing they see first is my skin color and the next thing is that they*

271

assume how I am as a person. And when they finally talk to me one on one, they realize that I don't speak, act or present myself as what they assumed I was to be, before they opened their mouths to have a conversation with me." I continued to explain. *"I'm different sir, and that's what makes them afraid of me. Not knowing the unknown can frighten a lot of people, especially those who judge someone before knowing someone, sir!"*

"Why do you think that is, Specialist Linson?"

"Look at me sir, I speak proper, I carry myself well and I don't talk with the slang that is expected of me as an African American male."

"I see. But why you?"

Once again, I felt like saying, "I'm bisexual." But instead, I played the game they wanted me to play, explaining what I could without telling the truth... *"Only one-word sir, Homophobic!"* I replied. *"If you can't understand something you don't know, homophobia takes over and a lot of people react negatively towards those whom they can't figure out. So not knowing who you are, they start to call you what they think best fits you, and in my case, gay or faggot. People are afraid of what they don't know, and they will jump to any conclusion to explain what they don't understand sir. And even if they do understand, they won't show others that they understand by standing up and doing what's right."*

"That's true," the Major replied. *"Hold on one minute."* As he got up and opened his office door and told the Sergeant to notify my Chain of

Command from Delta Company to come up here ASAP, then he came back and sat behind his desk and started with more questions.

"Why do you think people react to you the way they do? Why is it that everyone thinks you're gay?"

"Sir, it's because they judge me by my appearance and not as a person."

"What do you mean?"

"Look at me," I replied. *"I treat everyone nice and on top of that, I look good."* trying to put some humor into our conversation.

"But why do you think this is always happening to you, Specialist Linson?" the Major persisted. I realized I was stuck again in the Twilight Zone and did my best to answer.

"People are not used to meeting someone like me who is well mannered and well spoken. They're expecting to meet someone who has a speech defect and is uneducated, sir. And when they talk to me, they find out that I'm different from what they heard or assumed. They always jump to conclusions about what kind of person I am, and it always turns out to be gay. And that's not from asking me if I'm gay. It's from being uneducated and ignorant about people in the world, sir."

After a few more minutes had passed, CPT Ruckman and 1st SGT Griffin along with SSG Wright walked in and joined us. The Major started to explain why I was in his office and why he was holding my weapon... *"I want Specialist Linson to tell yall what he has been going through."*

For what seemed like the hundredth time, I explained and described the harassment and threats, and pointed out that they haven't done anything to protect me, after I brought it up to them several times before today. After I was finished telling them all my problems, 1st SGT Griffin asked me a question... *"Specialist Linson, you just told us the same thing happened to you in your last unit stateside. What happened, and why do you hate it when someone calls you gay?"*

"Because First Sergeant, soldiers tried to kill me before and on numerous of occasions, I was sexually assaulted and received death threats. And during all of this time, my last Chain of Command did nothing to stop it but swept it under the rug and moved me around within the Company. But this time around, I will not let that happen to me and I will defend myself to the fullest. Even if it requires me to lock and load on you and your soldiers, then I will! I will not be a victim of a hate crime while serving in Iraq or back in Germany for that matter, and while I'm still in the Army!" I explained to them all. *"You've given me 210 rounds, and I will use every last one to protect myself from anybody."*

SSG Wright quickly responded... *"Linson, I don't think you have it within you to do that to anyone of us."*

"Try me!" I quickly replied. *"Sergeant Wright, I know you have a daughter back in the states. Don't you?"*

"Yes, I do Linson."

"The only thing I want to do to you is to make you into a vegetable. I just want you to see your child and not be able to feel or touch her in any way."

"Linson, you're just mad at the moment."

"You damn right I am Sergeant Wright. How would you feel if someone here were to kill me?"

"I would feel bad Linson."

"Yea right! You have shown that you never cared about what's been happening to me since I came to Delta Company. And I know you don't want me to go to the promotion board because you and the other soldiers think I would sexually harass them."

"I didn't say that. Who told you that lie?"

"Sergeant Bass."

In an instant, my whole Chain of Command started to tell me that Sergeant Bass was a compulsive liar, and she was full of shit.

"Well Sergeant Wright, I trust her more than I trust any of you!"

"Well Linson, I can say none of us said that."

"You sure can't fool me Sergeant by the way all of yall been acting!"

After a few moments of silence, CPT Ruckman replied... "Linson, you're just mad and I know you wouldn't do such a terrible thing. I can't see it within you."

275

"Sir, when you push someone to their limits you don't know what they are capable of doing."

As they kept expressing their opinions about what I would and would not do, I just thought to myself... *"These people are the ones who need to be sitting where I'm sitting, getting their heads drilled."*

After hearing all their reasoning, I requested to speak to General Sanchez, the Commanding General of the 2004 Iraqi war at that time.

"Why?" they asked in unison.

"Because I believe all of yall are full of shit and nothing will come of this meeting."

The Major did his best not to laugh as he looked down towards the ground.

"Give us some time to fix this problem Specialist Linson," 1st SGT Griffin replied. *"You can talk to Command Sergeant Major Cook and Coronal Ross for the time being if you would like?"*

"No! I don't want to talk to them, First Sergeant!"

"You have to give us some time to work this out Linson."

"I have and look at this situation now First Sergeant."

After countless minutes had passed, I finally agreed to talk to CSM Cook. The Major gave my weapon and ammo to CPT Ruckman, who then returned them back to me. I was very surprised he returned my weapon back to me so quickly with no questions asked... *"Linson, can you step out of the office so me and your Chain of Command can talk?"* the Major asked me.

"Yes sir."

So, I got up and walked out of the office and saw SPC Doubs waiting in the lobby area with his NCO... *"How are you doing?"* he asked me. *"I'm doing much better. Thanks for asking."*

I looked over at the female Sergeant First Class and apologized for threatening to kill her and demanding her to reopen the clinic with a loaded weapon... *"Hey Linson, you were looking for help and I was in your way."* She replied.

When my Chain of Command finally came out of the Major's office, 1st SGT Griffin asked me to ride with him and the Commander back to the barracks. While we were on our way back, both of them explained to me that I was going to be moved to the orderly room and will be working under SGT Qunada and SPC Perizo and PV2 Chevez, and that they were giving me four days off to get myself back together again.

"AAAAWWWW! I hate these guys! God get me out of here before I do something crazy!" I thought to myself, while sitting in the back rethinking about locking and loading on the both of them.

For the next four days that I had off, I spent most of my time watching movies and sleeping the days away. During this time, SGT Qunada met with me and explained that I would be moved over to headquarters sleeping barracks, where I would live across from PV2 Strickland. When I heard that I was going to be living across from PV2 Strickland, I wasn't too happy to know that I was going to be sleeping near the only guy in the Company who had a severe hygiene problem. I knew something was up and I wasn't going to like it, not one bit.

After hearing what my new job was going to be, I met with 1st SGT Griffin who directed me to stay away from my old platoon and explained to me that... *"Private Strickland is to follow you everywhere, since you are reporting that everyone was harassing and threatening you, including soldiers from outside the Company. This arrangement was designed so you will have someone to report this to us as well, and not just one person. Also, you are now responsible for Private Strickland's hygiene and to make sure he has a clean uniform on every day."* 1st SGT Griffin explained. *"When I say he will follow you everywhere, I mean when you take a shower, he will be taking a shower. When you or him needs to take a shit, both of you will take a shit. When you are hungry, you both will eat together. Everywhere you go, he goes and wherever he goes, you go. You are now joined at the hip until further notice. Do you understand?"*

"No, I don't!" I replied. *"Why do I need to be in charge of another man's hygiene, First Sergeant?"*

"Because Linson, I believe you both can benefit from one another. Especially Strickland."

"What the Fuck!" I thought to myself. *"This is some bullshit!"*

"SERGEANT QUNADA!" 1st SGT shouted.

"Go get Private Strickland and bring him to my office."

"Yes, First Sergeant." SGT Qunada replied.

When PV2 Strickland arrived at the First Sergeant's office, it was also explained to him in great detail, that we were joined at the hip and what the punishment was going to be if we were not found together at any time.

I didn't like this arrangement and neither did Strickland, but as the month of August of 2004 wore on, PV2 Strickland and I became good colleagues. I helped him learn the great importance of personal hygiene and he helped me tolerate a lot of crap. And trust me, when I say CRAP, he smelled like CRAP when we first became joined at the hip battle buddies.

THE PAIN BEGINS

In the month of September 2004, I began to have painful compilations in my right pelvic region. When I went to be seen by the doctors on our FOB, none of them knew what was going on with me. At first, I was told I had an STD, since pain shot all over my growing area as well. Hearing what they thought was going on with me, I would disagree with the doctors every time they gave me a different antibiotic to see it that cured my pain. After a few long-drawn-out weeks of countless antibiotics one after the other, I was medevac to Baghdad Iraq for further medical treatment.

That night when the medevac Black Hawk helicopter flew in to pick me up, I was scared beyond all reason due to a lot of military helicopters were being shot down across Iraq around that time. Before we took off, the on-board flight doctor asked me if I wanted to lay down on the stretcher or sit up instead. Being that this was my first time in a Black Hawk, I didn't want to miss out on anything from wheels up and to wheels down. So, I told him that I wanted to sit up for the duration of the flight to Baghdad, although I was in extreme pain during the entire flight.

As we took off under the cover of that night's darkness, my heart was beating out of control as we climbed higher and higher above FOB Speicher and made our way towards the city of Tikrit. Never in my life have I ever been so excited, and nerve shaken from the sound of the Black Hawk and the hard banks and turns the pilots did. *"Wow! My GOD, Tikrit looks beautiful from up here!"* as we turned south towards Baghdad.

As the lights of the city vanished, the darkness of the night became our sanctuary, as I couldn't help but be mesmerized by the clear night skies and the billions of stars that shined all around us, as the cool air swiped through the cab of the Black Hawk. During the entire flight, I tried my best to stay awake, but I could not. After an hour or two, I woke up to us descending onto the hospital helicopter pad, where I saw three other medevac's landing at the same time. While I was being escorted off the Black Hawk and towards the entrance of the emergency room, I found myself in the midst of a Marine platoon that had been attacked by a few RPG's during a recon mission.

While I waited on my bed in the emergency bay, blood covered Marines in shredded uniforms surrounded me, and a few of them were walking around in a daze naked, as doctors rushed to get control of the ER. Three beds down from me, the doctors were operating on one Marine who kept repeating out loud, *"It's cold! I'm so cold!"*

Blood was everywhere, and the ward was rocked with screams from almost every bed around me. I glanced around myself and saw that I was the only person who wasn't covered in his own blood. But with all the commotion that was going on, my attention kept drifting back to the Marine who kept saying he was cold.

While the doctors kept operating on him, and the Chaplain was praying to him to hold to his faith, I started praying for him as well... *"Oh GOD, be with that Marine in his time of need. No one but you GOD can make it right, for today will not be his last but first of many to come. Oh GOD, stay beside him and be with him, and not just today but every day. Oh GOD, I know you hear his cries, and please GOD, work through those doctors to get him back on his feet again. For this is the day that he will not pass but be lifted up in your name forever more. GOD be with all of these Marines for they have been through great pain and suffering today. Come into this hospital and move everyone through their hearts and minds so that you will be lifted up above every name and every creation, day in and day out until your return for all of us. And GOD, help me to overcome whatever is wrong with me and bless me that I will live through this and become victorious in the end. In your precious name that I pray, AMEN."*

After the doctors had gotten everyone under control and most of the Marines rushed off to intensive care, the Chaplain walked over to me and looked me up and down and smiled... *"What's going on with you? You don't look like you're dying?"*

"HAHA, well sir, I don't need to be dying to be here." I replied.

"That's true. So, what wrong with you?"

In the short time that I had with him, I told him about my medical condition, and they did not know what was wrong with me. I also explained to him that they think that my testicles needed to be chopped off since they didn't know what was wrong with me.

"Wow," the Chaplain replied. *"Well, do you want me to pray with you?"*

"No sir, I got it. But there are other people here that need you more than me. I can pray for myself but thank you for asking."

"Any time Specialist Linson." As he smiled and walked off to the next bed.

After the doctors came to look over me, they sent me to get an ultrasound around my pelvic and groin area. After countless hours of test after test to determine that I wasn't going to lose any of my man hood, the doctors came up with the conclusion that either I had a hernia or a server case of a bacterial infection. During all the tests they performed on me, no one knew how my pelvic region became so dark red and swollen.

So, after I was given more antibiotics to try to fix what they thought I had, I was sent to the medical holding tent area, where they sent other military personnel who were not severely injured. After I had walked into the tent late that night, everybody was asleep, as I quietly picked out a sleeping cot on the left side of the tent where no one was. Early that morning after I woke up to see other military personnel who had came in while I was sleeping, I was surprised to see that I had Marine's on both sides of me. One Marine in particular, was sitting up looking at his family pictures in a daze as I sat up to engage him in conversation.

Since I have not talked with a Marine since AIT, I was eager to speak to one of them to know where he came from. Seeing that this one Marine was already up, I asked this Lance Corporal why he was here... *"I was in an IED (Improvised Explosive Device), roadside bombing, that killed my Gunny and our gunner, along with the other two Marines that was in my Humvee."* He explained to me. *"I don't know who I am. They keep telling me who I am, and I see my name on my uniform, but I don't remember anything before the IED."*

"Well Jones, everything will come back to you in time." I replied. *"Who are those people in that picture?"*

"I don't know. They said this is my mom and dad along with my brothers and sisters. But I don't know them, nor do I remember their names." as he started to cry.

"Hey stud, everything is going to be alight. No need to cry, trust me. It will all come back to you, and you will remember all of them no matter how long it might take. Just hang in there okay." I replied. *"By the way, my name is Howard Linson."*

After a few hours of sitting around and talking with this Marine, me and Jones became friends right from the start. For the four days that we spent around each other, we talked about our lives and what future we might have if we ever left Iraq. At times, I didn't know if he caught onto some of the things he told me about his childhood, and I often wondered if he knew he was starting to remember things subconsciously. But during our conversations, I never said anything to him when he talked about his home. The only thing I would do was to ask more questions about the things he remembered, to help him before we departed our ways.

Every day when we were around each other, I felt that I missed my calling when I first went to talk to the Army recruiters. When I went to chow (Eat) with the Marines, I felt more at home being around them, and not around anyone from the Army. Every Marine that I talked with treated me with respect. I realized, while I was around these Marines, I was supposed to be in the same branch of service as they were in. At times, a few Marines would ask me why I did not join up with the Marines instead of the Army, and the only response I could give them... *"I don't know."*

In the time that we spent around each other, Lance Corporal Jones would ask me how life was in the Army, and like anyone who would have asked me that question, I would lie and tell them only about the good parts and not the bad parts of what I was going through. I did not want to give any Marine that I talked with a bad impression about the Army or anything that pertained to degrading my choice of service.

When the day came for me and my new friend Jones to fly out, I realized I was not going to see him for a very long time, or possibly never again. No matter how much I longed to hold onto that time and moment, I knew that some good things had to come to an end. As soon as I found out when our flights were leaving, I looked on the board and saw that Jones flight was two hours before mine. I could not bring myself to believe we were going our separate ways, since he was heading back to the states and mine was taking me back to the pits of hell from which I had escaped from, for a short period of time.

Now that I knew I had only a few more hours to spend with Jones, I went back to the medical holding tent where I found him slumped over on his cot staring at the ground. As I sat down next to him, I asked him what was wrong... *"They're discharging me out of the Marines and sending me home to these people that they call my family. I don't even remember my own mother's name or any of them."* As he looked up at me with his eyes filled with tears, as he passed me his family picture so I could look at them again.

As I sat there hearing him cry softly with his face into his hands, I knew there was nothing I could say or do to make him feel any better... *"Hey Jones, everything is going to work out in time."* as I gave him his family picture back. *"Before you know it, you'll remember everything about them and yourself. When you do start to remember who you are,"* I added, *"don't forget about me."*

"I will never forget about you Howard. Your name is Howard Linson. You see, I remembered your name, but I don't know who these people are in this picture." as he continued to cry softly.

As I put my arm around his shoulder and shook him a little, as he looked back at me... *"Come home with me! Please."*

At that second, I did not know what to say as I looked into his eyes that looked very serious... *"You're the only person I know,"* he persisted. *"Your name is Howard Linson. See, I can remember. Come home with me, please! You're the only friend that I have, and I don't want to go anywhere without you."*

I looked into his eyes and saw that he was not playing around, as I replied... *"I can't go with you Jones. The Army wouldn't allow it, yet alone the Marines wouldn't either."* I replied, doing my best not to start crying myself.

As we sat there in silence, he looked down at the picture of his family, as I said to him... *"Go home and relearn your past and don't shy away from anyone who is in that picture, for they love you more then you will ever know."* I told him. *"GOD is with you every step of the way and he will never leave you alone, you hear me?"*

"Thank you, Howard. I will never forget you. Never!"

"And I will never forget you Jones."

When it was time for Jones to leave, I requested permission to walk onto the helicopter pad with him, so we could say our last goodbyes. Before we walked onto the pad, I pulled him to the side and prayed with him. After we prayed, I walked with him towards the Black Hawk that was taking him to the airfield where he would board another flight going home. Before he got onto the Black Hawk, I told him that we will meet again in the future, and to keep his head up at all times.

While watching him strap into his seat, I came so close to jumping into that Black Hawk with him and strapping myself in with super glue. In those few seconds before the pilot had closed the doors, I longed to fly the hell out of Iraq with the first chance I got, but I knew I had to face my problems alone. *"Bye Howard."* he shouted out loud. *"Bye*

Jones." As I started walking backwards waving at him, as he waved back to me, and before I knew it, he was air born and gone.

"Aw boy! Why didn't you just go with him?" I mumbled to myself, as I walked off the helicopter pad, looking down at the ground.

For the rest of that day before I flew out, I knew that I had to stay strong within myself and look forward to better days ahead. No matter how bad my situation might become, I knew I had to have faith that GOD was with me every step of the way.

When it came time for me to fly out, walking alone to my Black Hawk seemed as if I was being escorted to be executed. Walking out and onto the helicopter pad, I almost broke down knowing that this Black Hawk was taking me back to a place where bad people were waiting for me. But no matter how I felt at the time, I was determined to win this fight.

In the days that followed my return from Baghdad, my physical problems became worse. I could not move my right leg without experiencing sharp pain, throughout my entire pelvic region. 1ˢᵗ SGT Griffin kept telling me that I was trying to get out of the deployment by fabricating my health problems, and that my pain was more mental than physical. Every time he would tell me this crap, I so long to hit him dead squared into his face.

Shortly after my return, and countless times that I went back to the clinic to get seen by the doctor who was diagnosing me every time I went back, told me that my Chain of Command told him I would be denied another medevac out of FOB Speicher for further treatment. He also explained to me that my Company Commander and First Sergeant told him that I had to wait until I returned to Germany to get seen any further about my health problems.

Along with my health issues, I continued to face harassment from other soldiers outside of Delta Company, because of the gay rumors. Every time I experienced any harassment, I kept reporting the incidents to my Chain of Command, as well as PV2 Strickland who witnessed these incidents. A lot of NCO's and soldiers were very annoyed that PV2 Strickland was reporting them to our First Sergeant, and in most every section within Delta Company, their Chain of Command did not want me nor Strickland around their working areas.

After countless reports, 1st SGT Griffin called me into his office alone... *"Why can't you just shut up and be a team player Linson, and just go with it?"*

"What do you mean just go with it, First Sergeant?"

"You need to have thicker skin like a cow when dealing with other soldiers when they ask you for sexual favors. You're either going to go with it or not. If so, shut up and be a team player."

I did not know how to respond to 1st SGT Griffin's remarks. *"Did this man just tell me to shut up and suck these soldier's dicks, like they have been asking me too?"* I thought to myself... *"First Sergeant, I do have thicker skin than a cow, but I'm tired of the harassment regardless if they want me to be a team player or not!"*

"Well, it doesn't look that way Specialist Linson."

"So what First Sergeant! Who cares if I do or don't, I'm still going to receive the same amount of harassment regardless!" I added. *"When am I going to see Command Sergeant Major Cook, like yall promised me several weeks ago?"*

"He's busy with other matters." 1st SGT Griffin replied.

"Other matters? Okay First Sergeant, I need to see him today!"

"No, you will see him later this week!"

"I'm sure I will First Sergeant!"

At that moment, I did not show how upset I was towards my First Sergeant, but I had a different plan in mind as I walked out of his office and out of Delta Company, with PV2 Strickland in tow. After I was dismissed out of my First Sergeant's office, I told PV2 Strickland what 1st SGT Griffin had said to me about not being a "team player." PV2 Strickland was shocked to hear that First Sergeant wanted me to just "go along" with the sexual harassment I was getting. I told PV2 Strickland that since CSM Cook was too busy to talk to me, I was going straight to CSM Cardoza, the Brigade Command Sergeant Major instead.

As we started walking towards Brigade Headquarters, PV2 Strickland was laughing his butt off at the fact that I was going to see CSM Cardoza without telling anyone in our Chain of Command... *"If the Chain of Command starts to dick you around Strickland, then you have to take matter into your own hands and go above their heads to take care of situations yourself."*

"True, true," PV2 Strickland replied.

When we arrived at CSM Cardoza's office, he was in a meeting with the Brigade Commander, COL Henderson. While we sat and waited outside of CSM Cardoza's office, PV2 Strickland was still laughing about how we were up in Brigade Headquarters about to talk with the Brigade Sergeant Major.

"Perhaps one day, we'll be sitting outside the general's office in Division Headquarters."

"HAHAHA, dude you're crazy as hell."

"Hey, that's why it's called an open-door policy Strickland. Read up on it and you will know all about it."

After CSM Cardoza was finished with his meeting, he quickly recognized me from back in Germany, when I was a BOSS (**B**etter **O**pportunity for **S**ingle **S**oldiers) representative for Bravo Company.

"Hey Linson, what brings you to my office today?"

"Sergeant Major, I'm here to use your open-door policy." As he looked at me with a concern look on his face, as he replied to me... *"Does your Sergeant Major know you're up here to talk to me?"*

"No, Sergeant Major. I was told from my First Sergeant that he was too busy to talk with me, since a month ago, when I requested to speak with him. So being that he is too busy to talk with me on neck leveled serious bull shit, I'm now here to talk to you about it Sergeant Major."

"Oh really?" CSM Cardoza replied, sitting down at his desk.

In the hour that it took for me to tell him everything that was going on, me and PV2 Strickland explained why we were "joined at the hip." After getting an earful, CSM Cardoza asked me... "Why didn't they move you to a different Battalion? I would have approved a move if I knew what was going on, back in Germany."

After his reply, I told him that CSM Cook had talked about sending me to 201st SPT out in Vilseck Germany, but at the last minute he moved me to Delta Company instead. After CSM Cardoza thought to himself for a few minutes, he looked up at me and said... "I'll take care of this matter myself." He replied. "You will hear back from me soon, Specialist Linson."

"Okay Sergeant Major."

"For the time being Linson, keep your head up and your noise clean, until you hear back from me."

"Will do, Sergeant Major," as me and PV2 Strickland got up from his desk and walked out of his office.

Come the next day, 1st SGT Griffin ordered me and PV2 Strickland into his office. When we arrived alongside with SGT Qunada, 1st SGT Griffin was beyond pissed off at us. Looking at his face that went from beet red and dark purple, as he started to scream at us both… *"WHY DID YOU TWO GO TO BRIGADE AND TELL COMMAND SERGEANT MAJOR CARDOZA WHAT WAS GOING ON IN MY COMPANY?"*

Since PV2 Strickland was speechless, I explained away… *"First Sergeant, all of yall have been dragging yalls feet on this open-door policy business when I requested to talk to the Chain of Command a month ago. And since you accused me of not being a team player, I knew I had to take this matter over and above all yalls heads, ASAP!"*

1st SGT Griffin face quickly went from beet red to dark purple again after I told him that. While looking at him changing colors in front of us, I wanted to tell him to breathe, but didn't want to cause a fight within his own office. When he regained his composure, he looked at me and said… *"Well Linson, you got your wish. Sergeant Major Cook and LT Col Ross wants to see both of yall in the Battalion meeting room, NOW!"*

On the inside I was laughing my butt off, now that I blew up the hornets' nest with C-4 explosives.

SGT Qunada was ordered to take me and PV2 Strickland up to Battalion, as soon as we were dismissed out of the First Sergeant's office. At that point I had made up my mind to talk to COL Henderson next, no matter what CSM Cook and LT Col Ross had to say to me.

293

After reporting to them both, I explained to them what was going on, and that me and PV2 Strickland were getting the shaft from everyone. I expressed to them both that the only way to get things done was to use the Brigade's Chain of Commands open-door policy, just to get things moving within the 701st that they could not get done right.

CSM Cook and Lt Col Ross did not swallow that too well, but CSM Cook assured us that we would not have any more problems again and said that CSM Cardoza wanted to have a follow-up talk with us ASAP after our meeting. At that time, I was glad to see that someone from the 1st Infantry Division was taking care of business the right way.

After being driven back to Delta Company, SGT Qunada told us that 1st SGT Griffin wanted to see us after the Company's Chain of Command's meeting. I knew that my First Sergeant was bound to have a heart attack from the bomb shell that I dropped on him and his Company.

When First Sergeant finally came out of the Company meeting, he slammed his office door behind him... *"Get at parade rest."* He ordered both of us. *"I'm pissed the fuck off with you two. I can't believe that yall didn't have faith in your Chain of Command. But you know what,"* he added, *"you two are going to be on permanent guard duty for the remainder of our tour in Iraq."*

At that second, I did my best not to laugh right in front of him... *"So, this was their way of dealing with the situation?"* I thought to myself. *"Stick us on guard duty far away from everyone else, until we redeployed back to Germany? What a lame duck bullshit plan."*

After hearing First Sergeant explaining where we needed to be that following morning, I told him that CSM Cook told us that we needed to report back to CSM Cardoza ASAP.

"Why?" 1st SGT Griffin asked me.

"Because Sergeant Major Cook said so!"

"GET THE FUCK OUT OF MY OFFICE THE BOTH OF YOU AND LEAVE THE DOOR OPEN!" he shouted.

"Yes, First Sergeant." I replied, biting my bottom lip, trying not to laugh at him.

While we walked towards Brigade Headquarters, PV2 Strickland was surprised to see how well things went for the both of us, since we decided to go above our Chain of Commands heads... *"Sometimes Strickland, when your Chain of Command is doing their best to cover up their dirt, you have to be the one to uncover it, no matter how bad it might get for you. Always do the right thing, no matter how bad it gets."*

After we reported back to CSM Cardoza, he asked us what the outcome was. I explained to him that we were going to be put on guard duty until we had returned to Germany... *"So, they wish to bury the problem,"* he replied.

CSM Cardoza expressed how disappointed he was in how my Chain of Command had handled my situation, which had gone too far and out of control. He explained to us, that we needed to report to him every week until we redeployed back to Germany, but not outside of our Chain of Command. After we had acknowledged his orders and were dismissed from his office, I felt very satisfied to be reporting to the Brigade Sergeant Major but still wanted out of 701st MSB because I had experienced far too much to become complacent around these people.

During our time on guard duty, me and PV2 Strickland did our best to make the best out of our situation of being put "out of sight and out of mind." Come November 2004, PV2 Strickland went home for R&R for two and a half weeks, and during this time, it felt good to be away from him, but at the same time, it felt strange being away from him. Since we were around each other for so long, I sort of missed him and wanted to have someone to talk to, or for that matter, just to be around someone. But none-the-less, it felt good to walk everywhere without having to keep up with someone or slow down for anyone.

One particular night around two in the morning, I got up to go use the restroom, and decided not to take my flashlight with me since the moon was bright enough that I could see without it. On the way back to my living area, I saw two other shadows walking away from my old living area towards one of the abandon blown up Iraqi barracks with no flashlights themselves. *"What are they up to?"* I asked myself being nosey. Since I was already up and about, I decided to follow these two individuals quietly to see where they were walking to.

After seeing their ghostly shapes disappear into the building, I decided to walk around the other side where most of the windows were blown out... "SHHUUUU! AAWW, AAWW!" The noises came from one of the rooms, as I got closer to where they were.

"What in the world are they doing in there?" I asked myself.

Walking up to the window slowly, I heard more and more sounds of sexual moaning and a lot of movement coming from one of the rooms. Putting my back up agents the outside of the wall, as I stood next to the window where I saw a faint light from within. I turned and looked into the room and saw two male soldiers from Delta Company tearing into one another like buzzards on roadkill and flies on shit... *"Is that Private Murrey and PFC Richardson?"* I asked myself, as their faces kept moving around the flashlight on the ground. *"Holly shit it is! What the fuck! These two numb nuts are some of the ones who are going around telling other people that I'm gay, but here they are fucking the shit out of each other. What the hell!"* as I watched briefly as their sexual encounter became more erotic.

Walking away slowly, not to let them know that someone was watching them, I kept thinking to myself... *"Why are these guys telling everyone around me that I'm gay, but here they are dicking each other down?"* As I got further away from the room, my steps became wider and faster as the anger within myself came stronger with every step that I took... *"So, they wish to put the attention on me so they can do what they want to do without letting everyone around them know that they are the ones who are gay! This is some fucked up shit!"* as I kept walking back to my living area.

As I quietly walked back into my sleeping area, I was pissed off beyond all measure. These were some of the bastards who tormented me every day, while insisting they were straight. *"Why the hell were they scapegoating me? What the fuck!!"* as I laid back down on my sleeping bag.

Since I wasn't the kind of person who would expose the two of them, and since no one would believe me if I did, I decided to keep it to myself. As the days went by while PV2 Strickland was gone, my harassers became increasingly aggressive asking me for sexual favors and I was not going to become a "desert hoe" just to make it all stop. "Become a team player."

When PV2 Strickland came back from R&R, we both were happy to see one another, believe it or not, we gave each other huge hugs whenever we met back up with each other. After Private Strickland got settled back in, I told him everything that had gone on since his departure, and I also told him about the two soldiers that I saw duking it out over in the abandon barracks. He was mostly shocked when I told him who it was that I saw but not surprised to know that I was being sexually harassed as soon as he left.

Come December 2004, it was my turn to head home for R&R, and I was more than excited to know that I was going to be home for Christmas with my family. On the airplane ride home, I felt overwhelmed and filled with joy as I sat on my flights going home that month... *"How can I get out of this deployment?"* I kept asking myself on the way home. *"I don't think you can. We only have three months left and its back to Germany."* I told myself.

Touching down in Jackson Mississippi, I felt the need to run off the airplane as fast as I could, as soon as the doors opened into the terminal. As I walked through the terminal gates, my heart kept beating faster and faster as I got closer to the check-in area where I knew my momma was going to be waiting for me.

When I walked around the corner, I saw my momma from afar, as I took off running towards her, and to my surprise, my sister Hillary was standing next to my mom along with her boyfriend waiting for me. While I wrapped my arms around them both, a huge sigh of relief came out of me as I hugged them both as I took in deep inhales... *"Get me home quick, so I can get the hell out of this uniform."* I told my mom.

After my two weeks of R&R had passed, and it was time for me to head back to Iraq, my mom who always knew about my problems in the Army told me... *"Hang in there Howard. Everybody's prayers are with you, and GOD is with you."* At that time of hearing those words coming out of my momma's mouth, I almost started crying as I checked my bags in at the airport. *"Oh GOD, be with me here and now and for always."* As I hugged my momma goodbye, as I started to proceed through the terminal gate waving back towards her. I kept wondering where life would take me from here as I lost sight of her when I arrived at my gate to board my flight.

With every step that I took, I kept having flash back of my first day going into the Army and wishing I could turn back the hands of time and stop myself from enlisting into the Army that day.

As I walked towards the door of the airplane, I slowed down my walk and stared into the airplane as countless passengers boarded the flight. During the time of just standing around contemplating if I should get on or stay off, I kept trying to tell myself that everything was going to be alright and that the only thing I needed to do was to take another step and another and all of this would be over soon. *"Keep moving Howard, and don't stop."* I told myself as I summoned enough energy to step onto the airplane.

After a day and a half of flying all over the world, I was back in Iraq and back on guard duty, and the days seemed to pass much faster since it was time for a new rotation to come through and replace us.

Shortly after my return, 1st SGT Griffin told me and PV2 Strickland that we didn't have to be around each other anymore, but since we were so use to each other's company, we decided to stay around one another until we redeployed back to Germany.

CAREER ON THE LINE

It was Mid-February of 2005, as the snow crunched beneath my shoes as I walked towards my car that was in the vehicle storage area on Harvey Barracks in Kitzingen Germany. Smelling the faint scent of pine trees in the frigid cold air, it seemed like I'd been gone for far too long from here. *"Where is my car?"* as I kept walking around looking for my car that was covered in snow. *"It's cold out here…Oh, there you are,"* as I opened the truck to get my ice scraper out.

SCRAP, SCRAP, SCRAP….as I kept knocking off the snow and ice, while looking around at all the other vehicles covered in snow. Taking in and letting out a deep exhale, I stopped and watched the steam from my breath going up into the freezing cold air… *"Where are you, Howard?... Are you still in there somewhere?"* I asked myself, looking up towards the dark gray clouds, as it started to snow all around me. *"Okay, here we go…. Damn, my car won't start."*

Shortly after getting my car jumped off, I found myself driving down the Autobahn, in a zombie like state of mind, while passing the things I remembered and used to enjoy before I went to Iraq. I knew I had survived the pits of hell, but I did not feel like the same person who used to drive around in this car anymore. Looking around, there I was, making my way through the cities and towns that I used to hang out in, where my German friends were still living. *"Come on heater, warm this car up...Where are you, Howard? Are you still in there somewhere?"* I kept asking myself.

Heading towards Nurnberg Germany, I began to relax and enjoy the comfort of civilian life, knowing that I had made it back and I was not in uniform for the first time in a long time. But something was not right within myself, and I did not, or more like, I could not feel anything anymore. I knew I was back and in one piece, but I felt dead and useless from within, as I kept telling myself... *"Keep moving and don't stop, this isn't the end, Howard."*

On the days that I had off, I went to the bars and clubs shortly after my return. I felt very uncomfortable being around a lot of people, as I had not before. The bigger the crowd, the more I felt like hiding in a corner. With all my life changes, I realized I needed to think about my future and where to go from this point on... *"Do I get out of the military over here and try to find a job as soon as I got back to the states, or do I reenlist one more time and get out of the military state side?"* I kept debating with myself.

In my first formation back in Germany, the rear-d First Sergeant for Delta Company asked our small one consolidated platoon... *"Who would like to go work over in DTA (Drivers Training Academy)?"* Looking around the formation seeing that no one was raising their hands to volunteer their service in DTA, I quickly raised my hand and volunteered to do the job. Since I did not want to stand around people I did not like in the first place, I figured this was my chance to move away from all of the bull shit and have yet another new start away from Delta Company. When I was told to report to DTA directly after formation, I wondered if anyone would give me hell from leaving the orderly room before they came back from Iraq, or would they make my life a living hell as soon as they had returned from Iraq?

Walking up the stairs to the DTA area, in the same building where SFC Ford's EEO office was at, I introduced myself to the NCOIC of DTA, SSG Douglas from Bravo Company... *"Oh Lord, it's you."* He looked up at me, smiling. *"So, what brings you to DTA Linson?"*

"Well," smiling back, *"I was told that you needed a soldier up here to help you out."*

"Damn, it's about time they sent someone over here to help me out. Let me show you what we do up here in DTA, Linson."

While SSG Douglas showed me around the DTA area, I thought it would be great if I could remain up here for the rest of my time in Germany. But what would happen when the rest of 701st MSB returned from Iraq, and I was once again faced with a new forced relocation? I thought to myself, while being shown what DTA was all about.

But as time went by, I became very knowledgeable about my new job and loved training soldiers and civilian on how to drive around Germany in their POV (**P**rivately **O**wned **V**ehicles), or military vehicles when it came to convoys on the autobahn and out in the field.

By the time April of 2005 had rolled around, all of the 701st MSB was back in Germany, and I knew if they wanted me out of DTA, I would have been moved already. And since no one wanted me in their platoon or Company for that matter, DTA became my new home. Within myself, I felt I was no longer the fundamentally cheerful person I once was before the deployment. It took me a long time to relax and calm down after the months of hostility and always keeping my guard up. However, I knew my time would come when I would get the chance to challenge those who had caused me a great deal of mental pain.

When all of Delta Company was settled back into our old barracks, we were preparing to move out of them and into the new barracks that were finished being built next to the DTA building. I was shocked to know that one of the males that I saw that night out in Iraq, who is now a Specialist, was going to be my roommate, or more like the person who shared the bathroom with me, SPC Richardson. At first, I didn't want to alert him to the night that I saw him and PV2 Murrey going at each other like mad men, but I knew my day would come when I had the chance to confront him.

One day while I was walking to go and check my mail, I saw SPC Richardson walking alone in my direction, apparently deep in thought. I knew this would be the perfect time to ask him about his hot steamy night I saw him with PV2 Murrey... *"Hey Richardson, how are you doing today?"*

"I'm doing good," he replied. *"How are you Linson?"*

"Hey, it's another German day," I said, laughing.

"Yeah, tell me about it. So, what are you up to later today?"

"Nothing much. You know I don't hang out with anyone around here."

"Why not?"

"You know why Richardson. No need to act like you don't know what kind of hell I've been going through around here."

Richardson looked at me nervously... *"Yea, you're right. Yeah man, I'm sorry you're going through that kind of stuff here, but just to let you know, a lot of us like you but..."*

"But what?"

"You know..."

"No, I don't know. Why don't you tell me what I should know?"

"Well, it's what people are saying about you."

"Oh, okay. Are you talking about when I saw you and Murrey fucking each other out in Iraq when you thought yall were alone that one particular night?"

For a few seconds I almost enjoyed Richardson's stunned expression.

"What? What do you mean?" he stammered. "We didn't do...I don't recall...You saw us?"

"Yes! And you were hilarious." I did my best not to laugh. "You moaned like a girl dude."

Richardson looked away after I had made that comment.

"What happened between you two?" I asked. "Yall seemed to be madly in love with one another."

"He's a player. But don't worry about that Linson."

"Well let me ask you this. Why were you harassing the hell out of me all these years about me being gay? That's fucked up, dude. How in the hell are you going to say I'm doing all this shit, when it's yall fucking each other and making it look like it's all me? You know, I really wanted to kill you out in Iraq." As my tone became irritated questioning SPC Richardson.

"Look Linson, I can only say I'm sorry for putting you through that, but I gotta go. Hey, can we hang out later?"

"Fuck that hang out shit and I'm sorry shit!! Do you know what kind of hell you put me through, motherfucker!!"

"Look, it wasn't intentional, it's just.... Look, I always liked you but.... Can I come to your room later to talk about it tonight?"

"Fuck that! If you're going to be gay or bi and see someone like yourself being teased or harassed, maybe you should stand up and say something or stop it!"

"Look, I don't know what more I can say, but I'm sorry Linson." As SPC Richardson quickly turned away and walked off towards the barracks. As I watched him walk away, I saw how trapped he was within himself. I knew that one day he would come out of his own cave and face his own oppression. Although I had already forgiven him for his actions back in Iraq, I would never forget what him and all his buddies did to me.

For the most part when I was not on duty, I kept to myself during the rest of my tour in Germany after all my military friends that I used to hang out with, were all gone back state side. By this time, I was going to a few small villages that I had never heard of, just to find new ways to release the stress in my life when I did not have anyone to talk to.

While at work or walking around post, I managed to keep my composure around military personnel who I wanted to scrub off the face of the earth. At times, something deep within myself kept telling me... *"You haven't reached the end yet, keep moving."*

One week when I had no classes to teach, SSG Moody from Bravo Company, dropped by my office and asked me if I wanted to return to Delta Companies warehouse. Not to sound too angry by the question he had asked me, I simply replied... *"No Sergeant Moody, I'm enjoying my new surroundings very much, and having only one NCO to report to is the best thing that's ever happened to me since I've been in 701st."*

"Okay, I understand." SSG Moody replied. *"Oh yeah, by the way, I'm your new squad leader. They transferred me to Delta Company, and they sent SSG Kerlly over to Bravo Company."*

The only thing I could do was smile and say... *"Well Sergeant Moody, welcome to Delta Company. I hope your stay here is as pleasant as mine."*

"Yeah right! Well, I don't know what they want to do with you, but I think they want to keep you up here and away from the rest of the Company."

"That's fine with me Sergeant Moody. My life is a whole lot better since I've been up here and away from them."

"Well, that's good. I'll tell First Sergeant Griffin that you wish to stay up here, and I'll see if I can get you to the promotion board after everything calms down."

"That's cool with me Sergeant,"

After meeting my new squad leader, I wondered if he would be any different from the others I had in the past. As time went on and the days grew longer, so many soldiers that I knew had left Germany and went back state side. Soon I was within the last year of my second contract with the Army, and I had to decide to either stay in or get out. In my mind, I wanted to stay in and PCS back to the states and then get out of the Army from there. But the only thing that was hurting me from reenlisting was my physical health, and since I have not done any PT in over a year, I knew they would use that against me.

Giving SSG Moody time to talk with 1st SGT Griffin about my chances of going to the promotion board, I managed to catch back up with SSG Moody and asked him about what 1st SGT Griffin had told him... *"Specialist Linson, I don't know if you knew this already, but the First Sergeant put it out to all of us NCO's within the Company, that you will not be eligible to reenlist or go to the promotion board, and that you will ETS* (Estimated Time of Separation), *out of the Army from here."* He replied.

"What! No, no, no! I'm not trying to get out of the Army while I'm over here in Germany. I want to stay in for a little bit longer." (Despite all the problems, reenlistment was still my choice to make and not theirs.)

"I'm sorry Linson, this is what the First Sergeant put out and so did the Company Commander."

"And he said I couldn't re-up also?"

"Yep!"

"Why?"

"Well, do you remember what happened out in Iraq?"

"I remember everything."

"Well, it seems you burned a lot of bridges while you were out there, and a lot of people want to see you fail. Why do you think we're keeping you over in DTA and not back within the ranks with the rest of your fellow soldiers?"

"Sergeant Moody, this isn't right, and nor do I care if I nuked the hell out of a lot of people's bridges. Yes, I've been through a lot, and they know why as well. My leadership and work ethics show that I'm more than ready to become a leader in this man's army. I've never been brought up on any kind of disciplinary chargers and the gay thing is something they're holding against me, just to keep me from advancing."

"Well Linson, if you want to go to the board, the only person you need to convince is First Sergeant Griffin. He's the one who's stopping you from going to the board."

"Okay, I'll do that. Since I'm already talking to you now, let Sergeant Wright know that I'm heading over to First Sergeant's office to talk with him."

"Okay, I'll let him know. Good luck."

While I drove over to Delta Company, I kept telling myself to calm down and to not show how angry I was, for that would only make matters worse for me… *"Knock, knock."*

"Come in," 1st SGT Griffin yelled out. *"AAWW, Specialist Linson. What can I do for you today?"*

"First Sergeant, I was told that you don't want me to go to the promotion board."

"Yes, I said that Specialist Linson."

"May I ask why?"

"Look Linson, you burned a lot of bridges back in Iraq and the main one you burned was the one between you and me. I didn't appreciate what you did to us back in Iraq." He explained. *"Look, I know you're a good leader, but none of the NCO's in the Company want to see you make E-5, and neither do I."*

It was the same old hypocrisy all over again. I was a "good leader," but not good enough to stay in the Army, yet alone be promoted.

"First Sergeant, the Army isn't about who we want to see succeed or who we want to see fail and nor is it about our personal feelings towards each other. It's about what kind of leaders we promote to lead soldiers in and out of combat and in garrison."

"That's true Linson, but you will never get the chance to experience that for as long as you're wearing that uniform."

"Excuse you, First Sergeant!"

"I don't like you Linson, and I'm not the only one who feels that way."

"First Sergeant, I don't care if you or anyone in your Company likes me or not. Every single one of you put me through hell and you know it. If you say I can't go to the promotion board, what about me reenlisting?"

"That won't happen either. Look Linson, you're not going to the promotion board and you're not going to stay in my Army anymore. So, enjoy the time that you have left and keep your noise out of trouble. You're dismissed!"

After calmly walking out of his office and to my car, I felt like I could not breathe. While I sat stationary in my parking spot, I thought about ways on how I could change my current outcome... "What have I done in the past to help myself overcome things like this? Senator Cochran!" I thought to myself. "Damn, I should have contacted him a long time ago."

As that day came to an end, I found myself once again typing a letter to my Senator about what I was going through and how I needed his help again. After I sent the email off to him, another idea came to mind, "Go and talk to CSM Durr," our new Battalion Command Sergeant Major. So, the next day, I told SSG Douglas that I was going to talk to CSM Durr about my issues, and since we worked in DTA, we reported straight to the Sergeant Major about everything that went on in DTA. I knew from the moment that I needed to talk with CSM Durr, I didn't have to tell my Chain of Command in Delta Company, that I was heading over to Battalion to go and talk to him… *"Go for it!"* SSG Douglas told me.

When I met with CSM Durr, he wasn't pleased to know that he had been left in the dark about who I was, and why I was really working in DTA and not in Delta Company. A day or two later, after me and CSM Durr had talked, CSM Durr called me into his office for a second meeting and told me that he had spoken with 1st SGT Griffin who explained to him that I had not taken a PT test in over a year, and I had a few health problems as well. Those were the reasons why I could not re-enlist or go to the promotion board.

"So, what do I need to do, Sergeant Major?"

"I don't know," as he sat behind his desk and shrugged his shoulders. *"I would move you to another Battalion, but you don't have enough time before your enlistment is up. So, with that said, what do you think we need to do Specialist Linson?"*

"I can take a PT test Sergeant Major, but I have to get my doctor to change my profile so I can. But other than that, that seems to be the only thing that is the problem like my First Sergeant told you."

"Well Specialist Linson, the ball is in your court; let's see what you can do with it."

"Trust me Sergeant Major, I can go far with it."

"Let's see. You only have five months until your ETS."

"Let the games begin." I replied.

"I'm giving you one month to get in shape and pass your PT test and tape test, Linson. If you can't pass either one of them, have a good civilian life."

"Is that a challenge Sergeant Major?"

"Yes... You say you want to become a leader in my Army, well here is your chance soldier. Let's see how you measure up."

"To the top Sergeant Major. All the way to the top!"

"Okay Linson, make me into a believer."

As I left his office, I started putting my pieces in place, wondering how I could counteract these people and all their cruel ways. But I kept thinking about the letter I sent to my Senator, and I knew he would come through for me. Whenever I knew he did respond, the chance to prove them all wrong was going to be my win or theirs.

Making it back to my office that evening, I called over to the warehouse where SSG Moody was in his office, and I told him what CSM Durr had instructed me to do.

"Yea I heard about what you two talked about," SSG Moody replied over the phone. *"But even if you pass the PT test, First Sergeant said he will still not let you go to the promotion board or re-up, Linson."*

"Yea, I figured that much Sergeant Moody. But I'm not worried about that right now. My day is coming very soon."

"Even if it does Linson, they will win, and you won't."

"Are you sure about that Sergeant?"

"Okay Linson, if you think you can win, let's see you try."

"Let the games begin Sergeant." As I hung up the phone and started to fiddle with my fingers.

Knowing that I had to lower my profile restrictions to a level where I could work out and get back in shape and lose as much weight as I could in three weeks, I told my doctor that I wanted to stay in the Army and asked him if there was a way to completely suppress the pain in my pelvic region so I could do PT again… *"Yes, there is a way, but you might not like it,"* he replied.

After I had explained to him why I wanted to stay in the Army, he suggested a three-phase steroid injection that would completely neutralize the nerves that went into my pelvic region. So, when I started working out again, I wouldn't fell a thing… *"Would you consider three steroid injections?"* Without hesitation I quickly replied, *"Yes I would."*

Soon after I received my three injections over a period of two weeks, my health status went from 20% to 100%. But later down the road, I suffered the consequences of that decision.

Without hesitation, I started working out anticipating the Congressional investigation that I imagined was on the way. Still, I knew that when the investigation had arrived, the challenge of me passing everything was going to be on the four fronts of everything. If I fail just one part of the qualifications that was to allow me to re-enlist and go to the promotion board, that was going to be their ammo to kick me out of the Army for good.

A week and a half before my PT test, SSG Moody showed up at DTA wanting to speak to me when I was in the middle of teaching my class. As soon as I saw him walking towards the entrance of my classroom, I knew it was time to answer up for the letter that I emailed to someone of real authority. After putting my class on a ten-minute break, I walked up to SSG Moody as he quickly told me... *"Sergeant Major Durr and First Sergeant Griffin wants to talk with you ASAP."*

"Okay, but it will have to wait till I'm finished with my class today."

"I don't think they want to wait until you're finished with your class Linson."

"Well, we only have another hour left, and after that I'll be up there."

As Sergeant Moody turned and walked away, after my class started to filter back into the classroom, I started to think about how they felt when they received a congressional investigation about my problems within the 701st. Thinking about what they thought as soon as this investigation came down, I started to laugh softly to myself... *"Hehehe, I've got them. I will never give in or fail."* I thought to myself as my students started to ask me why I was smiling so hard.

Walking towards Battalion Headquarters, after I had dismissed my class for the day, I was full of anticipation of what was to come next from this Chain of Command. *"Yes, yes, yes! Now it's time to turn the tables back on all yall."*

After walking into the Battalion Headquarters, SSG Moody was standing outside of the Battalions meeting room waiting for me to show up... *"It's about time you got here,"* Sergeant Moody replied. *"I was wondering if you were ever going to show up Linson."*

"Well, you know, I had to teach first."

"In this case, I don't think so," SSG Moody replied irritated. *"Let's go."*

As I followed SSG Moody into the meeting room, I walked up to CSM Durr and 1st SGT Griffin and reported to them.

"Specialist Linson reporting as ordered."

"At ease Specialist Linson," CSM Durr replied.

"Look Linson," CSM Durr said, *"we're going to let you go to the promotion board this month and that's only if you can pass your tape test and PT test. Did we not discuss this already?"*

"Yes, we did Sergeant Major. But I was told, even if I was to pass everything, I wasn't going to be able to do any of what you were telling me I could do."

"I don't know where you got your information from, but this is the deal, you contacted your Senator about what has been going on here in the 701st and we have to answer it all. I myself don't understand why you went and told your Senator about this and not let us take care of this matter ourselves."

"Sergeant Major, for years on end, I have been fighting those same words over and over again, and in the end, your words and everyone else's words didn't even measure up to a hill of beans. If you say nothing of what I reported is true, then why have I been tucked away in DTA since we returned from Iraq?"

"I can't answer that Linson. I wasn't here when all of this was going on and I can assure you, like I just told your First Sergeant, you will be given the chance, like everyone else has, to prove to us all that you're ready to become a leader. Do you still agree to what our terms are, Specialist Linson?"

"Yes, Sergeant Major I do."

"Okay Linson... Sergeant Moody."

"Yes, Sergeant Major."

"You have one week to get this soldier ready for his PT test and the promotion board. If he fails any part of his tests, I will hold you *personally responsible for his failure. Do you understand me, Sergeant?"*

"Yes, Sergeant Major." SSG Moody replied looking nervous.

"There you go Linson, now all the balls are in your court. Let's see how well you do now. Also, by the way, I will be leaving 701st as your Command Sergeant Major and Sergeant Major Brown will be replacing me until further notice. I will let him know what is going on with you and I know he will hold you up to the same standards and agreement as I have."

"Sergeant Major Durr, I will be ready for anything yall can throw at me."

"Okay Linson. I'm from Missouri, the show me state. So, show me what you're made of."

"I will show you and everyone in here Sergeant Major."

"Okay, we'll see what you can do since you want this so bad. You're dismissed soldier.... Sergeant Moody, make sure he's ready for my board."

"Will do Sergeant Major."

After me and SSG Moody walked out of the room, I looked over at SSG Moody... *"Don't worry Sergeant Moody, I'm not going to let myself or you down."*

"We'll see about that Linson. You have one week to get ready for the PT test. Do you need help in any areas?"

"Yes. In the run I will need all the motivation that you can give me. It's been a long time since I've ran two miles or for that matter, PT."

"Okay, I'll help you, but you won't get any shortcuts out of me. If you really want this, you'll work your ass off for it. Do you understand me Linson?"

"I do Sergeant Moody."

"Okay, I'll see you a week from today and we will all see how much you want this E-5 rank you keep talking about."

After accepting this huge challenge, I knew that this was going to be my time to shine, and since I was determined to make it, I wasn't going to give up the fight that I had been fighting for far too long. After all the years of being told that I would not be able to succeed in this man's Army and being falsely accused of all types of behaviors and all the harassment, humiliation and threats that I had to take from all walks of life in this uniform, I knew this was my last and only chance to prove to myself and to everyone, that I was not the person they thought me to be.

While I was working out for my PT test, SSG Douglas was already discharged from the Army for medical reasons and my new NCO from Bravo Company became SSG Holden, who told me that before SSG Douglas had left, he explained to him why I was in DTA and what I've been going through while in the 701st MSB. During all this time when I was getting ready for my PT test, SSG Holden told me that I needed to pass my PT test and put all of those who thought negatively about me to shame.

I was so nervous walking into the gym that morning when it was time for me to take my PT test. All my Chain of Command showed up to observe me taking the test, and while I was stretching out to get ready, I prayed to GOD to help me pass everything, and to be what they said I could not be.

After I had passed the pushups and sit-ups, it was time for the two-mile run, which I had to complete in less than 15 minutes and 54 seconds. While I stood on the starting line, SSG Moody stood next to me and whispered... *"Everyone's betting you won't finish the run in time."*

"Oh really? Well, they're about to lose every red cent they own." I replied, looking down at the long stretch of road I had to run on.

"On your mark! ... Get set! ... GO!" SSG Wright, shouted out loud.

I took off running with SSG Moody at my side. At first, he told me to slow down and keep a steady pace next to him, and to speed up whenever he said to. Round and round, we went. I felt so lightheaded and out of breath before the run was over... *"Don't stop!"* Sergeant Moody yelled out to me. *"Keep moving Linson! Do you want them to win? Do you want them to be right about you?"*

"NO!" I shouted while trying to gasp for air.

"SO, GET YOUR ASS IN GEAR SOLDIER!"

"One lap to go," I kept thinking to myself, while I was gasping for air.

"Come on Linson! You have two minutes to make it around before you fail! MOVE YOUR ASS NOW!" SSG Moody yelled out to me.

Gasping for air, we took off at a dead sprint. My heart was pounding away... *"COME ON! ONE MINUTE TO GO! YOU'RE HALFWAY THERE! MOVE YOUR ASS, SOLDIER!"*

"Push yourself Howard," I kept saying to myself.

As we turned the corner towards the finish line that was 200 feet away, I heard SSG Wright yelling out loud, "15:45, 46, 47, 48, 49, 50...

"MOVE YOUR ASS!" SSG Moody yelled out to me.

"51, 52, 53, 54"

"You made it Linson!" SSG Moody yelled out to me.

I made it across the finish line at 15:54.

"I made it!" I shouted in my mind as I started to throw up all over the place.

While bent over holding onto my knees, SSG Moody came up to me and grabbed me by the arm... *"Walk it off Linson. You did it soldier, you did it. Walk it off big Sarg (A nick name for Sergeant). Now it's*

322

time for you to show them, you're ready for the promotion board
soldier."

Still gasping for air, I looked around and saw nothing but disappointed faces staring back at me. I could not show how happy I was because I was out of breath and throwing up all over the place.

Back in my room, I called my mom and told her the great news... *"See Howard, I told you. God is with you and what's his, is already yours baby. So just go in there and know you're already a winner sweat heart."*

"I will momma, I will." I replied. *"I love you so much, momma."*

"I love you too baby."

A couple of days later after I had passed my PT test and tape test, SSG Moody was helping me with my Class-A uniform and asking me questions for the promotion board.

(Tape test is to see how much body fat a soldier has. And to make sure that he or she is within regulations that pertain to their height and weight requirements)

"Don't worry Linson, you already passed the board."

"How do you know that, Sergeant Moody?"

"Because I know, Sergeant Linson."

Sergeant Moody didn't know, but he gave me a lot of confidence at that time... *"Sergeant Linson. Those words have a nice sound to it, and I never thought I'd ever hear it coming from someone else's mouth besides my own,"* I thought to myself.

Three days later, it was time for me to go to the promotion board. I was a little nervous as I stood around waiting for my turn to go in front of the board. Looking around at everyone else who was eager to get this done and over with... *"Why so long? Did I do this to myself or was this done to me?"* I kept asking myself, watching soldier after soldier walking into the board for a few minutes and walking out from the promotion board excited.

"Okay Linson, when I go in to present who is coming in next, count down from thirty and knock on the door three times." SSG Moody explained to me.

Watching SSG Moody walking in and close the door behind him, I started my count down, "30, 29, 28..."

"Knock, knock, knock." Nervous as hell.

"COME IN!" a voice called out from the room.

Walking up to the center of the room where I was told to stand, as I saluted the members of the board... *"Specialist Linson reporting to the promotion board as ordered."*

CSM Brown stood up and looked at me up and down and saluted me back.

"Parade rest...Attention...Left Face...Right Face...About Face... Left Step...March...Right Step...March...Quick Time...March... Soldier...Halt...About Face...Stand At...Ease!" ordered CSM Brown.

"Welcome to the promotion board, Specialist Linson. How are you doing today soldier?"

"I'm doing good Command Sergeant Major Brown and members of the board."

"That's good. So, I hear you're ready to become a Sergeant. Is that true?"

"Yes, that is true Command Sergeant Major Brown and members of the board."

"Okay. Well, your uniform looks good, and you look sharp today. You've passed the board Linson. You're dismissed."

As I stood back to attention and rendered a salute to the board, I was wondering why they did not ask me a single question. After getting a salute in return, I did an about face and walked towards the door from which I had entered and looked over at Sergeant Moody with my eyes and saw him smiling at me as I walked out of the room.

Walking out and closing the door behind me, I was stunned and confuse on why my turn in front of the board was so short and sweet... *"How did you do Linson,"* other soldiers started to ask me.

"I guess I did great," I replied.

The door opened back up and SSG Moody came out... *"Congratulation's Sergeant, you made it. Come outside with me."*

Letting out a deep sigh after we were outside, I looked at my squad leader and said... *"Thank you, Sergeant Moody for being there for me when no one else wanted to be."*

"Hey big sarg, that's what a leader is supposed to do soldier. But do me this huge favor whenever you put on your stripes."

"What's that, Sergeant Moody?"

"Don't act like the ones who have done you wrong all these years to your soldiers but be like the ones who have done right by you." As he shook my hand and told me he had a meeting to head off to.

As I watched him walk off into the parking lot, I kept telling myself, *"I will be just like him when it comes time for me to put on my stripes and take care of soldiers. That's a leader right there."* As I watched my squad leader walking off towards his car in the distance.

Walking back into the Battalion's staff duty area, after reflecting my years in the Army, I asked myself... *"Why did it take so long for me to get here? More importantly, where do I go from here?"*

While standing around waiting for the board to be over with, the first thing that came to my mind was to re-enlist and head back stateside, where I could reassess my life's direction going out of the Army.

After a few days had passed, I discussed my options with the companies re-up NCO about my choices back state side. Since I was short on time when it came to my ETS date, I knew my choices were going to be small. After waiting for SGT Qunada to come back to me with what was on the table, I picked Fort Hood over Fort Carson Colorado since I already knew Fort Hood and did not wish to be in the mountains but in the south instead.

After picking which post I wanted to go to next, SGT Qunada asked me who did I want to swear me in, and to everyone surprise, I picked our new Battalion Commander, LT COL Rain.

So, two weeks later, I was standing in front of the whole Battalion repeating my re-enlistment oath out loud. After a round of applause, LT COL Rain's asked me if I had anything to say to everyone. And you know what, of course I did...... *"Everybody under the sound of my voice listen up! To everyone who told me not to reenlist and to get out of the Army and go home, do me and everyone else around yourselves a huge favor. Take your own words of discouragement and distrust and apply them to your own career. I'm sick and tired of everyone in my Chain of Command, who constantly told me that I didn't belong here anymore and to get out of their Army. Do all of us good soldiers a huge favor and ETS the hell out of the Army yourselves and rid us of your horrible and venomous leadership, and yall's ignorance and stupid ways of thinking......Thank you."*

As yells of cheer and hooah came from within the Battalion as everyone started to give me a huge round of appliance. I looked over to the Coronal and said... *"I'm finish sir."*

"Wow," he replied. *"Okay, I guess that was a little different."*

As I looked around, most of the soldiers that I knew were laughing their butts off, but the rest weren't laughing at all...mostly from Delta Company. After the Battalion Commander had dismissed everyone, he turned and looked at me... *"Is there anything I need to know, Specialist Linson?"*

"There's nothing you need to worry about, sir. I'm almost gone from here."

"Okay, if you say so Linson."

As I turned and walked away from the Battalion formation, and made my way back towards DTA, a few soldiers that I knew ran up to me and congratulated me on my re-enlistment and my remarkable speech. Soldier after soldier came up and told me how impressed they were that someone finally had enough balls to stand up to their leaders. I did not gloat over what I said but reminded myself that I was still stationed in Germany and had two months to go until I had to report back to Fort Hood Texas, again.

Looking back over the years, while I was walking back to DTA, I realized that it took me five and a half years to be promoted to Sergeant from Specialist, and in most MOS's, that's way too long for being an E-4.

During this time of my military career, all the 1st Infantry Division was packing up and moving back state side to Fort Riley Kansas, while I stood in my office for the last time and looked around my empty classrooms, wondering what my next unit would be like. But this time around, I was going to be a Sergeant, and I would oversee my own soldiers. I thought to myself, while turning off the lights for the last time in DTA.

As I locked up my classrooms and the building all together, I knew I had to change my whole outlook about the Army if I was going to be a good leader to those who were looking to make this a career choice... *"Would this time be different for me?"* I started to ask myself, while walking towards my barracks.

"Would the demons of the past finally be put to rest?" As I looked around my post for the last time, before heading back state side.

DÉJÀ VU

There I was, getting processed into Fort Hood at the 21ˢᵗ Replacement Center once again. Standing in early formation, one cool morning, in the month of April 2006, I looked to my right at a soldier who looked lost and confused... *"Good morning, my name is Howard Linson. How are you this morning?"*

"Oh hello. My name is Nowak."

"Well Nowak, welcome to the United States Army. What's your job in this man's military?"

"I'm a light wheeled mechanic."

"Really?"

"Yep, and I can't wait to work on some military vehicles."

As I started to laugh out loud... *"Well, don't worry about that. As time goes on, you'll get your far share of them all."*

"What's so funny?"

"I've been in for eight years now, and let me tell yea, working on these vehicles around here, isn't what you'll enjoy the most out of your

military career. Trust me on this one, you'll dislike it after a few months of trying to fix the same vehicle over and over again."

After a few minutes of talking with PV2 Nowak, one of the Sergeants from 21st replacement yelled out loud, "LEFT FACE!"

"Well Nowak, here we go. I hope you're ready for this."

"FILE FROM THE RIGHT FORWARD…. MARCH!"

As we walked into the building to hear more speeches about Fort Hood and all it had to offer, I found myself rethinking about a conversation that I had with SFC Ford before I left Germany. While I was out processing 701st, she pulled me to the side… "Specialist Linson, I know you been through a lot since you been here, and in all this time, we tried to figure out why this was happening to you. Out of every soldier within the 701st, you had the most hell since day one." She told me. "When you get to your next duty station, I need you to look into the mirror and ask yourself why people react to you as they have your entire military career. Also try to make some changes about yourself to see if that will help at all."

"Change myself? I had changed for so many people throughout the years, what was there left to change? Wasn't it the Army that needed to change and not me?" I thought to myself.

Standing there listening to her speak about what she thinks I should do as an individual, I kept telling myself that no matter how many times I had changed for a group of soldiers, the outcome has always been hell for me. "Keep moving," a voice kept telling me in my mind. "Keep moving and it will all work out soon."

After coming back into reality and realizing I was sitting in a meeting hearing about the same bull shit about Fort Hood, it was time to hear what Division we were going to be assigned to... *"Linson."* The NCOIC from 21st Replacement called out my name.

"Here!"

"1st Cavalry Division, 615th ASB (**A**ir **S**upport **B**attalion).*"*

"Wow, aviation," I thought to myself. *"Never would have thought 88 Mike's were in aviation."* But knowing that my first unit at Fort Hood was something I didn't expect, I took my new assignment with caution.

After getting a makeshift map of where my new unit was located on East Fort Hood's airfield, I told the NCOIC in charge of our group I knew where my unit was located and that I will drive myself over to 615th ASB and report in myself instead of waiting for a unit liaison to come and pick me up.

Upon arriving at 615th ASB Headquarters, I kept telling myself that this was going to be a fresh start, and to do my best not to get caught up in anything he said, or she said crap within the ranks of my new Company.

Walking into the Battalion's S-1 office, I was told by the S-1 clerk that I was going to be assigned to Alpha Company 615th, under the command of CPT Freeman and 1st SGT Shelton.

I was a little stunned to hear my new Company Commander's name, which was the same last name as my first Battery Commander's last name when I was in 3-16th FA. At the time I did not pay too much attention to the fact that last names are very common within the military. But later that day, it all played out in a way I could not believe.

Standing around asking questions about what the unit's upcoming plains for Iraq or Afghanistan in the near future was going to be, the S-1 clerk replied... *"We're going to Iraq in six months. Did you just come back yourself?"*

"Yea, about a year ago,"

"How was it over there?"

"Not good, not good. You haven't been yet?"

"No, I haven't but I hope this time around things work out for you, Specialist Linson."

"Ha! I hope so too."

"Trust me, I know it will," she added. *"Also, one of your NCO's from Alpha Company is on their way up here to pick you up and take you over to where the Company is located at."*

"Okay." I replied.

As soon as I turned around to head back towards my seat, a female NCO by the name of SGT Bailey was looking at me dead into my face.

"Hello Specialist Linson. I'm Sergeant Bailey from 4th Platoon Alpha Company. You'll be in the same platoon as me."

"Oh really?"

"Yes. We're the only 88 Mike's in Alpha Company, or should I say the only ones in 615th."

"Well Sergeant, I'm happy to be here."

"That's good," she answered. *"Did you drive over here?"*

"Yes, I did, and I will follow you where you need to take me."

"Okay, just follow me."

"Will do." I replied, wondering why I reenlisted for this bull shit all over again.

As I followed her to the unit's location, I was very surprised to see that my new unit was located in the same exact location where 3-16th FA was. *"What kind of a coincidence is this?"* I asked myself. *"To return back to the same location where the 3-16th FA was after almost four years of being gone. Wow, keep moving!"* I told myself.

When we arrived at Alpha Company 615th location, I was introduced to my Platoon Sergeant, SSG Delapaz, who also introduced me to the rest of the NCO's within the platoon and the lower enlisted personnel there in. After getting all the platoon together to introduce the newcomer to the platoon, SSG Delapaz announced that I was being promoted to Sergeant later that month.

Standing there looking around at faces I never seen before, I felt disgusted around these people who did not know the slightest thing about me, and the people who I really wanted to be around me, were the ones I left back in Germany and not these soldiers and NCO's I had no relationship with. But when the day came for me to be promoted to Sergeant, it did not feel right when I stood in front of my new Company when their NCOIC from the training room started to read out loud my promotion orders. To me, I felt bad that the ones who had helped me to get this far were not there to see me pinning my stripes on.

While standing in front of the Company, while 1st SGT Shelton was pining on my E-5 rank, I knew this was going to be my last enlistment contract with the Army. But in the back of my mind, the nagging feeling that I was not going to finish my new tour of duty lingered on. At the time, I did not know why that thought was floating around in my mind, as I looked passed 1st SGT Shelton at faces, I did not know staring at me while I got promoted to Sergeant.

As I watched the whole Company giving me a round of applause, I kept telling myself... *"No matter how bad you feel, keep moving Howard."*

After getting settled back into the same barracks that I was in before, from time to time I had the urge to go back to the clubs and hang out where I used to go. But this time around, Fort Hood seemed different than it did back in the years when I was here my first time around. Nothing to me felt the same anymore. People that I knew were no longer around, and the mentality that I once had, had been demolished to a distant faint whisper of my past as I drove around Fort Hood and Killeen on my time off.

While getting to know and learn the behaviors of the soldiers within my platoon, I knew something was way out of place, either with myself or around me. Within my platoon, the soldiers and NCO's of 4th Platoon were fraternizing with each other on a level of insanity. If another soldier did not get along with another soldier, that soldier's NCO made sure that the soldier in question was put on a type of duty that involved harsh physical labor. But since I was the new NCO to the platoon, I just stood back and observed the actions and behaviors of everyone, just to get a better outlook of what I had to work with and change over time.

As the weeks went by, I recognized a few male soldiers kept checking me out in my platoon and from other platoons within Alpha Company. Every time that I saw someone winking at me, I did my best to ignore the stare downs and jesters that I received from NCO's and lower enlisted males and some females from time to time. But every time that this kind of behavior happened towards me, the first thing that kept running through my mind was… *"Oh no, not again. Maybe they're just curious about who this new Sergeant is."* I would try my best to convince myself that they were not flirting with me, but later that was not the case.

To my surprise after being in my new Company for under a month, more than five male soldiers came out to me, and a few had told me that they wanted me as their sexual partner. Immediately after I was getting sexual advances all over again, I started to hate my new duty assignment for fear of more retaliation from soldiers who I said no too. What made it worse was that some of these soldiers were in my platoon and under my command.

In the time that I was getting gestures after gestures from male soldiers, SFC Ford's question kept repeating through my mind... *"What are you doing to make these soldiers react to you the way they do?"* No matter how hard I tried, I could not answer that question every time that question ran through my mind.

So, one day, one of my soldiers named PFC Ethel, kept telling me how happy he was when I first showed up in the Company, and that he liked me since day one. Standing there hearing him telling me how he felt about me, I decided to ask him one simple question... *"What did I do to you, to make you feel this way about me?"*

"You just showed up and that's all it took for me to like you," he replied.

"Wow, no one has ever told me that before." I replied in shock.

"Hey what can I say, you're an attractive guy and when I first saw you, I wanted you."

"Really?"

"Yes. That's all it took."

"So, you're telling me, I didn't come on to you or flirt with you in any way?"

"No."

"Nothing I did prompt you to act this way towards me?"

"Nothing you did or said made me come out to you. From the first day I saw you, I knew you were either gay or bi."

"It shows?"

"No! But when you are, you just know."

"Yea that's what they say. But I'm confused to the core. You're not the only one who came out to me."

"Oh really. Who else?"

"Not telling you dude. Not looking to start any rumors around here, yea know."

"Yea, that's one thing we have too much around here already."

"Tell me about it."

This was a strange conversation I was having with my soldier. To me while we walked around talking about everything, it was the same old story, I did not come on to him, I did not talk a certain way or walk a certain way, and I surely did not act a certain way. So why was this happening to me all over again? I kept asking myself, while listening to my soldier talk about other soldiers he's been with, within the Company.

At times, I wanted to take some of these female and male soldiers up on their invitations, but I also knew if I had done that, that would cause me a great deal of trouble as an NCO. So, to not stir anything up, I allowed these soldiers throughout Alpha Company to tell me stories and make sexual suggestive remarks towards or around me. I figured if I allowed them that much, they would not retaliate against me, like soldiers did in my past.

I was not sure at the time, if I should have stopped them from telling me about their sexuality or how they personally felt about me, but at the same time, I kept hearing SFC Ford's questions repeating over and over again in my mind… *"What are you doing to make these soldiers come on to you? Why are they picking you to come out too? What are you doing or showing these people, that makes them think you're bi or gay?"*

To this day, I cannot answer those questions.

As the days grew longer and the time got closer for us to head over to Iraq, I found myself thinking about how this rotation was going to be, now that I was going back over to Iraq as a Sergeant.

Since I was living in the barracks and had my own room, from time to time, my soldiers would come around to chat or hang out on the weekends, and sometimes during the weekdays when there was nothing else to do. One four-day weekend in the month of August 2006, one of the soldiers in my platoon from 1st squad by the name of PFC Ortiz, came to my room with a large pepperoni pizza that he had bought, and asked me if I wanted some.

"Sure," I replied. *"Come on in."*

While me and PFC Ortiz sat down and ate some of his pizza, PFC Ortiz asked me if he could tell me a few personal things about himself... *"Sure Ortiz. You can talk to me about anything, no matter what or how severe it is."*

"Okay," PFC Ortiz replied. *"Well Sergeant Linson, I'm bisexual."*

"Okay...So why are you telling me Ortiz?"

"Because I feel I can come to you about anything."

"Yes, you can Ortiz. Most leaders don't listen to their soldiers anymore these days."

"Well, that's not all Sergeant Linson."

"What's up?"

"Well, I don't really know how to say this."

"Just let it come out, like the way you just came out to me." I told him smiling.

"Well, it's like this," he started to studier. *"I like you a lot, and I think you're the best NCO that has ever came to our platoon."*

"Wow, that was nice of you to say that Ortiz. But why me?"

"I don't know," he replied.

Then out of nowhere, PFC Ortiz came onto me and asked if we could do something sexual together. Shocked and overwhelmed by his aggressive mannerism, I quickly turned him down and told him to get a hold of himself while pushing him away from me. As I told him to calm himself down, while scooting away from him, in an instant, SFC Ford's questions kept repeating in my mind, and so I asked PFC Ortiz what made him pursue me. And just like before, he gave me the same answer the last soldier gave me… *"You just showed up and that's all it took."*

After I made it clear to him that nothing was going to happen between us two, he asked me if he could confine within me another one of his secrets… *"And please don't tell anyone about this,"* he added.

"What's that?"

"Sergeant Linson, I have a drinking and drug problem."

"When was the last time you did drugs Ortiz, and what do you define to be a drinking problem, high speed?" **(High Speed is a terminology that a lot of soldiers and leaders, within the military, use to tell other personnel that someone that they know is a good worker.)**

341

"Well, it's like this," PFC Ortiz explained. "There's this guy I'm seeing back home, and me and him had done EX (Ecstasy) together when I went home this weekend, and also last weekend I was drunk off my ass and drove his car into a lake."

"And why all of a sudden, you're just now telling this to your Chain of Command Ortiz?"

"Because none of the other NCO's besides you really listen to us and cares about us. Everyone else wants to demote us and try to embarrass us in front of everyone."

"Well, since you brought this matter up to me, how would you like for me to help you?"

"I don't know," as PFC Ortiz started to cry. "I think I might end up hurting someone soon with my drinking problem, and drugs are starting to take over my life."

As I sat there and watched PFC Ortiz cry, I knew I had to help him get on the path to recovery.

"Hey Ortiz, have you heard of the Army ASAP program (**A**rmy **S**ubstance **A**buse **P**rogram)?"

"Yeah."

"Come Monday morning, me and you will visit them and get this program going for you in your life. And just to let you know, this will stay between the two of us, unless you want Sergeant Delapaz and the First Sergeant to know?"

"No, no. Please don't tell them," PFC Ortiz pleaded with me. "I don't want them to know what I've done."

"Okay, I will do that. But come tomorrow, we'll get the ball rolling onto the right path, okay."

"Thank you, Sergeant Linson." As PFC Ortiz stood up to leave my room. "You can have the rest of the pizza. I'm full."

"Thank you, Ortiz. Everything is going to be alright." I told him, walking him to the door.

As I watched PFC Ortiz walk out of my room and down the stairs, I could not believe what I just heard from one of the most well-regarded soldiers in the platoon... "Well, you said you wanted to become a Sergeant and take care of soldiers, didn't you?" I thought to myself, thinking of what to do the next day. I knew I could not let PFC Ortiz down, as I'd been let down over the years as I sat back and recapped over the conversation we just had.

Come the next morning before the Company's PT formation, I approached PFC Ortiz and explained to him... "We're heading over to the substance abuse program building after PT this morning, Ortiz."

"No, that's all-right Sergeant Linson." he replied. "I can go on my own. Have you seen Sergeant Delapaz?"

"Yeah, he's right over there."

As PFC Ortiz thanked me and started walking towards SSG Delapaz and asked him if he could speak to him after formation… *"Sure thing,"* SSG Delapaz replied.

At the time I did not give it much attention or thought to why PFC Ortiz had changed his mind so quickly about me taking him to the ASAP program. I guessed PFC Ortiz wanted his Platoon Sergeant, SSG Delapaz, to take him and not me. But towards the end of the day SGT Haymond, PFC Ortiz's team leader, approached me and said he needed to talk to me about PFC Ortiz… *"What happened in your room yesterday afternoon with Ortiz, Sergeant Linson?"*

"Nothing." I replied. *"Ortiz came to my room with some pizza and told me about some problems he had been going through and asked me for my help. Why?"*

"Well, at any time did you ask him if you could suck his penis?"

"Excuse me? What did you just say?" I replied in an irritated voice.

"Calm down Sergeant Linson."

"I am calm! What the fuck did you say to me?"

"Hey, hey! I said calm down! That's what he reported to me and Sergeant Delapaz after PT this morning."

"Sergeant Haymond, fuck that! That soldier came up to my room and explained to me that he was going through some hard times back

at home and he needed my help, and I offered to take him to the ASAP program after PT this morning."

"So, you didn't ask him if you could sleep with him also?"

At that moment, my mouth fell wide open... "Are you fucking serious?"

"That's what he told me when I talked to him."

"Where's that fucking soldier at?" I replied, in anger.

"Calm down, Sergeant Linson. The rest of the NCO's in the platoon would like to talk to you about this also. Everyone is waiting in the Platoon Sergeant's office, over at the Company."

"Okay, let's do this. Lead the way!"

After SGT Haymond and I arrived at the empty Company's orderly room, SGT Gardner my squad leader, asked me to tell them all what had happened in my room yesterday. After I told them what me and PFC Ortiz had talked about, SSG Delapaz asked me if I would tell my side of the story in front of PFC Ortiz... "Yes. Where is he?" I replied.

SGT Haymond went to the back of the Company and brought PFC Ortiz into the orderly room. As soon as he stood at parade rest, SSG Delapaz asked him to tell everyone his side of the story... "No Sergeant, it doesn't matter anymore," PFC Ortiz replied.

"What the fuck do you mean it doesn't matter anymore soldier?" several of us NCO's asked him in unison.

"Look, Sergeant Linson came on to me in his room yesterday and asked me to take off my clothes," PFC Ortiz said. "That's all I have to say."

"THAT'S BULLSHIT!" I yelled out loud. "That's a fucking lie!"

SSG Delapaz asked me to repeat my version of what had happened in front of PFC Ortiz. After I was finished telling everything that was said between us, including about his sexuality, PFC Ortiz could not look me in my face, as he kept looking towards the ground while he stood at parade rest.

"Well?" SSG Delapaz asked him. "Look at me soldier! You have one more chance to tell us all the truth. Did Sergeant Linson ask you for any type of sexual favors yesterday?"

"I don't know Sergeant."

"What the FUCK do you mean you don't know soldier?" I screamed at him.

"I mean I don't know," PFC Ortiz stammered. "It's just that I..."

"I what?" SSG Delapaz asked.

"Well.... I just don't know."

"You don't know what soldier!?" SSG Delapaz demanded. "You're going to take a drug test first thing tomorrow morning. And if we find any type of substances in your system, we're going to bring you up on charges for lying to and about a Noncommissioned Officer."

346

"No, Sergeant!" PFC Ortiz quickly replied. *"Sergeant Linson didn't come on to me."*

"WHAT THE FUCK SOLDIER! DO YOU KNOW WHAT KIND OF PROBLEMS YOU JUST STARTED FOR ME?" I yelled out loud towards him.

"Sergeant Linson, please step outside," SSG Delapaz ordered me. *"Better yet, everyone besides Ortiz and his squad leader step outside now."*

"I'm sorry, Sergeant Linson," PFC Ortiz said as I exited the orderly room pissed off.

While I stood outside with the rest of the NCO's, they told me that the rest of the platoon had heard Ortiz's story earlier that day, and that none of them knew he had lied to them about it as well. After I had heard what was said, I kept pacing myself back and forth across the grass, trying to calm myself down before SSG Delapaz called us all back inside for our last meeting with PFC Ortiz. After a few minutes had passed, SSG Delapaz stepped outside and asked all of us NCO's to come back inside. On the way in, I kept a good distance away from PFC Ortiz when I returned into the orderly room... *"Sergeant Linson, PFC Ortiz has something he has to say to you."* SSG Delapaz announced.

"I'm sorry for lying about you. It was very unprofessional of me to make up a false sexual charge against you, Sergeant Linson."

"You know what Private!" I replied. *"It's because of shit like this, good NCO's turn into bad NCO's. You just took my good name and*

dragged it into the ground, because you thought it would be cool or some shit! You know what, I forgive you and accept your apology. But from this day forth, you stay the hell away from me and my room. If it doesn't pertain to the Army, don't even think about bothering me. Do I make myself clear soldier?"

"Yes, Sergeant Linson." PFC Ortiz answered back.

"Where do we go from here? SGT Gardner asked SSG Delapaz. *"The other soldiers think Sergeant Linson sexually harassed this soldier."*

"Don't worry about this, Sergeant Linson," SSG Delapaz replied. *"Private Ortiz is going to explain to the whole platoon tomorrow morning that he lied about you, and he will also apologize to every soldier individually."* SSG Delapaz looked over at PFC Ortiz, *"Do I make myself clear Ortiz?"*

"Yes, Sergeant" PFC Ortiz replied.

"Okay everyone, it's been a long day. I'll see yall in the morning. Sergeant Linson, go sleep this off. Everything will be alright." SSG Delapaz replied.

Not saying a word in response, I took off walking towards the barracks alongside with the other NCO's, who also stayed in the barracks, who kept trying to tell me... *"Don't let this get to you. We're going to fix this problem, and before you know it, all of this will be in the past and forgotten."* They kept telling me.

But knowing the outcome of my past, I just gave them my best fake smile as we kept walking towards our barracks. But once again, I found myself stuck in the same issues that I had experienced in the past 8 years I've been in the Army. *"This will not bring you down,"* I kept whispering to myself. *"Just keep moving. This is not the end."*

That following morning, PFC Ortiz apologized to the entire platoon and to me again after the PT formation, but I knew this episode wasn't over yet. Knowing the outcome of my experience with this same issue, I knew it was not going to end well for me in the months to come. Looking over the platoon, there was too much drama and fraternization within the ranks for any of this to just disappear quickly after he had apologized to everyone.

So, since I did not belong to any of the cliques within the platoon, from that day forth, I kept to myself and did not allow any soldier to tell me anything personal about themselves and I kept all conversations to a military professional level. And again, the same questions kept coming into my mind… *"Why you?"* SFC Ford asked. *"Why do people keep coming on or coming out to you?"*

THE END OF THE ROAD

Come September of 2006, I was bound for Iraq for the second time around. I flew out on an advanced party with some of the NCO's from every Company within the 615th ASB, to get everything ready before the rest of the Battalion showed up into Kuwait. Once again, I found myself back in Camp New York and at times, my past experiences kept flashing back through my mind, as I relived my steps around Camp New York from my first deployment.

For the first time in a long time, things were simple, and I did not feel or think that someone was going to shoot me in the back when I was not looking. I could say, since I was a Sergeant now and not a lower enlisted soldier, the drama of having to be bothered with the E-1 to E-4 rank structure was gone. After our first two weeks had passed while in Kuwait, my mind set about being deployed all over again changed when the rest of the Battalion arrived in Kuwait. Although I kept my distance from many of the soldiers in my Company, the tension between me and PFC Ortiz's friends began to grow. I found out through SGT Gardner that PFC Ortiz was one of SSG Delapaz's boys within the Platoon Sergeants' clique, and that SSG Delapaz and PFC Ortiz were mad about what had happened back at Fort Hood... *"I'm not worried about them Sergeant Gardner."* I told him.

"You should be Sergeant Linson," he replied before he turned and walked away from me.

"Okay, so here we go again," I thought to myself. *"What's going too happened this time around?"*

By turning down the sexual offer from PFC Ortiz and other soldiers within the Company, I only caused more problems for myself.

After all of our Company had arrived in Kuwait, the soldiers who were flirting with me back in the states became more aggressive in Kuwait, just like my first time around. Soldiers and some NCO's would grab themselves to reveal hard-ons through their uniforms whenever they called out my name to get my attention. And yet I still felt I had done nothing to attract this type of attention or behavior from these military personnel.

A week later after the Battalion had arrived in Kuwait, I was walking back from the mess hall (Cafeteria), when SGT Ashmade ran across the street towards me before I could cross over and head to where my Battalion sleeping area was at. As soon as he approached my location, he started to tell me what he was ordered to do… *"Hey Sergeant Linson, Sergeant Delapaz wants you to stay over on this side of the road until he comes over to talk to you."*

"Why?"

"I don't know, he just ordered me to tell you this."

"Okay, well I would like to know what's going on."

"I don't know big sarg, but he's mad about something you've done."

"Something I've done," I replied. "I haven't done anything."

"Well, that's going to be between you and Sergeant Delapaz and Sergeant Gardner."

"What the hell is going on now?"

"I can't talk about it, Sergeant Linson. Sergeant Delapaz is going to talk to you about it." SGT Ashmade replied before heading back over the street to talk with SSG Delapaz.

Standing by myself, not having a clue about what was going on or what was said for SSG Delapaz to order another Sergeant to tell me not to cross the road. I waited for about twenty minutes until SSG Delapaz and SGT Gardner finally walked across the street to talk to me. As they approached me, I felt like swinging away at them both... "What's going on, Sergeant Linson?" SSG Delapaz said.

"I don't know. Why don't you tell me why you don't want me to cross this road, Sergeant?"

"Well Sergeant Linson, we'd hope you would tell us first." SSG Delapaz responded in a sarcastic manner.

"Sergeant Delapaz, if I knew what was going on, I wouldn't be standing here surprised and dumb founded don't you think."

"You know exactly why we're talking to you right now Sergeant Linson. You wish to give it a try on why you can't come over to the tents right now?"

"Didn't I just tell you I don't know what's going on?"

"Okay Sergeant Linson, since you're acting like you don't know what's going on, let me tell you. More than eight soldiers have reported to their NCO's that you're standing around in the shower trailers watching them take showers and that you've been watching them undress and get dressed before and after they are finished taking showers." SSG Delapaz explained. "Also, one soldier from first platoon came up to me crying with his Platoon Sergeant, telling me that you asked him to meet you in the Porter John after he took a shower. Now explain that to me Sergeant Linson."

"Excuse me?" I replied in disbelief looking back at my two NCO's. I knew by the looks that they gave me, I was already guilty as charged.

"Sergeant Delapaz, what you just said doesn't make any sense. Listen to what you're saying, none of it sounds right, nor does it make any sense!" I replied in a harsh tone.

"Well, we had this problem back in Fort Hood with you and PFC Ortiz Sergeant Linson, and now we have it with other soldiers in this platoon and in other platoons within the Company. Do you wish to explain?"

"How in the fuck can I explain something I didn't do Sergeant Delapaz?"

"Sergeant Linson, I need you to stop lying and start telling us the truth. Are you going around trying to use your rank to get sexual favors out of certain male soldiers?"

"How can I tell the fucking truth when you and Sergeant Gardner already think I'm guilty?" I replied. *"What the fuck you just said I'm doing isn't me!... Look Sergeant Delapaz, if I was standing around in the showers asking people for sexual favors, and watching countless soldiers take showers where other Officers, NCO's and soldiers from other Companies and Battalions take showers, don't you think you'd have more than just eight soldiers reporting me for the same thing, you dumb fuck!"*

"Watch your language when you talk to me Sergeant!"

"No! Fuck you Sergeant Delapaz and fuck you too Sergeant Gardner! Yall are telling me that I'm going around trying to use my rank for sexual favors towards lower enlisted men. No, fuck that and fuck you bitch! I want to talk to the First Sergeant about this shit!" I replied in anger.

"No!" SSG Delapaz replied. *"You will talk to me first."*

"Fuck you, you short fucking bastard! I'm not going to stand around here in the middle of this damn desert and let you accuse me of homosexual acts! Especially when we're all carrying live ammunition! Fuck you, you piece of shit and that goes for you too Sergeant Gardner!" I looked at them both.

"AT EASE SERGEANT!" SSG Delapaz yelled out loud.

"Fuck you're at ease dip shit!" You're accusing me of things I wouldn't dream of doing! Listen to yourself dumb ass! Nothing that you are saying to me makes any sense."

"Sergeant Linson, you need to calm down." SGT Gardner tried to order me.

"Okay, okay! First of all, FUCK YOU Sergeant Gardner. Let me tell you both something. Sergeant Delapaz, if you think I'm out here doing all these things you say I'm doing, then someone needs to put a gun to my head and blow my fucking brains out. I know and GOD knows I'm not out here doing this shit!" I demanded to them both.

"You know what Sergeant Linson. When someone is guilty, they always go into a defensive mode." SSG Delapaz replied.

"You know what Staff Sergeant Delapaz, this conversation is over. I'm going to the First Sergeant and there's nothing you can do about it. If you get in my way, I'm going to fuck you up bitch!"

"Sergeant Linson come back here!" SSG Delapaz grabbed my arm and yanked me back towards him, as I turned and shoved him down to the ground… *"YOU TOUCH ME AGAIN,"* I shouted, *"AND I'LL BE THE LAST PERSON YOU'LL SEE BEFORE I BUST YOUR FUCKING HEAD WIDE THE FUCK OPEN!!"*

Immediately, SGT Gardner stepped in between the two of us and told me to back away from SSG Delapaz.

"THAT'S IT SERGEANT!" SSG Delapaz shouted, as I was walking away from them. *"I'M BRINGING YOU UP ON CHARGES!"*

"Charge this bitch!" as I flipped my middle finger up at them as I kept walking towards the tents.

Walking at a quick pace, SSG Delapaz and SGT Gardner ran past me towards the First Sergeants' tent, to make it there before I did. When I made it to the tent where the Commander and First Sergeant were at, SSG Delapaz and SGT Gardner were already talking with 1st SGT Shelton and CPT Freeman. When I walked up to the Commander and tried to speak to him, he ordered me to stand 100 feet away from them and wait until he had finished speaking with SSG Delapaz.

I knew at that point when I was ordered to move away from everyone, that they would believe SSG Delapaz and SGT Gardner's before hearing anything I had to say. After waiting a few minutes for them to finish talking, 1st SGT Shelton approached me... *"Walk with me, Sergeant Linson,"* he said. *"We need to talk and give your weapon to the Commander."*

As I followed him into the dark towards where all the field generators were located at, I kept wondering why we were walking away from everyone who stood in the light, and we were walking off into the dark.

Turn after turn, around generator after generator, 1st SGT Shelton came to a stop, turned around to face me and took out his weapon (M-9 pistol), locked and loaded one round into the chamber and took it off of safe and put his weapon into the side of my head... *"WHO THE FUCK DO YOU THINK YOU ARE THREATENING TO KILL MY SOLDIERS,*

SERGEANT!?...I WILL BLOW YOUR FUCKING HEAD CLEAN OFF YOUR FUCKING SHOLDERS RIGHT FUCKING NOW, MOTHERFUCKA!" 1st SGT Shelton kept yelling. *"WHAT THE FUCK ARE YOU THINKING SERGEANT!?"*

"FIRST SERGEANT, DON'T DO THIS!... IT'S ALL LIES!... I DIDN'T DO OR SAY WHAT THEY'RE ACCUSING ME OF!... FIRST SERGEANT, PLEASE DON'T!" I cried out loud, pleading for my life.

"SINCE YOU WANT TO END OTHER PEOPLE'S LIVES, I'M GONNA END YOURS FIRST! IS THIS WHAT YOU WANT, MOTHERFUCKA?"

"FIRST SERGEANT, DON'T PLEASE!... I DIDN'T THREATEN ANYONE." as my First Sergeant kept pressing his gun harder into the side of my head.

"THEN WHAT DID YOU SAY, MOTHERFUCKA?"

"FIRST SERGEANT, I TOLD SERGEANT DELAPAZ THAT SOMEONE SHOULD PUT A GUN TO MY HEAD AND BLOW MY BRAINS OUT, IF I WAS DOING WHAT HE SAID THEY WERE ACCUSING ME OF DOING...I DIDN'T SAY I WAS GOING TO KILL ANYONE!" doing my best to yell over the generators.

"OH, SO YOU WANT TO KILL YOURSELF?!... OKAY LINSON, I WILL DO IT FOR YOU RIGHT NOW BITCH!"

"FIRST SERGEANT DON'T!" I kept yelling, walking backwards, until he grabbed me by my collar and pulled me back towards him.

"WE JUST PROMOTED YOU TO SERGEANT NOT TOO LONG AGO, AND THIS IS HOW YOU REPAY US, BY THREATENING TO KILL MY SOLDIERS AND YOURSELF??" 1st SGT Shelton started to press harder against my head. *"GET ON YOUR FUCKING KNEES, MOTHERFUCKA!"*

"FIRST SERGEANT, PLEASE…."

"I SAID GET ON YOUR FUCKING KNEES BITCH!"

Getting down on my knees, as 1st SGT Shelton started to point and press the muzzle of his pistol into my right eye, as I thought my end was near. Looking up into his face, with the distant lights showing me his dark facial expression and to make out his dark eyes as they stared down at me, I knew right then and there, my First Sergeant was going to commit murder in the name of homophobia… *"FIRST SERGEANT, DON'T DO THIS!"* as I felt his weapon start to shake against my eye.

Looking up at him after a few minutes, life in those few minutes seemed to pass for a lifetime, as 1st SGT Shelton finally spoke… *"GET THE FUCK UP, SERGANT!"*

Reaching down and picking me up by my neck, he yanked me to my feet and dug his pistol underneath my chin, as I quickly moved my hand onto his wrist and started to squeeze his wrist, to relieve the grip that he had on my neck, being that he was chocking me… *"LET ME TELL YOU SOMETHING LINSON, YOU'RE DEAD MEAT. YOU HEAR ME?"* 1st SGT Shelton kept digging his pistol harder underneath my chin. *"I'M NOT THROUGH WITH YOU YET, YOU SON OF A BITCH!"*

By this time, we were now nose to nose.

"DO YOU WANT TO DIE, MOTHERFUCKA?"

"NO…. FIRST…. SERGEANT!" as I tried to speak out those words, as he tried harder to chock me out.

"THEN WHY DID YOU THREATEN TO KILL MY SOLDIERS?"

"I……. DIDN'T…… FIRST…... SERGEANT! WHY…… DON'T…... YOU…... BELIEVE…. ME?" I did my best to yell out loud.

A few seconds passed, as his pistol started to shake out of control underneath my chin.

Finally, he released his grip on my neck and put his weapon back on safe and slowly returned it to this holster… *"FOLLOW ME!"* he ordered.

As we walked back towards the tent area, I kept staring at the back of his head, wanting to kill him while he was walking ahead of me. But somehow, I managed to keep control of myself while rubbing my neck, thinking to myself… *"I need to tell someone quick about what just took place."* And the first person I thought of was CSM Vela, the Battalion Command Sergeant Major. When I first meet him, I knew he was a hard ass and did not take any shit from nobody, no matter what their rank was.

As we found our way out of the field of generators, I said in my normal voice… *"I'm not through with you either, First Sergeant. Not one fucking bit, you black motherfucka."*

When we finally returned to where the Commander was still talking to SSG Delapaz and SGT Gardner, I knew this would be my last and final fight in the United States Army.

1st SGT Shelton turned and looked at me… *"Take your ass to bed Sergeant! And come tomorrow, we will deal with you."* 1st SGT Shelton yelled. *"Sergeant Delapaz, I want you to keep guards on his ass all night! GET THE FUCK OUT OF HERE, SERGEANT LINSON,"* 1st SGT Shelton screamed. *"GET THE FUCK OUT OF MY FACE RIGHT NOW!"*

Before I turned and walked away, I saw the happy expressions on both SSG Delapaz and SGT Gardner's faces as if they were victorious.

Getting back to my sleeping area within the tent where 4th platoon was located at, I felt like screaming to the top of my voice and fighting everyone who was in sight. I did not believe for one second what had just happened to me. *"How does anyone fight back after an incident like this?"* I asked myself, laying down for the night.

Come the next morning, the entire Company had to attend an EEO class about sexual harassment. As I took a seat away from my platoon, SSG Delapaz approached me… *"Stay away from the enlisted soldiers in my platoon until further notice, Sergeant Linson. And if I see you within 100 feet of them,"* he added, *"I will have you locked away forever."*

"I'm not finished with you either, Sergeant Delapaz." I said to myself, while seeing that my soldiers were looking over at me, with concern looks on why I was sitting away from them all.

After the EEO class was over, I walked up to the Company's Equal Opportunity NCO and told her what 1st SGT Shelton had done and that I needed to talk to the Sergeant Major ASAP. Hearing what I had to say, she was beyond shocked to hear what had happened to me last night. She told me she had heard a little about what was going on but did not know the full story until now. So shortly after she had answered a few more questions from some of the personnel within the Company, she quickly escorted me to go see CSM Vela and explained to him the whole story, starting with the PFC Ortiz incident back at Fort Hood.

When I told CSM Vela that 1st SGT Shelton held his loaded pistol to the side of my head and threaten to end my life, CSM Vela was furious… *"HE DID WHAT?"* CSM Vela shouted. *"Stay right here. I'll be right back, Sergeant Linson!"* As I watched him walk out of the Headquarters sleeping tent, I knew I was going to be in a fight for my life.

It took CSM Vela a few minutes to return with my weapon and ammo in hand. *"Let's go see the Battalion Commander."*

After explaining everything to LT Col Hurshinger, he asked for my weapon from CSM Vela and looked at me and said… *"Can we trust you with this weapon, Sergeant Linson?"*

"Yes sir," I replied, as he handed me back my weapon and ammo, while the memories of my Commander from Delta Company 701st kept flashing through my mind, when he returned my weapon to me that day, I went to go see the mental health doctor.

"You're sleeping in this tent now Sergeant Linson," CSM Vela said. *"Go get your things and bring them over here, ASAP. Don't say a word to anyone or explain yourself."*

Walking back over to my platoon's tent area, it took less than five minutes for me to get all my stuff together and move into the Headquarters Company tent. After I had settled in from across where CSM Vela slept, he looked over at me and said... *"Sergeant, you look tired. Get some rest."*

"Roger that, Sergeant Major." I replied, putting my stuff down on the ground. Not really feeling like fixing up my sleeping area, I decided to lay down on top of some of my bags that I didn't even unpack. In a matter of minutes after rethinking about what I needed to do in the days ahead, I was out cold and did not wake up until the next morning.

In the weeks that followed my ordeal with 1st SGT Shelton, CSM Vela told me that I will be his new driver while we were in Iraq, and that my Chain of Command should have mentioned my situation to him long before we came on our deployment. Then I heard the words that had become bitterly stale to me... *"None-the-less, you're with me now. And if anyone from Alpha Company starts any problems with you, I don't care what time of the day it is, you come straight to me. I don't care if I'm asleep, you wake me up! Do I make myself clear Sergeant Linson?"* CSM Vela demanded.

After hearing the same old words coming out of CSM Vela's mouth, I told him yes after he had explained to me what I needed to do, but deep within myself, a war was growing stronger within me, and I was on the brink of losing my mind... *"I can't take this shit anymore! I can't!"* I kept repeating to myself. *"Keep moving Howard."* A voice kept repeating in my mind. *"Keep moving and don't stop!"*

As we left Kuwait and began to make our flights up to Taji Iraq, I was always by myself everywhere we went, since I was moved into Headquarter Company. I figured I was still new to the 615th ASB, and no one in Headquarters Company knew who I was, and for the most part, a lot of people from Alpha Company knew I was not with them anymore but did not know why at the time.

In the time that it took the 615th ASB to finally make it to Taji, I had plenty of time to think about ways to get out of this deployment and back to the states.

As we got settled into FOB Taji, CSM Vela put me in charge of an Iraqi shopping area that was not too far from the 615th ASB Command Center. As time went on, my stress levels started to go down, until one day when I was on my way back from the defac (Cafeteria), when SSG Delapaz cornered me and started to ask me a few questions... *"Sergeant Linson, what were you thinking when you decided to start sexually harassing my soldiers and use your rank to try to get what you wanted out of them?"*

"*Are you stupid or something, you ignorant fuck?*" I told him while stepping closer towards him. "*Didn't Sergeant Major Vela and First Sergeant Shelton tell you to stay the fuck away from me, bitch?*"

"*I don't care what they said Sergeant, I just want to know why did you sexually harass my soldiers? Are you gay?*"

"*You have three seconds to get the fuck out of my face before I put you in the grave where you stand, Sergeant!*"

"*Are you threatening me Sergeant?*"

Stepping into his face... "*What the fuck do you think asshole?*"

"*I just want to know why you did the things you did Sergeant?*" SSG Delapaz kept pushing the issue.

"*You know what, now I see that you really are stupid. Move the fuck out of my way.*" As I pushed him away from me with my shoulder while looking at him as I started to walk away.

"*WHY DID YOU TRY TO HAVE SEX WITH MY MALE SOLDIERS, SERGEANT LINSON?*" SSG Delapaz shouted at the top of his voice.

As I kept walking way, SGT Gardner and SGT Wallace, came around one of the sleeping trailers to see who was yelling out loud, and saw me walking towards their location... "*Yall need to get your fucking hobbit size NCO quick,*" I demanded. "*Where the fuck is yalls First Sergeant?*"

"*He's over in his trailer,*" SGT Wallace replied. "*What's wrong?*"

"You know what the fuck is wrong Sergeant! Don't even stand there acting like there isn't anything wrong Sergeant Wallace!" as I started off towards 1st SGT Shelton's trailer.

After arriving at 1st SGT Shelton's trailer, I found him sitting on his doorsteps talking to one of his Platoon Sergeants... "Sergeant Linson, what are you doing over here."

"First Sergeant, I know, and you know I'm not supposed to be over here, but I'm just letting you know what just happened between me and Sergeant Delapaz," I said, "and just to let you know, I will bring this matter up with Sergeant Major Vela."

"Okay Sergeant Linson, I will have a talk with Sergeant Delapaz and find out what happened." 1st SGT Shelton replied looking nervous.

"Okay First Sergeant. Just do me a big favor, tell that NCO to stay the hell away from me or next time it won't be nice." I replied, before I took off walking towards Battalion Headquarters.

After I had arrived at CSM Vela's room and told him what took place, he told me to head back to Alpha Company and bring back 1st SGT Shelton and SSG Delapaz, and to meet back with him in his office.

While heading back to Alpha Companies sleeping area, I felt as if CSM Vela was the real deal and I wished someone like him would have been in all my past units and just maybe I would not feel the way I did about the U.S. Army at the time.

Coming back with 1st SGT Shelton and SSG Delapaz a few steps behind me, we arrived at the Battalion where CSM Vela was waiting in his PT's... *"What the fuck are you doing to this NCO, Sergeant Delapaz?"* CSM Vela yelled out loud. *"Did we not tell you to stay away from Sergeant Linson?"*

"Yes, Sergeant Major you did." SSG Delapaz replied.

"So, what the fuck am I hearing that you asked him if he's gay? Do you want me to bring you up on charges SERGEANT?"

"No Sergeant Major. I just wanted to know why Sergeant Linson......"

"Shut the fuck up Sergeant Delapaz! I'm starting to think that Sergeant Linson is innocent and yall have been fucking with him since day one. Why are you fucking with him, Sergeant Delapaz?"

As the room fell into silence as we all stood there looking at SSG Delapaz, not coming up with an answer to Sergeant Major's question. I strongly believe that everyone knew right then and there, that SSG Delapaz had it out for me, since he could not respond to the question that was left open for an answer.

"First Sergeant Shelton," CSM Vela said, *"You better keep this NCO away from him and if I find out that this disobedient Staff Sergeant comes near him again, I will bust his ass back down to Sergeant before he knew what hit him...Do you hear me First Sergeant?"*

"Yes, Sergeant Major, I will see to it that he understands it clearly." 1st SGT Shelton replied.

When I heard 1ˢᵗ SGT Shelton say that I really wanted to say out loud, *"You mean the way you did me?"*

"Staff Sergeant Delapaz, this is your last and final fucking warning. Stay the fuck away from Sergeant Linson or it will be you in his place! Do I make myself clear Sergeant?"

"Yes, Sergeant Major," SSG Delapaz replied in a soft voice.

"As for you Sergeant Linson, the next time someone from Alpha Company comes up to you and starts demanding answers, walk the fuck away and don't entertain them or I'll hold you as equal and guilty as them. Do I make myself clear Sergeant Linson?"

"Yes, Sergeant Major. Very clear."

"Now all of yall get the hell out of my office and go to bed."

As we all left out of the Battalion, 1ˢᵗ SGT Shelton pulled SSG Delapaz to the side to talk with him, as I kept walking towards my trailer happy as hell. *"It's about damn time."* I thought to myself. *"But keep moving Howard."* A voice kept repeating in my mind.

As the weeks went by, things seemed to be calm in my world and in my area of responsibility until two of my soldiers, SPC Perusse and PFC Manlove from Alpha Company, snuck over to have a private conversation with me... *"Sergeant Linson, do you know what they're planning on doing with you?"* PFC Manlove asked me.

"No," I replied. "The only thing I know is that I'm not supposed to be around any of yall."

"No, Sergeant Linson. They're going to put you in prison for all the sexual charges that soldiers reported against you." SPC Perusse replied.

"What?"

"That's right. They interviewed a lot of us, and they said you have been brought up on charges for sexually assaulting 10 soldiers," SPC Perusse replied. "They told us that you will be sent to jail in a few weeks from today."

"What the fuck! Who is they?" as I looked at them both, as if they were frozen in time.

"You're telling us you didn't know about this?" PFC Manlove replied. "Sergeant Major Vela and some Officer we never seen before told us they already interviewed you and you confessed to sexually assaulting these soldiers."

"Bullshit I did!" I replied in anger.

"Most of us have already talked with CSM Vela and he expressed his feelings about what you did to us, and he assured us that you will be punished under the full law of the military justice system." PFC Manlove added.

"You know what Perusse and Manlove, thank you for telling me this. I see Sergeant Major Vela every day and he has never told me anything *about this or even asked me one question pertaining to this issue."* I replied. *"But you know what, thank you so much for sneaking over here and letting me know what's their next move is and now that gives me the chance to checkmate their asses."*

"What are you going to do, Sergeant Linson?" SPC Perusse asked.

"Well put it this way, in a few days you won't see me anymore."

"Where are you going? I don't want to see anything bad happen to you, Sergeant. That's why we came over here to let you know." PFC Manlove replied. *"A lot of us know your innocent, but Sergeant Delapaz and his clique are telling all of these lies about you and some of us had to let you know."*

"Put it this way yall, don't worry yourself about it. When you see that I'm no longer around, just know I'll be all right." Knowing that my soldiers were not happy about the situation I was in, I simply added... *"Hey fellas, I've come this far in life, and do you really think I'm gonna let these lame ass ducks, fuck with me again?"*

All three of us started to laugh... *"No Sergeant, we know you won't let them,"* they replied. *"Wherever you go Sergeant Linson, you take care of yourself."*

"I will yall. And again, thank you for the heads up." As my soldiers got up and both gave me a handshake and a hug and walked out of my office.

Watching them walk out of my building, I started to think quickly to myself... *"Okay Sergeant Major Vela, you slick motherfucka! You think you got me? Well, it's time to turn the motha-fucking tables back on you and everyone else."* I said to myself while standing up looking outside of my window at the Black Hawks and Apache's landing and taking off from the airfield.

Before this day, my pelvic pain had returned and the injections that I had received were only temporary pain reliefs to get me back out going again. But I knew at that moment while looking out of my office window, I had a way out of Iraq for good. Knowing their next move, I used my last and final chess piece, my "Queen", and I used her all the way.

In Mid-November of 2006, I walked into the medical clinic in FOB Taji and explained to the Colonel in charge of the facility that I was in severe pain. After showing him my thick sheaf of medical records that documented my years of pelvic issues, he ordered me a medevac to pick me up the following day.

During that whole day, I did not tell anyone where I was going. I knew if my Chain of Command had found out I was leaving for medical reasons, they would have stopped my departure immediately. I have seen it happened to countless soldiers who needed medical attention, and the only way they would have gotten it, was to be medivac out of Iraq. But instead, they were forced to stay in Iraq and later became disabled after they redeployed back home.

Soldier's Chain of Commands does not like it when their soldiers must leave any major deployments. So, to keep their numbers up for funding purposes, they deny a lot of soldier's proper medical attention just to keep a fake number of healthy soldiers on paperwork.

So that following morning I packed the most important things I needed to take with me when it was time for me to head over to the medevac helicopter pad... *"Just let them find out through Brigade, when they saw I signed out."* I laughed to myself.

While I was packing my things up in my trailer, there was a knock at my door... *"Who is it?"* I yelled out.

"Sergeant Major Vela wants to see you in his office ASAP," his gunner SPC Cyr yelled out. *"Like yesterday he wanted to see you, Sergeant Linson."*

"Okay, I'm on my way." I shouted back.

"Ha, ha, haaaa, oh shit they found out! Well, time to go and face the piper."

While I was walking up towards Battalion, I passed a few NCO's and soldiers from S-1 who kept asking me why I was being medevac'd out of Iraq... *"I have some medical issues yall,"* I replied as I kept walking past them.

Walking towards CSM Vela's closed office door... "Knock, knock, knock!"

"Come in!"

371

"You wanted to see me, Sergeant Major?"

"Get your ass in here now, Sergeant Linson!"

"Yes, Sergeant Major."

"Who the fuck told you, you could go on sick call Sergeant?"

"Sergeant Major, I'm in pain."

"Fuck your pain! Why am I just now hearing about your medical problems?" he demanded. *"Why am I just finding out that you're flying out in less than two hours, Sergeant?"*

"I don't know, Sergeant Major." I tried my best not to laugh but I could not hold it back anymore. *"HAHAHAHAHAHA!"*

"SHUT THE FUCK UP! WHAT ARE YOU FUCKING LAUGHING ABOUT, SERGEANT?"

"HEHEHEHAHAHAHA, I'm sorry Sergeant Major. I should have told you I was leaving."

"Get the fuck out of my office!"

"HAHAHAHAHA! Yes, Sergeant Major."

"GET OUT!" he shouted to the top of his voice.

As I was walking out of his office laughing, LT Col Hurshinger came out of his office to investigate what all the yelling was about. When he saw me laughing as I was walking out of the Sergeant Major's office, he asked me... *"What's wrong, Sergeant Linson?"*

"Nothing sir, HAHAHAHAHAHAHAHA" I replied still trying my hardest not to laugh, as I kept walking out of the Battalion Headquarters waving at everyone as I walked out of the front doors.

As soon as I got out into the open space, I took off running like a bat out of hell at a dead sprint back to my trailer to get my things together and took off running again to the medevac Black Hawk landing pad. *"Keep moving, just keep moving Howard."* I kept telling myself. *"Don't stop, keep moving."*

Being that I was not the only one catching this flight to LSA Anaconda, when the medevac Black Hawk landed, I was the first one on board and strapped into my seat.

Our flight took us straight to LSA Anaconda, which is now called Camp Victory, where I made my plea that I was beyond severe pain, and I could no longer serve out in Iraq. After being told that my only options were to return to Landstuhl Germany or stay one more night and try some painkillers, I quickly disagreed to the one night stay over, because a soldier's Chain of Command can make one phone call and that soldier will be back on a bird in a heartbeat, heading back to the post from which he or she came from with no questions asked.

So, I told every doctor that examined me that I've been taking pain meds for over three years now, and none had helped me recover. That being said, it was all stated in my medical records.

"Okay, you'll be on the next flight heading to Germany in an hour. Have a safe trip home Sergeant." The doctors replied.

373

"Don't worry, I will sir." I replied, trying not to burst out laughing again.

Speed walking out of the hospital, and to the out-processing manifest area, as I kept telling myself to get the hell out of dodge as quickly as I could... *"Yes, yes, yes. Let's get to Germany and make it a short lay over and keep moving."* I mumbled to myself, waiting in line to be signed onto the flight heading out of Iraq.

After arriving nine hours later into Landstuhl Germany, I had to report for an immediate checkup with the head General Surgical Doctor. While I sat at the Brigadier General's desk, who started cursing me out... *"You're a sorry piece of shit excuse for a NCO, Sergeant!"* he cried out. *"It's been almost three years since you had this problem and now here you are wasting my time and the Army's time. You can't even keep up with your soldiers! Oh yes, you're going back to Fort Hood, where you will be discharged, you broke down individual!! Now get out of my office!"*

"HAHAHAHAHAH! Yes sir. I'm a sorry piece of shit NCO, SIR. Yes, I am, sorry shit, sorry shit!" I busted out laughing out loud again... *"HEHEHEAHAHA."*

"GET OUT!" he yelled to the top of his voice.

"HEHEHEHEHAHAHAHAH! Yes, I will sir." I replied getting my records back from him, with a signed letter for me to get on the next available flight back state side.

Walking out of his office wiping the tears off my face from laughing so hard, I walked as fast as I could through the hallways of the hospital to make it to the manifest area where they were processing soldier's back state side. After waiting in line for a couple of minutes, I gave them my signed slip, and you know what? Wheels went up three hours after I had first landed into Landstuhl Germany, and I was heading back home to Fort Hood Texas.

"Yeah, keep moving, keep moving." I kept telling myself during the flight home.

It took some of us, who were heading back to Fort Hood, two and a half days from the time it took us to land stateside at Andrews Air Force Base and back in the air again heading home. When I made it back to Fort Hood and back to the 615th ASB rear-d location in the motor pool, the acting rear-d Command Sergeant Major, 1st SGT Lehmann, called me into his office and said... *"The Chain of Command missed you in Anaconda, and they missed you when you were in Germany. But we got you now and you know what Sergeant? You're heading back tonight, on the first flight out of here."*

"Oh no I'm not!" I replied. *"I have a medical profile that states I'm nondeployable First Sergeant."*

"We'll see about that Sergeant Linson. Who's your doctor and what's his or her name, so we can call and get you off that profile and back to Iraq?"

"Well First Sergeant Lehmann, you can try all you want, but I'm not going back to Iraq!"

"Oh yes you will, Sergeant Linson. Who's your doctor?"

"Sorry, you will not find that out until tomorrow when I go back for a checkup over at Darnel Hospital."

"Okay, when you do get their number, we need it so we can change your profile ASAP!"

"Yeah right, dip shit!" I thought to myself, as I turned around and walked out of his office after being dismissed. *"Keep moving and don't stop."* I kept whispering to myself.

Come the next morning, I was dropped off at Fort Hoods Darnel Medical Center and my doctor asked me if I wanted surgery or be medical discharged? So, thinking that I wanted to be operated on first before I had gotten out of the military, I told my doctor that I wanted surgery first to determine what was really going on inside of my body. And after countless MRI's day after day, a week later I had a date set up for surgery towards Christmas time in December of 2006.

During this time before I went into surgery, my Chain of Command tried over five times to put me on a flight back to Iraq, and every time I had missed my flight, they threatened me with an Article 15 for missing movement. But every time I did not show up, they would send me over to the rear-d Discom Brigade Chain of Command where I showed them my profile, stating that I was nondeployable. Let's say the 615th ASB rear-d command, did not swallow that too well every time I flashed that sheet of paper into their faces.

After I had my surgery, my oldest sister Heather was there to pick me up when I was released from the hospital, but I had to return less than 12 hours later because of an infection that spread across my abdomen and down both of my legs from my doctor messing up during my surgery. When I was finally discharged out of the hospital for the second time around, and was sent home on convalescent leave, was when my Chain of Command tried for the sixth time while I was on leave, to put me on a flight back to Iraq when I was not able to walk on my own.

SFC Vega, the Headquarters Company rear-d First Sergeant, told me… *"You need a wheelchair, so we can roll you onto the airplane and send you back to Iraq, to be court marshaled Sergeant."*

At the time, I was pretty pissed off when he told me that, but no matter which way they tried, they did not succeed in sending me back to Iraq.

After I had returned back from convalescent leave, one of the NCO's from Headquarters Company who worked in S-1 pulled me to the side to speak with me in person… *"Sergeant Linson, don't tell anyone I told you this, but they're going to send you back to Iraq regardless of your current profile and physical state. If you can, you need to request a medical discharge quickly before they will do all that they can, to send you back."* She explained to me.

"How long have they been talking about this?" I asked her.

"Ever since we found out that you were on your way back from Iraq." She replied. *"I also heard them say that they're going to put you into hand cuffs and leg irons before you leave out of here. And when you return to Iraq, they will read you your rights and what they will charge you with and send you to prison form there."*

"Oh really?" I replied with a calm voice, while thinking quickly on how to check mate their asses one more time... *"Thank you Sergeant for bringing this up to me, and trust me, I will do all I can to make sure that they will lose this battle."*

"Good Sergeant Linson. What they said you did out there doesn't make any sense, and I can see just from meeting with you and talking to you that you are not the person that they described to us. Now get out of here and get a medical discharge before they do what they want to do with you, okay."

"Okay Sergeant. Trust me, GOD got this." I replied looking back towards all of them, sitting around socializing with one another at their desks.

Walking out of the motor pool, I knew my Queen was still good and her wings were as strong as the day she was made... *"This is my time to check mate all of them and end this bull shit once and for all."* I said out loud, while walking to my car and making my way back up to see my doctor at the hospital.

After I had arrived back at my doctor's office, I requested a medical discharge before my Chain of Command could try to work around my doctor and force me back to Iraq in chains. During this time, I kept thanking GOD for working through my doctor who kept telling my Chain of Command "no" at every turn. And to my Chain of Commands surprise, my doctor agreed to start processing me for a medical discharge out of the Army.

During this time, it took two weeks to successfully out-process 615th ASB and moved over to the medical holding unit out in West Fort Hood. On my last day when I was finished out-processing 615th and getting all of my paperwork signed, I ran into Lt Col Hurshinger who was home for R&R, as I was walking out, and he was walking in...
"Sergeant Linson!"

"Colonel Hurshinger, how are you sir?"

"Hey, I'm home for R&R. I hear that you're getting med-boarded out of the Army?"

"Yes, sir I am. My health comes first before anyone and anything in this Army, sir."

"Yes, it does, Sergeant Linson. Look, who cares what they want to do with you back in Iraq. The best thing is that you're here and they're there. Do what you must do and keep moving. Don't let anybody stop you from getting where you got to be in life, okay."

"Yes sir. That's what I'm doing right now."

"It was nice to have you for one of my NCO's, Sergeant Linson. You have a good life and stay out of trouble."

"You do the same, sir. And keep your head down whenever you return back to Iraq. And oh, yea sir! Can you do me a really huge favor?"

"Sure, what's up?"

"Whenever you return back to Iraq, can you tell Sergeant Major Vela that I said I should have told you that I was leaving and hello?"

"HAHAHAHA, sure thing Sergeant Linson, sure thing. HAHAHAHAHA." We both started to laugh out loud.

Before we departed our own ways, I shook my Battalion Commanders hand and walked out of the 615th Air Support Battalion for the final and last time.

After nine years of active military service, on May 5 of 2007, I Howard Dewitt Linson at the age of 27 was medically discharged out of the United States Army, with an Honorable Discharge.

EPILOGUE: THE TRUTH YOU NEED TO KNOW

Hello everyone. Let me take the time and explain to you what the military or any political official who has been against the doing away of the "Don't Ask, Don't Tell" policy does not want you to know.

During my enlistment while serving in the United States Army, my journey from one unit to the next was not a sweet lullaby. I have lived through a time where countless soldiers of all races and backgrounds have been discharged under the Don't Ask, Don't Tell Policy, Army Regulation 600-20 Chapter 4-19, and section 654 of Title 10. Every one of these American Soldiers, were dishonorably discharged having shown; Loyalty, Duty, Respect, Selfless Service, Honor, Integrity and most import of them all, Personal Courage.

Regardless of what a group of people might think of a person's demeanor, none of what has happened to me should have happened. The United States Military has always had policies in place to protect service members from racism and unjust prosecution, but as you don't know, all these things are alive and kicking, in today's Armed Forces.

From childhood and into young adulthood, we see today in schools that kids are being bullied and harassed to the breaking point of suicides, based on the assumptions of their sexuality or who they are as a person. These same kids, who are all grown up and are now serving in today's military, are teaming up with people like themselves and ranging havoc on those who are seeking a better future for themselves or for their families.

Earlier in my book I spoke about a particular type of people who caused a lot of my troubles throughout my whole entire military career, "Homophobia's." When you take a Homophobic person and place them in a position of leadership that gives them the power over those who they suspect to be a certain way, life for that person or people will end up on the road I was forced to take.

Soldiers and civilians everywhere, Homophobia's are dangerous and unstable within themselves and are very unpredictable when they are faced with the fact that they must sleep or work next to someone who is perceived to be a homosexual or anything else that they do not like. Especially if you're a male.

As you have read from my experience within the United States Army, many of our leaders have told every person in uniform that, "A soldier who feels harassed or threatened for any reason should report the harassment or threats at once to his or her Chain of Command." One thing that they did not tell you is that the Command has the right to implement what he or she feels is necessary to handle the problem without conducting a thrall investigation into the nature of one's well-being.

That means, they can say that they have investigated the problem, or they have moved you to correct the issue before you will or will become an incident of a hate crime that they will do their best to cover up. Examples: Friendly Fire, Training Accident or Self Termination (Suicide).

Everything that I have written about is 100% truth and I have seen with my very own eyes what they can do, (Homophobia's). People will say… *"Why does the harassment continue, after the Chain of Command was notified?"* It is a simple answer, **"Unit Cohesion."**

An Officer who is in a Command position knows that a soldier can report threats, harassment or violence to the Command, free of harm or reprisal. Commanders are also supposed to take appropriate actions to protect the safety of soldiers who have reported threats or harassment. The Commander or The Chain of Command should include prompt investigation of the threat or harassment itself without singling that individual or individuals out. Threats or harassment based on a soldier's perceived, or alleged sexuality does not constitute credible information justifying an inquiry about possible homosexual conduct by the harassed soldier.

Humm, with over 14,000+ soldiers who have been discharged under Army Regulation 600-20, do you think that these steps were followed?

From the first day of Basic Training, drill instructors have told everyone to treat each other with dignity and respect, which has been the bedrock value that the military has had for decades passed. Although the Don't Ask, Don't Tell policy is on the way out of the Armed Forces, everyone needs to know that a soldier's sexual orientation is and has always considered to be a private matter and is not anyone's personal job to find out, no matter how they might assume they are or not.

Soldiers, if someone comes up to you and asks you if you're LGBTQ+ (Lesbian, Gay, Bisexual, Transgender, Queer, + non-cisgender), don't tell them. Just because the policy is going away or it perceives to be gone, don't disclose your private lives to them, because I promise you later down the road you will have problems.

For those who seek out gossip in the military and civilian world, a few things you need to know what is not considered credible evidence. 1. Rumors that a person is a homosexual. 2. People's opinions about a person's sexual orientation. 3. Seeing that person or hearing about that person going to a homosexual bar or reading sexual publications. 4. Seeing that person's marching in a gay rights rally. 5. The type of clothing that person wears. And most of all, 6. Anyone's way of speech.

Now, I have told you about Commanders thought process on how to take care of a situation based off the notation that someone is a homosexual, and I told you that it was Unit Cohesion that determined the outcome.

Well let me tell you what the military defines as **Unit Cohesion**...

Unit Cohesion – "as an important contributor to military performance and winning on the battlefield. Inquiries into cohesion have distinguished various types of cohesion as a means to better analyze how interpersonal dynamic impact the performance of small organizations – e.g., teams and small military units, such as squads and platoons." (MacCoun & Hix, CH 5. 2010)

Now you're asking yourself, what does that really mean?

It means, no matter what a person's (individual unit member), problem is within that unit, the overall mission is greater than the demise of that member's well-being.

In the military's eyes, get the job done and put the small things on the back burner, i.e., don't pay attention to those individual issues. And over the years it is shown that, when the Chain of Command ignores the issues within their "Unit," sexual assaults and death occurs.

One thing I want to add in there about this is that the bedrock of the Armed Forces policies will still be around, way after the Don't Ask, Don't Tell policy goes away. Now what I mean about that is, the armed forces must maintain personnel policies that exclude persons whose presence in the armed forces would create an unacceptable risk to the armed forces' high standards of moral, good order and discipline and unit cohesion that are the essence of military capability. The presence in the armed forces of persons who demonstrate a propensity or intent to engage in homosexual acts would create an unacceptable risk to the high standards of moral, good order and discipline, and unit cohesion that are the essence of military capability.

Soldiers and future soldier's do not disclose your sexual orientation for they will use other means to dishonorably discharge you in its entirety.

A little bit of history behind the Don't Ask, Don't Tell Policy.

The "Don't Ask, Don't Tell" policy was introduced as a compromise measure in 1993 by President Bill Clinton, who campaigned on the promise to allow all citizens to serve in the military regardless of sexual orientation. At the time, per the December 21, 1993, Department of Defense Directive 1332.14, it was legal policy that homosexuality is incompatible with military service and people who engaged in homosexual acts or stated that they are homosexual, or bisexual were discharged. The Uniform Code of Military Justice, passed by Congress in 1950 and signed by President Harry S. Truman, established the policies and procedures for discharging homosexual service members. The Clinton Administration on December 21, 1993, issued Defense directive 1304.26, which directed that military applicant were not to be asked about their sexual orientation. This is the policy now known today as the "Don't Ask, Don't Tell". The "Don't Ask" provision mandates that military or appointed officials will not ask about or require members to reveal their sexual orientation. The "Don't Tell" states that a member may be discharged for claiming to be a homosexual or bisexual or making a statement indicating a tendency towards or intent to engage in homosexual activities. The

"Don't Pursue" establishes what is minimally required for an investigation to be initiated. A "Don't Harass" provision was added to the policy later. It ensures that the military will not allow harassment or violence against service members for any reason. But harassment continues. (Schaefer, Ratner, Young, Rostker & Darilek. CH 2. 2010)

As it exits out of the door, DADT specifies that the "Don't Ask" part of the policy indicates that superiors should not initiate investigations of a service member's orientation in the absence of disallowed behaviors, though creditable and articulable evidence of homosexual behavior may cause an investigation. Violations of this aspect through unauthorized investigations and harassment of suspected servicemen and women resulted in the policy's current formulation as "Don't Ask, Don't Tell, Don't Pursue, Don't Harass." Efforts to repeal the policy, in effect since 1993, increased following the election of President Barack Obama in 2008, who advocated a full repeal (i.e., allowing homosexual and bisexual service members to serve openly) during his election campaign. On October 10, 2009, Obama stated in a speech before the Human Rights Campaign that he will end the ban but offered no timetable. As president, Obama said is his first State of the Union Address in 2010, "This year, I will work with Congress and our military to finally repeal the law that denies gay Americans the right to serve the country they love because of who they are." (Obama, 2010) This statement was quickly followed up by Defense Secretary Robert Gates and Joint Chiefs Chairman Michael Mullen voicing their support of a repeal of DADT. In 2010 the House of Representatives passed an amendment to the National Defense Authorization Act for Fiscal Year 2011 that would repeal the relevant sections of the law. When this stand-alone bill with identical language of December 15, 2010. Following a successful cloture vote in the Senate of December 18, 2010, the bill was passed and, on December 22, 2010, signed into law by President Obama. "The ability of service members to be open and honest about their families and the people they love honors the integrity of the individuals who serve, strengthens the institutions they serve, and is one of the many reasons why our military remains the finest in the world. (Slack, 2012)

Implementation: The passage of the repeal act does not result in the immediate repeal of DADT. Under the terms of the new law, the President, the Secretary of Defense and the Chairman of the Joint Chiefs of Staff must certify in writing that they have reviewed the Pentagon's report of the effect of DADT repeal, that the appropriate regulations have been reviewed and drafted and that implementation of repeal regulations "is consistent with the standards of military readiness, military effectiveness, unit cohesion, and recruiting and retention of the Armed Forces". (Senate Hearing, 2010)

Letter of support for maintaining DADT

Howard P. McKeon the ranking member of the HASC, at the time, wrote a letter to Secretary Gates and Admiral Mullen stating: "No action to change the law should be taken by the Administration or by this Congress until we have a full and complete understanding of the reasons why the current law threatens or undermines readiness in any significant way, whether a change in law will improve readiness in measurable ways, and what the implications for and effects on military readiness, cohesion, morale, good order and discipline are entailed with a change in law." (Lowrey, pg. 72, 2021)

Now that I have given you the history of the DADT and shown you that there are a lot of people in Command positions who don't like the fact that homosexuals can serve openly in what they consider to be their military. Let me further educate you on the oaths that Officers and Noncommissioned Officers have taken to ensure your well-being and their own. First let me explain the Officer's creed to you all...

"Always Ready"

I will give to the selfless performance of my duty and my mission the best that effort, thought, and dedication can provide.

To this end, I will not only seek continually to improve my knowledge and practice of my profession, but also I will exercise the authority interested to me by the President and the Congress with fairness, justice, patience, and restraint, respecting the dignity and human rights of others and devoting myself to the welfare of those placed under my command.

In justifying and fulfilling the trust placed in me, I will conduct my private life as well as my public service so as to the free both from impropriety and the appearance of impropriety, acting with candor and integrity to earn the unquestioning trust of my fellow soldiers-junior, senior, and associates-and employing my rank and position not to serve myself but to serve my country and my unit.

By practicing physical and moral courage I will endeavor to inspire these qualities in other by my example.

In all my actions I will put loyalty to the highest moral principles and United States of America above loyalty to organizations, person, and my personal interest.

To all soldiers and future Officers, and most importantly to all the parents that have kids in the military now, this is for you. The first sentence in the Officers Creed states how their thought process should be to the highest and best traditions of the United States of America, and to leave their personal beliefs and feelings at home.

2. Explains how an Officer should go by conducting him or herself in learning and knowing what the leadership of this country has in trusted them with, and to take charge of the care of soldiers under their command.

3. Explains that no matter what kind of background you come from, treat everyone with respect and dignity.

4. Explains how an Officer is supposed to set the example of physical awareness and to set the standards of how to maintain that appearance to all of the men and women beneath them.

5. Explains to us all, that no matter what changes come while serving your country as an Officer in the United States Armed Forces, you will implement the orders of the President and Congress within yourself and throughout your whole entire Chain of Command, all down to the lowest person. And anything less, would be a lack of loyalty to those appointed above you.

The Noncommissioned Officer Creed

"The U.S. Army NCO Creed"

No one is more professional than I. I am a Noncommissioned Officer, a leader of soldiers. As a Noncommissioned Officer, I realize that I am a member of a time honored corps, which is known as "The Backbone of the Army". I am proud of the Corps of Noncommissioned Officers and will at all times conduct myself so as to bring credit upon the Corps, the Military service and my country regardless of the situation in which I find myself. I will not use my grade or position to attain pleasure, profit, or personal safety.

Competence is my watchword. My two basic responsibilities will always be uppermost in my mind accomplishment of my mission and the welfare of my soldiers. I will strive to remain tactically and technically proficient. I am aware of my role as a Noncommissioned Officer. I will fulfill my responsibilities inherent in that role. All soldiers are entitled to outstanding leadership; I will provide that leadership. I know my soldiers and I will always place their needs above my own. I will communicate consistently with my soldiers and never leave them uninformed. I will be fair and impartial when recommending both rewards and punishment.

Officers of my unit will have maximum time to accomplish their duties; they will not have to accomplish mine. I will earn their respect and confidence as well as that of my soldiers. I will be loyal to those with whom I serve; seniors, peers, and subordinates alike. I will exercise initiative by talking appropriate action in the absence of orders. I will not compromise my integrity, nor my moral courage. I will not forget, nor will I allow my comrades to forget that we are professional, Noncommissioned Officers, Leaders!

Now for the NCO's creed. Civilians, soldiers and current and future NCO's listen up. As you know, the number of NCO's from top to bottom are not living up to the NCO creed. Let me break this down for those who are serving now and will be serving in the future.

1. First paragraph explains to all NCO's, no matter how far up the Chain of Command you have made it, you are a leader of SOLDIERS! This country looks up to you all, to take and bring their children back home and yourselves from any combat areas of the world and state side. As an NCO you will not use your rank for other means but that attended purpose to why you are in your leadership position.

2. Explains to everyone that it is your mission from day one to look out for your soldiers of all KINDS, no matter what you feel about them. No matter what the cause, you will always place them before yourselves and assure them and yourself, you are that leader they can put their trust in.

3. Explains, you will not allow Officers to do your job for you. It is your responsibility to make sure that you are the ones taking care of your soldiers and not your Officers when they are supposed to be focusing on the mission at hand.

4. Explains, respect does not come from putting on your E-5 rank on up to E-9, it comes from the trust and loyalty of those appointed above and below you. The Officer sets the distance, but you are the ones that set the pace. If you ever see your fellow NCO's diverting from who they're supposed to be while in or out of uniform, always and I mean always remind yourself and your fellow NCO's that you are all PROFESSIONALS and to always conduct yourselves as such.

So here we are now today, with the DADT gone out of the window, or so it seems for us who are standing on the outside looking In. But for those who are still on the inside, listen up. The "Don't Ask, Don't Tell" policy might look like it is gone for good, but in reality, it is still in place to protect "Unit Cohesion." You might be in right now and thinking you can express yourself through cloths or even through items that you can hang on your walls or shelves and around your body and POV's (**P**rivate **O**wn **V**ehicles), let me tell you something, **"DON'T!"**

It will take up to 25 and 35 years to filter out those who are in command positions that are still firmly against the repeal of the DADT policy to be completely gone. And until then, they will seek your hurt, pain or life even if it means discharging you under other regulations to satisfy their own demons.

Always keep your personal life to yourselves and regardless if someone asks you, watch your back at all times. Because if you're not watching your own back, I guarantee you no one else will.

Always keep your head's up and never let anyone tell you, you can't be what you want to be or make you look down when you're supposed to be looking up.........**Keep Moving and Don't Stop!**

"KEEP MOVING and DON'T STOP!"

Howard Dewitt Linson

NOTES ON SOURCES

Lowrey, N. (2021). Repealing Don't Ask, Don't Tell.
https://www.jcs.mil/Portals/36/Documents/History/Dec21/SHS_15_R
epealing_DADT.pdf

MacCoun, R. & Hix, W. (2010). Unit Cohesion and Military
Performance, in Sexual Orientation and U.S. Military Personnel Policy:
An Update of RAND's 1993 Study.
https://law.stanford.edu/publications/unit-cohesion-and-military-
performance/ &
https://www.law.berkeley.edu/files/csls/Unit_Cohesion_and_Military
_Performance_Ch5_MacCoun_Hix.pdf

U.S. Army Officer & NCO Creed's. (2022).
http://www.wiu.edu/coehs/military_science/cadets/officers_creed.ph
p & https://www.army.mil/values/nco.html

President Obama, B. (2010) State of the Union Address.
https://www.obamalibrary.gov/timeline/first-state-union-address

Schaefer, A., Ratner, E., Young, S., Rostker, B., & Darilek, R. (2010) The
History of "Don't Ask, Don't Tell".
https://www.jstor.org/stable/10.7249/mg1056osd.10?seq=1#metadat
a_info_tab_contents

Slack, M. (2012). From the Archives: The End of Don't Ask, Don't Tell. https://obamawhitehouse.archives.gov/blog/2012/09/20/archives-end-dont-ask-dont-tell

Senate Hearing. (2010) Committee on Armed Services United States Senate. https://www.govinfo.gov/content/pkg/CHRG-111shrg65073/html/CHRG-111shrg65073.htm

Young S. Command Sgt. Maj. (2019). Team Building and Unit Cohesion. https://www.armyupress.army.mil/Journals/NCO-Journal/Archives/2019/October/Team-Building-and-Unit-Cohesion/

ACKNOWLEDGMENTS

First, I want to thank GOD for being with me and for my loving family, who was there for me from day one. If it was not for the love that I received from GOD and from my family, I do not know where I would be today. Thank you!

Also, I would like to give recognition to Senator Chad Cochran, of Mississippi, for being there for me when things were at its worst. Senator, you have shown me that no matter how bad any soldier's problems can get, there will always be someone in an elected position that they can turn to, that can fix what most leaders cannot fix.

Finally, I want to give thanks to the people who made a major impact in my military career while I served in the United States Army. First to 1st Sgt Burns, who stepped up and protected me from countless military personnel, and for being that father figure when I needed it the most. Second, is to my best friend Spc Strittholt, for staying beside me through the thick and thin, when my life was at its wits. There has been no one who can mount up to you. Third, I want to thank Spc Hanenburg for also being my friend when everyone else walked away during my hard times within my military career.

Thank you all!

www.ingramcontent.com/pod-product-compliance
Lightning Source LLC
Chambersburg PA
CBHW031300310326
41914CB00116B/1764/J